ATKINS

Architecture & Urban Design

Selected & Current Works 2011

Published in Australia in 2011 by
The Images Publishing Group Pty Ltd
ABN 89 059 734 431
6 Bastow Place, Mulgrave, Victoria 3170, Australia
Tel: +61 3 9561 5544 Fax: +61 3 9561 4860
books@imagespublishing.com
www.imagespublishing.com

Copyright © The Images Publishing Group Pty Ltd 2011
The Images Publishing Group Reference Number: 980

National Library of Australia Cataloguing-in-Publication entry

Author: Atkins (Firm).

Title: Atkins: architecture and urban design : selected
                 and current works 2011 / Atkins ; edited by
                 Edwina Askew and William Grime; sub-edited
                 by Maya Thomas.

ISBN: 9781864704518 (hbk.)

Notes: Includes index.

Subjects: Atkins (Firm).
                 Architecture, Modern.
                 Industrial design.
                 City planning.

Other Authors/Contributors:
                 Askew, Edwina.
                 Grime, William.
                 Thomas, Maya.

Dewey Number: 720

Coordinating editor: Debbie Fry

Edited by Edwina Askew and William Grime
Sub-edited by Maya Thomas
Designed by Shaun Killa, Martin Pease and Gareth Kirkwood
Graphics by Vadim Charles, Donna Hawkins and Mukund Agarwal

Pre-publishing services by United Graphic Pte Ltd, Singapore

Printed on 150 gsm Quatro Silk Matt paper by
Everbest Printing Co. Ltd., in Hong Kong/China

IMAGES has included on its website a page for special
notices in relation to this and our other publications.
Please visit www.imagespublishing.com.

ATKINS

Architecture & Urban Design

Selected & Current Works 2011

Contents

Atkins across the globe

Aarhus	Cardiff	Dublin	Hoofddorp	Manila	Phoenix	Swindon
Aberdeen	Chelmsford	Edinburgh	Houston	Mansfield	Port of Spain	Sydney
Abu Dhabi	Chengdu	Epsom	Ipswich	Minneapolis	Portland	Tamworth
Alberta	Chicago	Esbjerg	Istanbul	Muscat	Princeton	Taunton
Aldermaston	Cleveland	Exeter	Jeddah	New York	Rotherham	Telford
Athens	Colchester	Farnham	Jönköping	Newcastle upon	San Francisco	Tunbridge Wells
Atlanta	Colombo	Fredericia	Kuwait	Tyne	San Juan	Västerås
Bangalore	Copenhagen	Galway	Leeds	Norwich	Seattle	Warrington
Beijing	Cork	Glasgow	Lisbon	Nottingham	Shanghai	Warszawa
Belfast	Croydon	Glastonbury	London	Orlando	Sharjah	Washington, DC
Birmingham	Cumbria	Gliwice	Los Angeles	Orpington	Shenzhen	Williamsburg
Boston	Dallas	Göteborg	Luxembourg	Oslo	Singapore	York
Bristol	Derby	Hamburg	Malmö	Oxford	St Asaph	
Bucharest	Doha	Helsingborg	Manama	Perth	Stockholm	
Cambridge	Dubai	Hong Kong	Manchester	Peterborough	Swansea	

THE **WORLD HAS NEVER SEEMED SMALLER,** OUR SENSE OF **CONCERN ABOUT THE ENVIRONMENT** HAS NEVER BEEN **GREATER,** AND THE **PACE OF TECHNOLOGICAL CHANGE** HAS NEVER BEEN **QUICKER.**

Atkins Now

by Robert Powell

The Burj Al Arab, an awe-inspiring resort hotel located at the southern end of the Arabian Gulf, is the icon of modern Dubai, as memorable as Utzon's Opera House in Sydney and Frank Gehry's Guggenheim Museum in Bilbao. Completed in 1999, the Burj Al Arab is a spectacular building marking the belated arrival of Atkins into the international architectural spotlight – one of the world's leading design firms, which has been in existence since 1938 and is well known for its engineering expertise, but whose architectural work had hitherto gone relatively unnoticed.

Until the last decade of the 20th century, the nature of Atkins' architectural commissions was in areas that did not readily attract media attention – power stations, steelworks, dams, railways, military installations – almost always in support of the much acclaimed engineering expertise of the company as a whole. While functional, pragmatic and a necessary adjunct to its engineering capability, the architectural output of Atkins had been so submerged in its corporate identity that the design community barely knew of its existence, and when the Burj Al Arab was revealed, the common reaction was one of astonishment.

The Burj Al Arab is the 'jewel in the crown' of the Jumeirah Beach Resort. Officially opened on 1st December 1999, the 321 m tower in the form of a giant sail is the tallest all-suite hotel in the world. It has been applauded as an epic design, stunning in its simplicity and clarity, which makes an unequivocal statement about Dubai's emergence as a regional hub and tourist destination.

The spin-off from the success of the Burj, in placing Atkins' architecture on the world stage, has been immense. Atkins designers have continued to win international competitions and commissions, and have built a solid reputation for high-quality architecture and masterplanning through thousands of projects and over 400 completed buildings over the last decade. Atkins is now one of the architects of choice in the Middle East and Asia, winning commissions in a highly competitive environment against more established and internationally-renowned design practices.

The company's confidence in its stature is such that it has become a leader in encouraging the built environment sector to adopt sustainable practices. Atkins coined the term Carbon Critical Design™, which is now synonymous with the push to prepare the world for a low carbon future, while projects such as the Bahrain World Trade Center stand as a beacon for this new way of thinking.

Atkins changes track

Architecture found its voice in Atkins during the 10 years spanning the turn of the century, helped by a major review in 2001 of the company's business structure. In 2003 the newly appointed chief executive, Keith Clarke, who comes from an architectural background, called for a 'design-based culture' to elevate the trajectory of the company. This new emphasis on product and excellence focussed the efforts of the Atkins design community to capitalise on its hidden strengths.

But, even before this, architecture had 'taken off' within the group, which is currently the second largest employer of architects in the UK and has more than 500 architectural staff worldwide. While it is an engineering based firm, Atkins now has a strong architectural focus, especially in the Middle East and China, and this focus is growing in the UK. "There is a new momentum driving Atkins. It is design-led, obsessed with 'raising the bar'," emphasises Shaun Killa, principal design architect in the Dubai office. It's a view shared by Keith Clarke, who enthuses of the multidisciplinary business "… when we are all pulling in the same direction, Atkins is unbeatable…".

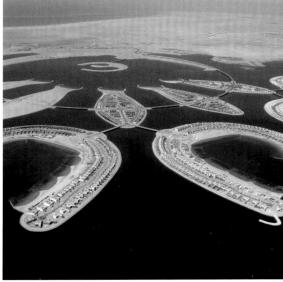

The origins of architecture at Atkins

Sir William Atkins founded the firm of engineering consultants, WS Atkins and Partners, in 1938. He was an innovative engineer; as early as 1934 he founded a contracting company, later to be called London Ferro Concrete, which specialised in the production of pre-cast concrete components. He was also an exceptional entrepreneur and his legacy, Atkins, is now the largest engineering consultancy in Europe and the eleventh largest design firm in the world, with more than 18,500 staff working in over 150 countries. The group has worked internationally for over 40 years and is renowned as a technical services provider in the fields of transport, design and engineering solutions, management and project services.

Atkins engaged a number of private architects to work with the firm in the early days but eventually decided to appoint an in-house architect. The first incumbent was Stuart Mobsby who was succeeded in 1964 by AG Shepherd Fidler who led the architectural division, known as Atkins Shepherd Fidler, until 1978. Shepherd Fidler was the former city architect of Birmingham and prior to that, architect of Crawley New Town. The acquisition of this influential public figure was indicative of Atkins' business acumen. He was quick to seize opportunities to network with the public sector, which was the source of much of the company's work.

In 1979, Mike Jeffries was appointed as the next head of the architectural arm of the company and remained with Atkins until his retirement as Chairman of the Board in 2005. Jeffries set about altering the perception that architecture was an adjunct of engineering and, in 1991, the company acquired Lister Drew Haines Barrow, a design-oriented London-based architectural practice. The effects were not instantaneous, but a breakthrough came in 1994 when Atkins was commissioned to design the Jumeirah Beach Resort in Dubai. Tom Wright, one in the crop

of young architects who had been brought on board from Lister Drew, grasped the opportunity to realise an 'iconic' design for the Burj Al Arab. But despite the huge success of the firm in the Middle East market, Atkins was still almost unknown to the international architectural fraternity and this situation continued for several years.

Atkins in the Middle East

"Dubai is an extreme example of urbanism. One of the fastest growing cities in the world today, it represents the epitome of sprawling, post-industrial and car-oriented urban culture."[1]

Atkins set up an office in the Middle East in 1976. Initially the company was involved in dredging Dubai Creek and infrastructure. Other contracts encompassed surveying and water-related engineering projects in mountainous Oman and road design in Abu Dhabi. In Kuwait the company tackled marine contracts and transportation projects, including the structural design of bridges.

The early work was exclusively engineering-based, but in 1982 Atkins acquired a small architectural commission – a private villa design in Dubai. Other architectural commissions followed and in 1985 Atkins established an architectural department in Dubai. The Standard Chartered Bank Building was commissioned and this was followed by numerous projects for the municipal authority. By the end of the 1980s, Atkins had an extensive portfolio that included police stations, the Officers' Sports Club and the Dubai Police College and Academy. Other projects followed in the 1990s, including the 19-storey Al Mussalla Tower, the Taj Palace Hotel, the 28-storey Al Salam Tower and the Bank Melli Iran Headquarters. The buildings were well received

1 George Katodrytis, "Metropolitan Dubai and the rise of Architectural Fantasy", in *Bidoun: Arts and Culture from the Middle East*, Dubai, August 2005.

and Atkins gained a reputation for reliability and appropriate design.

This somewhat modest acknowledgement of the firm's architectural design skills was altered dramatically in 1994, when, following a limited competition with some of the world's best design-led practices, Atkins was engaged to design the Burj Al Arab. Tom Wright summed up his thoughts on first discussing his design for the commission with the client: "It didn't take long to realise that Dubai wanted to be seen as a fast-developing, forward-looking, first world culture. This being the case, we decided to look to the aspirations of the people for our ideas, rather than basing them on the historical cultural context. It seemed reasonable to take the theme of this modern tourist destination and design the tower hotel in the form of a giant sail – not a historic dhow sail, but a modern, high-tech sail."

The project team was relocated to the UAE, where it remained for the duration of the entire Jumeirah Beach Resort Development project. That included the Jumeirah Beach Hotel and the Wild Wadi Aqua Park – an innovative water park that upon its completion won the World Water Park Association Award for outstanding design.

With a new business emphasis focussing on the growth of the Middle East architectural business, there followed a number of commissions won in design competitions against other world-renowned architectural practices, one effect of which was the growth of the Dubai office from 45 to 900 staff in the eight years to 2008. In the same period, the Gulf regional multidisciplinary teams grew from 250 to over 2,800 professionals in seven offices.

The prime catalyst for Dubai's growth was an aspiration to create a world-class business and tourism destination, a tax free commercial environment and a global transportation hub. Subsequently this was consolidated by the availability of freehold

accommodation and a sustained increase in the price of oil. The combination of Dubai's rapidly growing market and Atkins' new-found reputation for world-class design ensured that, after 1999, architecture was firmly established as one of the lead disciplines driving the business.

The Middle East practice has since designed and completed, among others, the 53-storey 21st Century Tower (the tallest residential skyscraper in the world at that time); the 50-storey Chelsea Tower; the 61-storey Millennium Tower; the 306 m, 63-storey The Address, Downtown Dubai; the 360 m, 66-storey Almas Tower and the five Executive Towers in the new Business Bay District, which average 40 storeys each. Ten towers have been completed in the Jumeirah Lakes Towers development, and five of the world's tallest 100 buildings have been designed by its Middle East offices and constructed in Dubai.

Since the recent slowdown in commercial activity, Atkins has diversified its geographical reach, taking on projects in the Kingdom of Saudi Arabia, India and eastern Europe, which are driven by economic diversification, the growth of tourism and infrastructure investment.

"Atkins' approach to architecture is not formulaic" says Shaun Killa, "but it does involve a distinct ethos, embodying several significant principles. The first is **Inspiration** where we strive to delight our clients by exceeding their expectations and developing the project brief to add value; then it's **Innovation** in architectural design, engineering and the challenges of reducing global warming. Next is **Building Efficiency** where floor plates of 75–80% efficiency are critical to the success in providing our clients with commercially successful developments. Fourth is **Carbon Critical Design™**, a concept created and trademarked by Atkins. Ecological concern is no longer an optional extra; it is woven into our design for every building and masterplan, from initial sketches

to construction. Next is **Integrated Multidisciplinary Design**, drawing individuals from the wide Atkins pool of architects and engineers with each team building on the successes and innovations of previous projects. Finally comes **Contextual Care** where particular attention is paid to the way in which new buildings are set into their context, how they relate to the ground and engage with their surroundings and the people that inhabit them."

The growing reputation of Atkins in the Middle East was given new resonance by the opening of the Bahrain World Trade Center in 2008. Shaun Killa's sail-shaped twin towers and triple turbines created a new icon for the region. A modern reinterpretation of the traditional wind tower, it is the first building in the world to integrate large-scale wind turbines as part of a commercial tower structure. It was followed by the Durrat Al Bahrain commission at the south of the island, masterplanned by Tom Wright.

Killa is passionate when speaking about architecture in the UAE: "The Dubai architectural studio grew from 10 to 140 staff within six years. At the same time our studios in Abu Dhabi (UAE) and Muscat (Oman) grew, and we opened new studios in Manama (Bahrain) and Doha (Qatar). This saw our architectural staff in the Gulf peak at 240 in 2008.

We have won significant commissions in design competition with other high-profile architectural practices from the UK and the USA, as well as receiving direct appointments that have further elevated our position in the region. Through our design and understanding of both our clients and the market, we have gained a solid reputation in the Middle East for designing expressive icons with timeless qualities, which also encompass efficient and commercial design aspects."

A conscious effort has been made to avoid the development of an Atkins style, and there is broad diversity among the designs created by its studios in the Middle East. Killa

explains that their design aesthetics have evolved over the years. Atkins ideologies stem from a multi-layered approach where buildings evoke dynamic movement, sometimes even defying gravity, engage the observer and result in clean-lined buildings with presence. Examples of this approach are evident in the cantilevered diamond exchange at the base of the Almas Tower or the floating half-disc of Iris Bay.

The buildings Atkins produces are not only pragmatic solutions to a client's brief, but opportunities to take design to the 'next level', where restraint is balanced on the fine line between too much and too little. Often, the initial idea can be seen to emanate from the subtleties of cultural expression, as in the folded *mashrabiya* foil of the Riyadh Tower, or the sails and Arabian wind towers inspiring the Bahrain World Trade Center.

Killa's drive and passion is mirrored by the collective approach of Joe Tabet in Abu Dhabi, Ray Phillips in Bahrain and John Croser in Oman. Architecture has driven the growth of the Middle East offices, supported by the Atkins competitive edge of having a seamless, in-house, multidisciplinary engineering team. The offices bring international teams with diverse cultural values from all over the world to the design process.

Although the bulk of the work is above 40 storeys, a high-rise specialism for which it is now renowned, Atkins is also well-established in other sectors such as hospitals, airports, schools, hotels and retail centres. As Shaun Killa adds, "We are constantly evolving and there is an insistence on design excellence in all aspects of what we do." This message is reinforced by Simon Crispe, architect and Atkins' Middle East regional commercial director: "Our aim continues to be for Atkins to create great buildings, for Atkins to continue to develop its architectural legacy and continuum of design excellence, founded upon the achievements of our first architects in the region more than 20 years ago."

Atkins in China

KY Cheung, a China-born, US-educated architect joined Atkins in 1998. He was pivotal in establishing the company's architectural practice and kick-starting the Atkins design name in China. He explains the context in which Atkins has prospered in Asia by pointing out that "during three decades of steady development China has provided a constant source of opportunities for the best international design companies". Since then, Atkins has been vying with the architectural elite in mainland China, initially from design offices in Hong Kong, to which were added offices in Shenzhen, Beijing and, in 2003, Shanghai.

The urbanisation process is the prime design generator. Already 45% of the population of 1.3 billion people live in an urban environment, and it is growing by 1% per annum. There is consequently a huge challenge to provide housing and regenerate existing cities. 90 million people live below the poverty line and a major challenge is to provide them with decent homes.

A breakthrough came with a commission for the Shenzhen Dameisha Airland Hotel (1998), a joint design project by KY Cheung and Tom Wright. This curvilinear set of hotel buildings is not a type widely seen in China, and the success of the project was instrumental in promoting Atkins' expertise there. Soon after, Atkins won an important international competition for the masterplan and detailed design of the Athletes' Village for the 2001 Summer Universiade in Beijing in 1999. These projects became the cornerstone of Atkins' entry into the China market. The significance of the Athletes' Village in particular should not be underestimated – it made a major contribution to Beijing's successful bid to host the 2008 Olympics.

Atkins' China division has doubled its staff from 2005 to 2010, and is now 1,000 strong. It mixes western and local staff to offer clients a combination of international expertise with local knowledge, extending the range of design options with a particular emphasis on sustainability. Close cooperation between Atkins' international offices make the best use of its multidisciplinary skills, particularly valuable for complex projects. The firm has now executed over 200 projects in China, from regional planning to individual buildings, many reflecting China's progressive urbanisation. As demand has moved beyond pure residential development, it has used its international experience to develop complementary projects in the fields of tourism, offices, commerce and transportation.

Despite the pressures of a large workload, the China offices have avoided a consistent design expression. Clients appreciate this rigorous dedication to finding a special solution that distinguishes their project from any other through creative interpretation of the site, brief, culture, climate and structural elements.

At the core of many cities are important projects that define the urban skyline with 'signature' buildings. Winning the landmark TEDA Towers against some of the world's best design practices helped to establish Atkins in China's northeast region. It subsequently won TEDA Centre, the 1.5 km long mixed-use development of 25 towers, now under construction. Within the more affluent coastal region are found most of its mixed-use projects, including Guangzhou East Tower, Shanghai Shi Liu Pu and the recent Xiamen Twin Towers, each responding to the brief with an appropriate design extending well beyond functional requirements.

Improvements in living standards have vitalised national as well as international tourism in China. Atkins has responded by designing resorts such as the Shanghai Harbour Crowne Plaza Hotel in Lin Gang, the dramatic cliff-edge Songjiang Shimao Wonderland Intercontinental Hotel and the Suzhou International Crab Market, which is dedicated to a famous local delicacy. More traditional luxury hotels include the Four Points Beijing, Chengdu Hilton, Jiayu Ningbo,

Zhanjiang Minda Sheraton, Wuhan Hiayu Landmark Hotel and the extensive 1,200 room Phoenix Hotel leisure and conference facility in Tianjin.

As an indispensable element of urbanisation, transportation affords many design opportunities in railway and airport expansions. Atkins has won five competitions for airport terminals, all of which are now either completed or under construction in Yinchuan, Taiyuan, Hangzhou, Changsha and Xian. All exceed modern technical standards while reflecting local cultural diversity and serving as gateways to their respective cities.

The urban planning and consultancy business was established in China in 1994, and has become a major component of Atkins' workload in China. Mark Harrison, planning director, says: "Masterplanning encompasses a multidisciplinary approach to development, economics, tourism and urban planning. Low-carbon planning enhances the process by addressing the issues of climate change and rapid urbanisation while improving quality of life." Working for both public and private sectors, Atkins has completed large-scale masterplanning projects in over 100 cities across China.

Representative projects include the 500 km² Shenfu Connection Area in Shenyang, which integrates the two northeastern cities of Shenyang and Fushun, and the Bao'an Central Business District, which lies between the airport and the core city of Shenzhen. The latter masterplan aims to achieve a 'vertical city', seamlessly connecting commercial development and pedestrian movement with mass transit stations.

The masterplan for the Oceania Point resort community of Xunliao in southern China covers a highly attractive coastal area of some 20 km². Taking the quality of the waterfront landscape as its starting point, the scheme is now under implementation.

The need to travel, in combination with the sheer scale of China, is resulting in the creation of highly accessible, multi-modal transport hubs, bringing together high-speed railway stations, metro stations, airports and ports. This accessibility can be harnessed to achieve city development goals beyond those of purely transportation. This is the approach taken in the masterplan for the Hangzhou High-speed Rail Station Area in eastern China.

Landscape design is a huge real-estate marketing tool. In China, 400 ha parks are commonplace. After winning several international competitions, Atkins has also become one of the best-known international landscape design firms in China. Some of its signature works include the 7.2 km riverfront park that lines the city gateway of Mianyang and the 27 km streetscape in Suzhou's high-tech industrial park.

Landscaping often drives design, and great importance is placed on the image, symbolism and expression of green environments. *Feng shui* also plays a big part in landscape design; for example, water equates with 'wealth' and 'abundance'. Symbolism is an important ingredient in every project and a grasp of Chinese mythology is vital to conceptual planning.

Atkins in the UK

In the UK, Atkins' architecture teams deliver a broad spectrum of building types and specialist knowledge to the education, healthcare, mass transit, commercial, leisure and public building sectors. Martin Pease leads the UK design teams and Tom Wright leads the UK International team. The latter specialises in high-profile international projects, particularly hospitality and commercial developments and water parks, for a range of clients around the world.

Recent projects include Regatta Jakarta, an Indonesian development completed in 2009, comprising a five-star hotel, 10 luxury apartment towers, two serviced apartment towers and a water park, across 11 ha. It is one of the most luxurious developments in the area and has already scooped an award in the coveted FIABCI Prix d' Excellence 2010. The Epsom design team also created an entirely new concept for the cruise industry in *Oasis of the Seas*, a luxury cruise liner launched in 2009 for Miami-based Royal Caribbean International.

Projects still in design include a concept for the 126 m Capital Fort tower and mixed-use development, which is set to make the financial and commercial centre of Bulgaria's capital city, Sofia, a worthy competitor for similar centres worldwide. Construction of Tom Wright's masterplan for the Durrat Al Bahrain island resort is well underway and is set to become one of the world's most distinctive island cities and a fine example of contemporary urban planning.

Atkins operates a network of regional studios dealing with projects within the UK, including London, Epsom, Oxford, Bristol, Warrington, Leeds, Newcastle and Glasgow, each headed by a design director. Education is a key market and Atkins has provided a wealth of design and specialist skills to schools, further education and higher education facilities.

Recently completed schools projects include Newcomen Primary School in Redcar, Cleveland, which makes innovative use of outdoor space by bringing it into the learning environment and enabling pupils to learn about their surroundings. The unique shape and glass-fronted entrance of Northwood Primary School in Darlington, Co. Durham, presents the positive statement to the community of being a building for the public and pupils alike.

Designs for tertiary education facilities are also developing clients' expectations for low-carbon, community-centred design. Lowestoft College, Sussex, has

a technically driven form that maximises passive, low-carbon design features.

The Atkins team in Glasgow is working on a major mental health development, NHS Tayside, that is set to transform the environment in which mental healthcare is delivered in Tayside and the north of Scotland. At the other end of Britain, the design for Anchor Care Homes provides a benchmark facility for the care of the elderly.

Within the commercial sector, the success of The Hub, an exemplar of sustainability (and Atkins' South West regional office), demonstrates an ability to overcome low-carbon challenges in any context. The project has already won 'Building of the Year' in the Best Corporate Workspace category of the British Council for Offices annual awards 2010, and was shortlisted for the 'New Build of the Year' award 2010 in CIBSE's annual low carbon awards. Elsewhere, developing an airtight storage facility for the British Library was a technical *tour de force*; now, following the success of the project, Atkins' Leeds-based team is developing a specialist newspaper archive facility.

Emulating the Chinese experience, the mass-transit sector is providing exciting challenges. Atkins' London office, in concert with some world-class partners, is undertaking part of the £16 billion project to deliver Crossrail, the new high-frequency railway for London and the southeast of England that is due for completion in 2017. The team is playing a key role in multidisciplinary joint-venture contracts to design Tottenham Court Road Station, Custom House Station and the common architectural component finishes for Paddington, Bond Street, Liverpool Street, Whitechapel and Custom House stations.

Atkins in North America

With the acquisition of PBS&J in North America in late 2010, the architecture team in the US provides a full range of building design services to the federal,

higher education, leisure, aviation and civil market sectors. Benton Rudolph AIA, who leads the North American design practice in five US offices, says: "Our focus is on our clients – we create exceptional buildings through design excellence, considering the full life cycle of buildings. Technology (BIM) and sustainability are at the core of this model, but architecture within the context of a very diverse environment informs our solutions."

With a growing reputation in all markets, the Federal Design Studio has been honoured with multiple awards for the recently completed Energy Demonstration Fitness Center at Tyndall Air Force Base, Florida. This is the first LEED Platinum building in the United States Air Force.

The recently completed Wizarding World of Harry Potter at Universal's Islands of Adventure in Orlando, Florida has rapidly become a signature project of the Leisure Design Studio. The recent selection as the architect for the University of Texas (Austin) 'Super Computer' Building anchors an exceptional reputation in US higher education work.

With this acquisition, a wider range of design skills in complex mixed-use, commercial, retail, hospitality and sustainable masterplanning is also offered by Atkins within North America. Faithful and Gould, a subsidiary of Atkins, is well established in the US and further extends Atkins' services to project management, economic feasibility, program management and project cost control. Combining the new North American team with Atkins' established reputation for design excellence further establishes Atkins as a leader in architectural excellence.

Embracing diversity

Atkins is now the second largest global architectural firm according to the BD Top 100 of World Architecture 2010. Its huge output, spread across four continents and 150 countries, raises

the question – is there an Atkins 'style', in the sense that a building by Frank Gehry, Richard Meier or Santiago Calatrava is instantly recognisable? When, to the educated eye, the corporate output of many other internationally acclaimed architects has a certain quality that defines it as the product of a specific design culture, can the same be said of Atkins?

Atkins' designers believe that design solutions from its international studios must fit into the time, place and culture in which they are located. There is a continuing discourse within the firm about the value of icons. Charles Jencks, critic and author, contends that "metaphors are liable and open to idiosyncratic interpretation, but they have to be taken seriously as the primary way architecture communicates in an age of iconography."

Conversely, writer Peter Buchanan holds that icons are "disruptive of contiguous urban fabric; they fail in the contemporary task of re-stitching the city and recreating a sense of place." For many architects appropriate architecture is place-specific, contextual, led by the client's brief and driven by issues such as ecological awareness and sustainable design. These factors drive much of the work of Atkins in the UK. Philip Watson, design director, resolves the matter by explaining: "Our philosophy is not to produce a style of architecture, but to consider the particular conditions of each project to produce buildings that have narrative – resonance with their landscape, climate, culture and people. It's about trying to create a unique sense of place that will evolve and absorb new stories over time."

In China, the metaphor is a key feature of architecture, as is *feng shui*. A project that conveys in its form, orientation and architectural image promises of fortune, wealth, longevity and good health will invariably be attractive to a Chinese client. Atkins always attempts to root a project in the local culture; the lotus flower, for example, was the inspiration for the transportation hub in Songjiang.

This concern with culture and context has served Atkins well, enabling it to succeed in diverse markets in world terms, but more importantly, enabling it to produce architecture of integrity, appropriate designs of which it can be proud. This concern also integrates well with sustainable design. Atkins' recent designs for carbon-zero cities in Arabia, for example, approached from first principles, produced solutions that bear a striking resemblance to the traditional Arabian desert town – narrow streets, tall buildings, enclosed courtyards, shady landscaping. There is a close correlation between culture, context and sustainability, clearly vindicating Atkins' determination to incorporate all three in their resolutely contemporary approach.

The future – Atkins Now

"Our aspiration is to take our place at the top table of world architecture, and our architects are leading the way," says Keith Clarke. "The Burj Al Arab was the first milestone on the journey: Atkins provided all the expertise, from the concept, through the marine engineers and ecologists who surveyed the seabed and protected the marine environment, to architecture, engineering, lighting design, cost and project management – all the skills were available in-house. It's that capability and commitment to the total project we need to promote. Few other companies in the world can match Atkins' range of multidisciplinary skills."

Atkins is now producing cutting-edge architecture in which every project adopts low-carbon design principles and contextual integration. Already it has excellent credentials in the spheres of high-rise architecture and city masterplanning, and a diverse and outstanding portfolio of architecture. The quality of Atkins' design is now recognised by a profession that is notoriously reluctant to acknowledge that a corporate firm

can consistently produce excellent design. There is a new spirit driving Atkins architects and a passion that is palpable in every studio.

Atkins architecture is a well-kept secret. This book is intended to rectify that curious situation and celebrate the richly diverse architecture emerging from Atkins offices worldwide.

The writer: Robert Powell is an architect and urban planner. In 1984 he joined the staff of the National University of Singapore where he was Associate Professor of Architecture and Urban Design until 2001. He was the editor of *The Singapore Architect* from 1997 to 1999 and *Space* magazine from 1999 to 2001. He is the author of 25 books on architecture and urban design including *The New Asian House* (2000), *Singapore Architecture* (2003), *SCDA Architects : The architecture of Soo Chan* (2004) and was co-author of *The Stadium* (2005). He writes for several international architectural journals including *Architectural Review* (UK), *Architectural Record* (USA), *Monument* (Australia) and *Dialogue* (Taiwan).

Sustainability
and Carbon Critical Design™

THE GREATEST CHALLENGE IS NOT KEEPING PACE WITH CURRENT LOW CARBON THINKING, BUT **PREDICTING WHAT IS COMING NEXT.** FOR ATKINS, IT'S **NOT JUST A MORAL DECISION, BUT ONE THAT IS BUSINESS CRITICAL.**

The need...

With the planet under stress from the activities of mankind, a sustainable approach to design and construction is needed. From habitat destruction to over-harvesting of resources and pollution of the land, sea and air, the built environment has a direct, if not immediate, impact on the world.

The most significant effect is on the climate, primarily through burning fossil fuels and the greenhouse gases this emits. Up to half of these emissions are due to the construction, powering, heating, cooling and demolition of building developments.

Those emissions associated with the construction, refitting and demolition phases are called embodied carbon emissions (after carbon dioxide, one of the main gases involved) and those associated with running the building are operational carbon emissions.

Fortunately, through the work of the United Nations, people around the world, from consumers to political leaders, are becoming increasingly aware of this. Global trends reveal that buildings and urban developments that address environmental concerns,

particularly through energy and water efficiency, are increasing in demand over those that don't.

Even so, only around 10% of new developments are designed with sustainability in mind, and thus many countries are improving their building and development control legislation to require more stringent environmental performance standards. Additionally, eco-town type projects are being conceived to provide leadership, education, experience and to set the right example.

Atkins' test rig is set up on the roof of its Middle East head office to monitor a number of manufacturers' and technologists' photovoltaic (PV) panels, providing groundbreaking research into the performance of solar panels in the Middle East.

... and the benefits

The typical response from responsible design professionals in the built environment industry is to design 'sustainably', or at least in a way that is environmentally benign. Such a building and its infrastructure will be designed to take advantage of its local environment to provide comfortable conditions and to minimise its energy and water consumption. It will be efficient to heat, cool, light and operate. It will make sparing use of materials, and these materials will come from local sustainable sources that have low embodied energy, do not release toxins and can be recycled or reused. It will not pollute, nor will it adversely affect local flora and fauna. Indeed it will restore the biodiversity that was lost as a consequence of the development taking place.

The next step, and one that we strive for, is to design buildings and urban environments not only to be benign but to make a positive contribution. These living buildings restore the environment by cleaning and replenishing local water supplies, enhancing local habitats, absorbing CO_2 and, in the best cases, producing excess clean energy for use elsewhere.

And they give back to the people who use them. They speak to our inherent connection with the local culture and the natural world because we are, and always have been, a part of it. Whether it is through indirect reminders, such as organic forms, fractal patterns or enticing streetscapes that encourage us to explore, or more direct reminders such as gardens, water, natural light and fresh air, a development designed to be sustainable will be a pleasing, changing, invigorating and healthy place. It will positively stimulate the human sensory system and help improve quality of life.

The many 'live, work and play' communities within the new eco-towns cut down on the need for personal transit and, through their particular identity, character and charm, build stronger social structures. In the same way, energy and water engineering is devolving to a community level where heat and electricity is generated locally and used to power buildings and industries in the immediate vicinity, without costly transmission losses.

Heating, cooling and power generation processes are being integrated to maximise efficiency, and then further integrated with liquid and solid waste treatment processes to generate electricity. The waste from one process becomes the nutrient for the next: we call this 'community integrated energy and water' and in the future it wll be combined with smart electrical grids, renewable micro-generation and large-scale renewables to provide a holistic solution with a fraction of today's carbon footprint.

Environmentally successful and socially successful, a truly sustainable design is also (despite general misapprehension) affordable: if not immediately cheaper than 'business as usual' (and the evidence is that it generally IS cheaper, due to passive design, infrastructure with reduced capacity and other synergies), then always affordable in terms of through-life cost and added value. The question, then, is what is most important? Cost? People? The environment? Or a combination of all three?

Environmental
Visible natural environments on which we depend

Sustainable natural & built environment

Sustainable economic development

Social
Nurture communities that nuture your business

Equitable social ecology

Economic
Sufficient income, strong brand and reliable relationships

Getting the balance right

In this context, we believe the most important design considerations are the following:

- **Carbon Emission Minimisation** – embodied and operational;

- **Waste** – during manufacture, construction, operation, end of life and as a fuel;

- **Materials** – sustainable sources, durability, environmental toxicity, locality, recylability;

- **Water** – efficient sourcing and use, reuse, pollution and contamination control;

- **Site and Habitat** – site selection, local habitat and biodiversity;

- **Indoor Environmental Quality** – thermal comfort, air quality, odours, lighting, acoustics;

- **Human Experience** – health, happiness, inclusiveness, connection with nature, culture;

- **Local Community** – access to amenities, social integration, enrichment of life, freedom from imperative to travel;

- **Economics** – first cost, whole life cost, whole life value, return on investment, relative performance, wealth and job creation.

Aside from carbon emissions, this list is in no particular order; the relative importance of each item will change for every development, depending on local conditions, client needs and building function, but they are interlinked. Construction materials, for example, need to be selected based on cost and availability, as well as embodied carbon, opportunities for reuse or recycling, and the environmental impact of their manufacture.

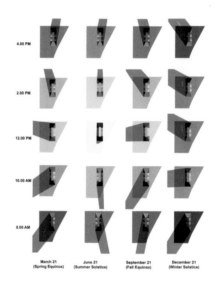

4.00 PM			
2.00 PM			
12.00 PM			
10.00 AM			
8.00 AM			

| March 21 (Spring Equinox) | June 21 (Summer Solstice) | September 21 (Fall Equinox) | December 21 (Winter Solstice) |

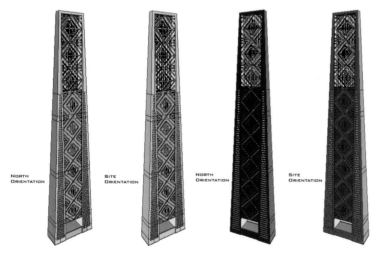

NORTH ORIENTATION   SITE ORIENTATION   NORTH ORIENTATION   SITE ORIENTATION

Wh/m2
1100000+
1030000
960000
890000
820000
750000
680000
610000
540000
470000
400000

In setting a new benchmark for Dubai, the DIFC Lighthouse Tower aspires to be a LEED Platinum-rated, low-carbon commercial building. Atkins was commissioned to carry out a separate sustainability design study to identify innovative ways of achieving this goal. Design provisions include passive solar architecture, many low-energy, low-water engineering solutions, recovery strategies for both energy and water, and integrated renewables (including PV panels) within the façade.

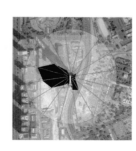

THE DIFC LIGHTHOUSE TOWER, DESIGNED BY ATKINS, IS SET TO BE DUBAI'S FIRST LOW CARBON COMMERCIAL TOWER, AIMING TO REDUCE ITS TOTAL ENERGY CONSUMPTION BY UP TO 50% AND WATER CONSUMPTION BY UP TO 40%, COMPARED TO A TYPICAL DUBAI DESIGN.

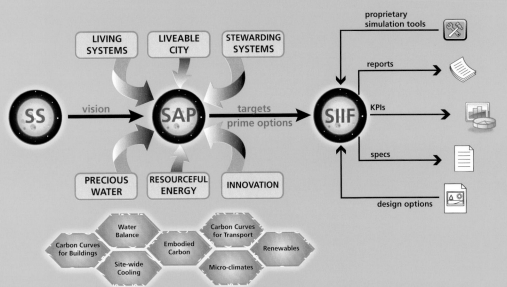

There is no standard formula that defines the sustainability design criteria for a project. Every project is different, and so the bias and depth of the sustainability measures have first to be agreed upon. To achieve this, Atkins starts the design process with a sustainability design workshop with key stakeholders to ascertain the sustainability balance for the project.

This is developed into a **"Sustainability Strategy" (SS),** which defines the vision, ensures common understanding of the aims throughout the design team and provides an assessment standard for all major decisions in the design process.

From this a **"Sustainability Action Plan" (SAP)** is created. Essentially this is an expanded set of key performance indicators (KPIs) with targets that, if met by the design and construction team, will result in the achievement of the sustainablity strategy.

Finally, a **"Sustainability Identification and Implementation Framework" (SIIF)** is set up. The SIIF identifies the many design options that are possible and, through its management processes, ensures that they are properly assessed from a 'sustainability' perspective, along with other criteria such as first cost, through-life cost, buildability, programme and aesthetics.

The SIIF provides a number of output reports, ranging from design team performance with respect to SAP targets to high-level specifications for sustainable solutions.

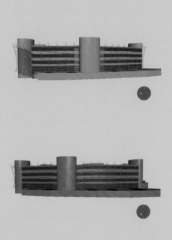

The unique form of the new Law, Business and Design School at Northumbria University City Campus East incorporates an intelligent double skin, comprising solar *brise soleil* shading and solar collectors. These shield the building from 50% of the sun's radiation, optimising natural daylight while capturing solar energy to heat water for the building.

Atkins sustainability and Carbon Critical Design™

In 1987, Gro Harlem Brundtland, in her report *Our Common Future*, defined the concept of sustainable development and brought to the world's attention the urgent need to address this issue. Since that date, Atkins has developed and retained expertise in this field. Aside from experts in both building and holistic urban sustainability, Atkins has over 1,000 staff who have sustainable design expertise as their specialism. This community has collaborated using a virtual network called SusNET for the last decade.

However, producing and delivering integrated and holistic sustainable solutions for built environment projects is difficult because of the many interdependent and often confrontational issues that face design teams and stakeholders. There have of course been notable successes, but in general the construction industry has been unable to deliver sustainable solutions as a matter of course due to the complexity of social networks and technical integration challenges.

Atkins accepts that the single most important issue facing the construction industry today is the need to reduce greenhouse gas emissions to prevent excessive climate change, and recognises that the design of the built environment plays a pivotal role in this. When faced with the decision to either strengthen its capability to design all projects sustainably or find an alternative and more pragmatic route, Atkins has chosen the latter. This is because the rate of improvement in sustainable design proficiency is low, due to its complexity and the behavioural changes it needs, and is not on the same timeline as that being set by the climate change agenda. In short, we will not get there in time.

Atkins has identified all those components of sustainable design that are in some way connected with greenhouse gas emissions and climate change, and has separated them into a new design layer called 'Carbon Critical Design™'. Compared to the complicated, interactive multiple layers of sustainable design, Carbon Critical Design™, while quite complex in itself, is manageable and something that the construction industry can modify design methods and products to reflect.

Atkins embarked on a 'hundred week journey' to Carbon Critical Design™. This programme, aimed at all staff, was devised to raise awareness, provide training, develop 'carbon tools', provide knowledge transfer and to engage clients. It created an environment in which designers and stakeholders are able to collaborate and produce carbon critical designs for every project.

Developing tools for a low-carbon future

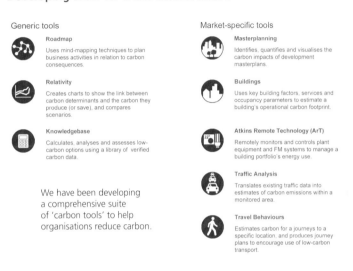

Generic tools

Roadmap
Uses mind-mapping techniques to plan business activities in relation to carbon consequences.

Relativity
Creates charts to show the link between carbon determinants and the carbon they produce (or save), and compares scenarios.

Knowledgebase
Calculates, analyses and assesses low-carbon options using a library of verified carbon data.

We have been developing a comprehensive suite of 'carbon tools' to help organisations reduce carbon.

Market-specific tools

Masterplanning
Identifies, quantifies and visualises the carbon impacts of development masterplans.

Buildings
Uses key building factors, services and occupancy parameters to estimate a building's operational carbon footprint.

Atkins Remote Technology (ArT)
Remotely monitors and controls plant equipment and FM systems to manage a building portfolio's energy use.

Traffic Analysis
Translates existing traffic data into estimates of carbon emissions within a monitored area.

Travel Behaviours
Estimates carbon for a journeys to a specific location, and produces journey plans to encourage use of low-carbon transport.

Atkins now has a series of leading-edge 'carbon tools', all with outputs calibrated in carbon emissions and designed by designers, for designers. They have a pragmatic structure that makes them intuitive and the design tools of choice. They are largely used at the planning stage of projects to ensure that designs start off in the right direction, avoiding potential disappointment, when final solutions are simulated or constructed, with performance compared to original targets.

Where do the tools fit?

	Business planning	Planning and conceptual design	Detailed design	Build and deliver	Operate and maintain	Decommission and replace
	Alternative terminology from the delivery phases of market-specific lifecycle processes such as GRIP, RIBA, CADMID, MADMIT, HA Major Projects Life cycles, etc	• Appraisal • Design brief • Concept • Design development • Pre-feasibility • Option selection	• Technical design • Production information • Assessment and demonstration	• Mobilisation • Construction to practical completion • Construction test and commission • Manufacture	• Asset operation • In-service • Migration	• Shutdown • Disposal • Termination
Roadmap (Generic tools)						
Relativity						
Knowledgebase						
Masterplanning (Market-specific tools)						
Buildings						
Atkins Remote Technology						
Traffic analysis						
Travel behaviours						

Primary purpose
Secondary benefits

We designed the tools to provide complete coverage of the client's project delivery process.

A carbon critical initiative does not cancel allegiance to sustainability; indeed it provides a good foundation upon which sustainability may flourish and should be seen as a bridging initiative to address climate change. Carbon Critical Design™ directly reflects the policies of the governments in most of the world's developed countries, whose bias is shifting towards addressing climate change.

Design hierarchy

To manage operational carbon emissions, Atkins' approach to design, while very integrated as a consequence of a multidisciplinary team configuration and operational ethos, follows a hierarchy that focuses first on passive design before focussing on improving the efficiency of systems. Then it considers the recovery of energy and water.

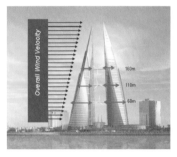

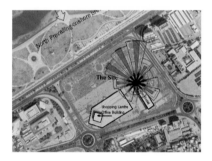

embodied carbon and provide spin-off benefits for operational carbon.

These design systems deal with carbon emissions that have become the first measure of design success, followed by quality of life and value – neither of which should be compromised by the approach to the first. By adopting the carbon emissions hierarchy and combining it with community integrated energy and water, overall construction costs tend to reduce, as sustainably designed buildings require

less utility infrastructure to service them and being optimally designed, minimal solutions can prevail.

Beyond that, options based on whole-life costs are assessed, considering operational, maintenance and replacement costs, as well as the initial construction cost. By incorporating revenue from emerging carbon emission reduction incentives, where available, the client can save significant expenditure in comparison to a business-as-usual design.

Operational Emissions Hierarchy

Once a development's operational carbon footprint has been minimised, the team considers how to go beyond low impact to positive impact, and considers renewal: renewable energy, aquifer recharge and so forth.

As developments become more efficient in operational carbon terms, embodied carbon emissions are proportionally increasing and receiving far more attention. Atkins' design approach to these is again four-fold, but not sequential. The criteria it uses to guide a design are 'minimal + local + durable + recoverable'. Careful application of these in the right balance will significantly reduce

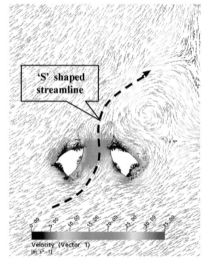

The Bahrain World Trade Center is the world's first example of large-scale integrated wind turbines on a commercial building.

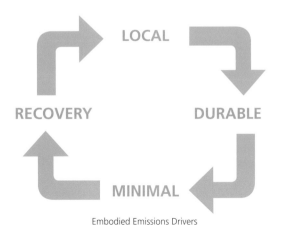

Embodied Emissions Drivers

Atkins architects and engineers undertook months of meticulous research, including extensive dialogue with specialist turbine manufacturers during the concept feasibility study and design development stages. Technical validation included the incorporation of environmentally responsive design elements, different wind regime analysis of turbine performance and SARM analysis. Results from the simulation modelling yielded the production of the final design.

Tools of the trade

Atkins has a dedicated team specialising in advanced building physics and predictive simulation of buildings. This involves building virtual prototypes of buildings and testing their performance, and the performance of their systems, under a range of climatic conditions (typically using real weather data).

From daylight levels and glare to thermal comfort both inside and out, from energy consumption to carbon impact, Atkins optimises designs based on reliable data and a rational and auditable process.

Atkins Carbon Critical Building tool is used to execute carbon emission modelling during the initial stages of the design process.

Assessment methods

Since the early 1990s, Atkins has been involved in the development of many buildings and the development of environmental assessment methods, and this continues.

Beyond development, Atkins also has many trained professionals in the various building rating systems in use around the world, including LEED accredited professionals, BREEAM, BREEAM Gulf and BREEAM healthcare assessors. We have similar credentials with CEEQUAL for civil engineering and public-realm-based projects.

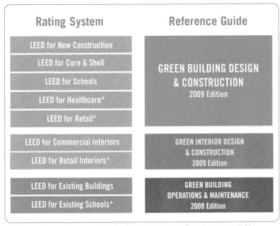

Rating System	Reference Guide
LEED for New Construction	
LEED for Core & Shell	GREEN BUILDING DESIGN & CONSTRUCTION 2009 Edition
LEED for Schools	
LEED for Healthcare*	
LEED for Retail*	
LEED for Commercial Interiors	GREEN INTERIOR DESIGN & CONSTRUCTION 2009 Edition
LEED for Retail Interiors*	
LEED for Existing Buildings	GREEN BUILDING OPERATIONS & MAINTENANCE 2009 Edition
LEED for Existing Schools*	

* These rating systems are under development or in pilot. Once they are available supplements will be sold for the new LEED 2009 Reference Guides.

How to design a carbon critical building

So what is a carbon critical building?

Buildings consume energy and water and are constructed or altered from materials that have to be sourced, processed, shipped, assembled and eventually demolished and disposed of, or recycled. Some buildings generate power in the form of heat or electricity from renewable energy sources that are integrated into them. All of these processes can be measured by assessment of carbon emissions.

Energy and water consumption are connected with the operation of a building and the associated carbon emissions are known as 'operational emissions'. The energy consumed during the life cycle of materials, along with chemical reactions such as the curing of concrete, produce carbon emissions and these are known as 'embodied emissions'. Typically operational emissions outnumber embodied emissions by about five to one, so most designers and regulatory authorities are concentrating on the reduction of operational emissions as the first priority.

A 'carbon critical building' is one that has lower life cycle carbon emissions when compared with local design practice, but which in achieving this does not compromise quality of life or value.

For operational emission reduction, the first objective is to design and orient a building envelope such that heat gains and reliance on air conditioning are minimised in summer, winter solar gains provide beneficial heating in cooler climes and daylighting opportunities are maximised, but not at the cost of more cooling or heating. The second objective is to design buildings and their systems to be more efficient, so that they demand less energy and water. The third objective is to take advantage of opportunities to recover energy and water. By incorporating these three elements a building's operational carbon emissions can be reduced significantly.

Embodied carbon emissions can be reduced by favouring local materials, through the selection of more durable materials, by using fewer materials, by choosing low carbon materials, by minimising waste and by paying attention to reuse and recycling. Some natural materials such as timber have absorbed CO_2 during their growth period and as such have carbon emissions locked in them, making them carbon negative.

Offsetting allows us to further reduce our carbon critical building's emissions. This includes initiatives such as integrated or remote renewable energy sources and other allowable measures such as the sponsoring of energy and water efficiency programmes in adjacent developments. Zero carbon buildings are those where all building emissions are offset.

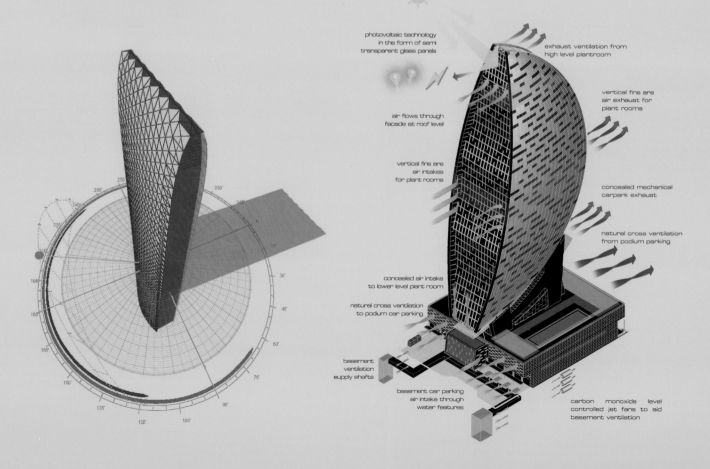

photovoltaic technology
in the form of semi
transparent glass panels

exhaust ventilation from
high level plantroom

air flows through
facade at roof level

vertical fins are
air exhaust for
plant rooms

vertical fins are
air intakes
for plant rooms

concealed mechanical
carpark exhaust

natural cross ventilation
from podium parking

concealed air intake
to lower level plant room

natural cross ventilation
to podium car parking

basement
ventilation
supply shafts

basement car parking
air intake through
water features

carbon monoxide level
controlled jet fans to aid
basement ventilation

Measuring a carbon critical building

By their very nature, carbon critical buildings tend to aspire to the broader values of sustainability, and as such we use three primary KPIs to assess them:

1. Annualised carbon emissions
2. Building environmental assessment method (BEAM) rating
3. Value

Carbon emission targets are set in $kgCO_2e/m^2/year$, on the basis of 'operational only' or 'operational and embodied'. Given that the design strategies that flow from the mitigation of emissions can amount to 60% of all sustainable design strategies, it is plain that the first KPI is a good proxy for sustainability. Atkins' engineers measure the efficacy of their design solutions by assessing carbon emissions throughout the design process using the Atkins Carbon Critical Design tools.

There are many BEAMs, such as BREEAM, LEED, Estidama Pearl and Green Star. One is normally selected and Atkins' sustainability consultants work with designers to develop and obtain certification for a solution with the right bias that achieves the target. Particular attention is paid to credits connected with 'quality of life' to ensure these are not compromised by the first KPI.

Value is measured in a number of different ways, starting with construction cost and project whole life cost (WLC), then moving to more holistic methods where true value is assessed in terms of WLC and less tangible factors such as increased business performance, user health and so on. Achieving the optimal value point, and, indeed, the definition of value, varies for each project and requires close stakeholder consultation.

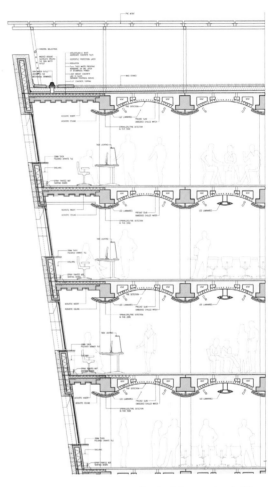

A potential zero carbon building.

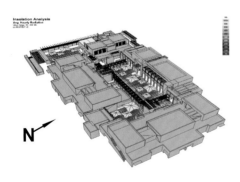

Macro and microclimate studies to optimise design conditions for buildings and microclimates between buildings.

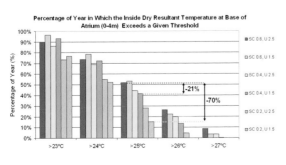

Designing thermal comfort.

Dubai Promenade Hotel.

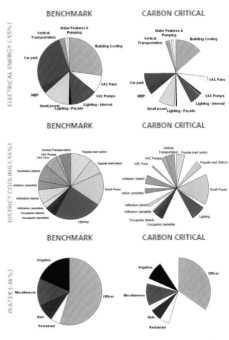

Example of energy and water savings possible with a carbon critical building.

How we design a carbon critical building

The design process flow diagram below shows the carbon critical design model for a low or zero carbon building. It is designed to be integrated into the sustainable design strategy and follows the normal stages of design, but also includes a pre-concept stage in which the SS and SAP are defined and initial design targets set using the Atkins Carbon Critical Design™ and planning tools.

For each design stage the design model considers the passive, efficiency, offsetting and embodied aspects of the Carbon Critical Design™ and indicates the interrelations of the various design tasks with these four aspects. It also considers the broader aspects of sustainability and the building certification process.

The strategy revolves around a robust carbon critical definition in the SAP, the use of carbon critical tools and expert judgment to set achievable design targets at a very early stage in the design process. As the design develops and more detailed analysis is executed, the SAP targets and even the SS can be revisited.

With the conclusion of the concept design stage, a detailed 'basis of design' for the subsequent stages will have been produced, and, given that this is developed from two iterations of the carbon critical tools assessment and a series of engineering and design studies, it will provide a strong foundation for design development.

Shading and solar access studies to optimise solar shading in summer and solar heating in winter.

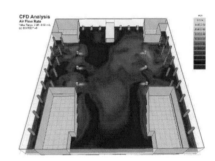

Computational Fluid Dynamic (CFD) studies to simulate and optimise natural and forced air movement and associated thermal conditions.

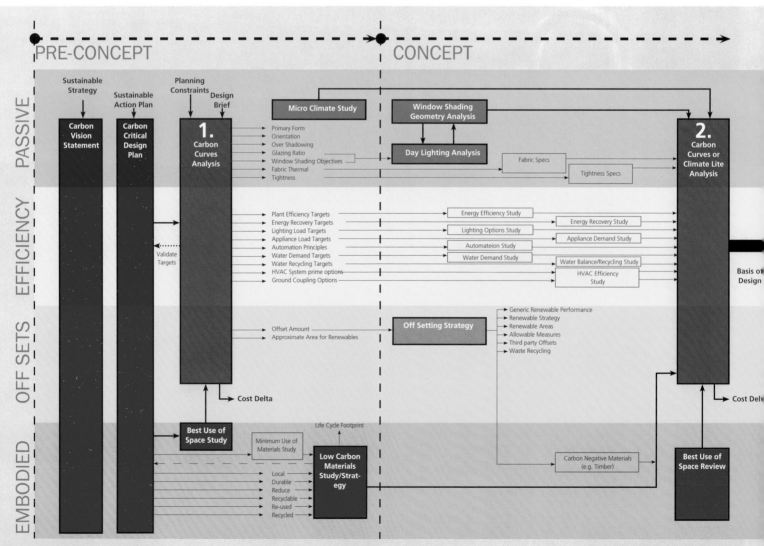

Academia and industry

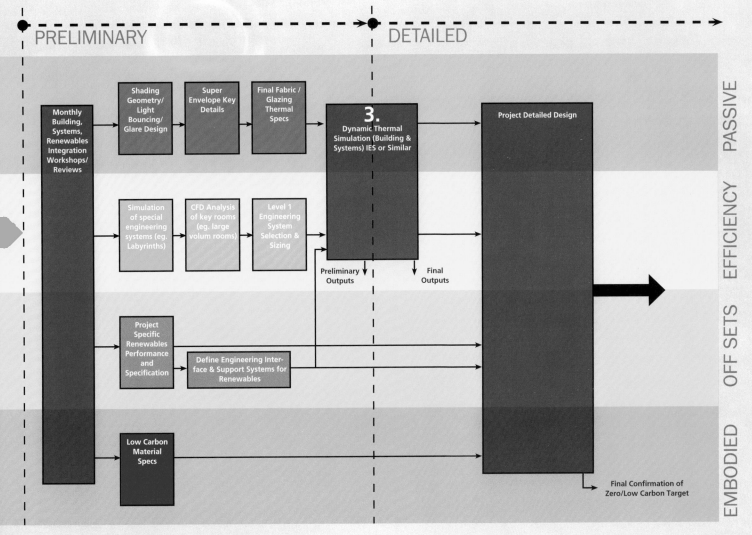

What really sets Atkins apart is its strong links with both academia and industry, providing up-to-date knowledge of the latest technologies, as well as advance details of future initiatives. Atkins has strong ties to Cardiff University, a world leader in sustainable building research; Hong Kong Polytechnic, the developer (with Cardiff University) of Hong Kong's building environmental assessment methodology, HK-BEAM; and the British University in Dubai, where we sponsor the chair and senior lecturer of Sustainable Design of the Built Environment.

A long track record

As well as a corporate philosophy centred on Carbon Critical Design™, expertise in optimising design, numerous 'green building' assessors and strong links with other organisations, Atkins has a long track record of delivering green projects around the world. Examples are summarised in the following chapters of this book.

Solar insolation studies identify key treatment zones and energy harvesting opportunities.

If we had to devise a problem, the complexity and scope of which humankind would find the hardest to address, it would look like **Climate Change**.

Adapting to it is vital, but in particular, the mitigation of damaging greenhouse gases or carbon emissions represents a huge challenge.

With buildings accounting for 45% of all carbon emissions, those involved with building design have to rise to the challenge and develop new ways of working and designing to meet the needs of the future. This has to be substantially underway by 2020 and largely complete by 2050.

In design terms, this is right now, and we have no time left to waste before we embark on the journey. It will not happen by 'just trying harder', or worse still, with only some of us 'just trying harder'.

PRELIMINARY | DETAILED

Monthly Building, Systems, Renewables Integration Workshops/ Reviews

Shading Geometry/ Light Bouncing/ Glare Design → **Super Envelope Key Details** → **Final Fabric / Glazing Thermal Specs** →

3. Dynamic Thermal Simulation (Building & Systems) IES or Similar

Project Detailed Design

Simulation of special engineering systems (eg. Labyrinths) → **CFD Analysis of key rooms (eg. large volum rooms)** → **Level 1 Engineering System Selection & Sizing** →

Preliminary Outputs | Final Outputs

Project Specific Renewables Performance and Specification → **Define Engineering Interface & Support Systems for Renewables**

Low Carbon Material Specs

Final Confirmation of Zero/Low Carbon Target

PASSIVE | EFFICIENCY | OFF SETS | EMBODIED

HOTELS

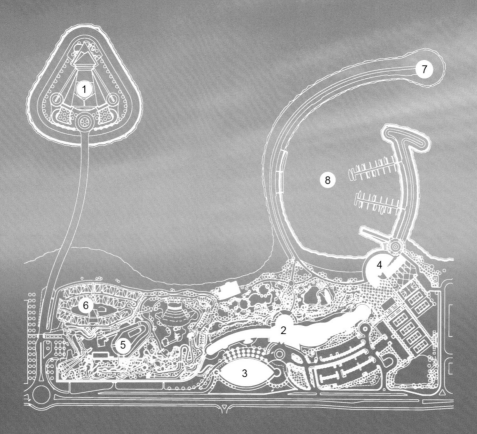

1. Burj Al Arab
2. Jumeirah Beach Hotel
3. Conference Centre
4. Sports Centre
5. Wild Wadi Aqua Park
6. Beit Al Bahar
7. Marina Restaurant
8. Marina

Jumeirah Beach Resort
Dubai, UAE

HOTELS

Client
Confidential

Area
12.25 ha

Type
Masterplan

Status
Complete

Date
1993–1999

Jumeirah Beach Resort is a project of crucial importance to both Atkins and Dubai. Atkins began working on the masterplan of the Jumeirah Beach Resort in 1993 and still maintains an involvement in the project.

The Jumeirah Beach Resort makes a strong statement about the ambitions of Dubai. The Jumeirah Beach Hotel was the first stage of the 12.25 ha development. It opened in 1997 and has since been consistently rated the 'Best Resort Hotel in the World' by *Business Traveller Magazine UK*.

Much féted at the time, it paved the way for the second major hotel on the Jumeirah site, which opened some two years later – the Burj Al Arab.

If the Jumeirah Beach Hotel made Dubai's reputation as an international destination, the Burj Al Arab consolidated it.

Newly arrived visitors can make use of the conference centre, the Wild Wadi Aqua Park, the Beit Al Bahar villas, a sports centre, a world-class marina and the associated restaurants that are all sympathetically integrated into the resort's amenities.

Atkins was responsible for concept through to detailed design for the entire enterprise, coordinating complex programmes and providing imaginative, outstanding solutions to every technical challenge.

Burj Al Arab
Dubai, UAE

HOTELS

Client
Confidential

Area
111,500 m²

Type
321 m, G+56 super
luxury hotel

Status
Complete

Date
1994–1999

The Burj Al Arab is for many people the defining image of Dubai, in much the same way that the Eiffel Tower serves Paris. Each symbolises its city in a way we have come to call 'iconic', even though both were designed well before the word became ubiquitous.

The Burj Al Arab would have been an extraordinary building wherever it had been located, but much of its impact and renown comes from its appearance in the right place at the right time – Dubai 1999.

Its spectacular sailing aesthetic is reflected in its offshore location, and its appearance off the Jumeirah Beach, which has its own outstanding hotel, made the whole Jumeirah Beach complex a destination that no self-respecting world traveller could ignore. Whether one chooses to experience the delights of a stay inside it, or simply to gaze at it from the beach, it has come to define the pinnacle of luxurious world travel and the central role that Dubai plays in that enterprise, both literally and figuratively.

The Burj Al Arab stands on an artificial island 300 m offshore. That location, and the trip across the private bridge to reach it, reinforces the Burj's exclusivity. Furthermore, its true size only becomes apparent as one approaches it. At 321 m, this is the tallest single structure hotel in the world, its 57 storeys providing access to 202 suites.

The alternating bands of deep and pale blue glass each enclose two storeys, reflecting the duplex layout of those suites, but at the same time reducing the visual impact of the height from a distance. All that disappears as one approaches over the bridge, and the blue bands recede behind the magnificent Teflon® sail that seems to billow above the visitor, filling their field of vision with a clean, sharp sculpture in white against the blue Dubai sky and sea. At night an internal lightshow suffuses the sail with colour, producing an equally impressive but quite different spectacle. Arriving at the Burj Al Arab is always an experience.

As well as a unique exterior form, the Burj Al Arab is famous for being the world's first super luxury hotel. At the entrance, one's eye is drawn by installations featuring fire and water in an elegant display before the sheer height of the atrium seduces the attention.

At 182 m it is the world's tallest hotel atrium, and provides the triangular core that is fronted by the translucent sail around which two walls of balconied landings provide access to suites. The two-storey high lobby aquarium extends down into the Al Mahara underwater restaurant, while some 200 m above sea level the Al Muntaha sky view restaurant and the famous helipad are cantilevered out over the waters of the Arabian Gulf.

Part yacht, part building, the Burj Al Arab has stretched perceptions of what a hotel might be. In the process it has helped define Dubai as a centre of luxury and hospitality, and has grown in the affections of the city's inhabitants as a result.

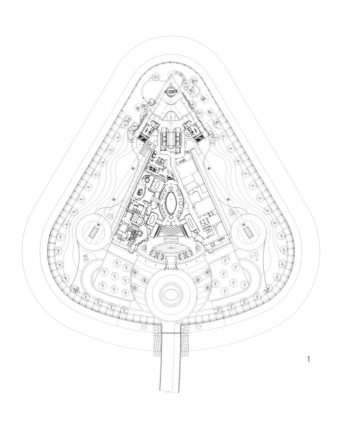

1

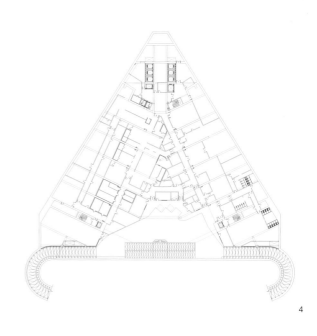

4

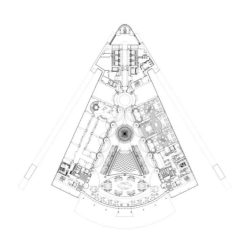

2

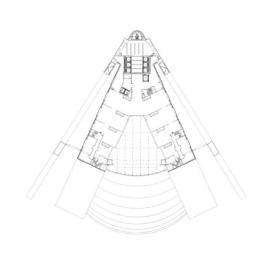

5

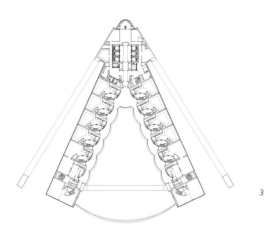

3

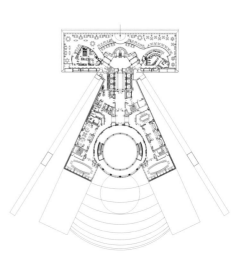

6

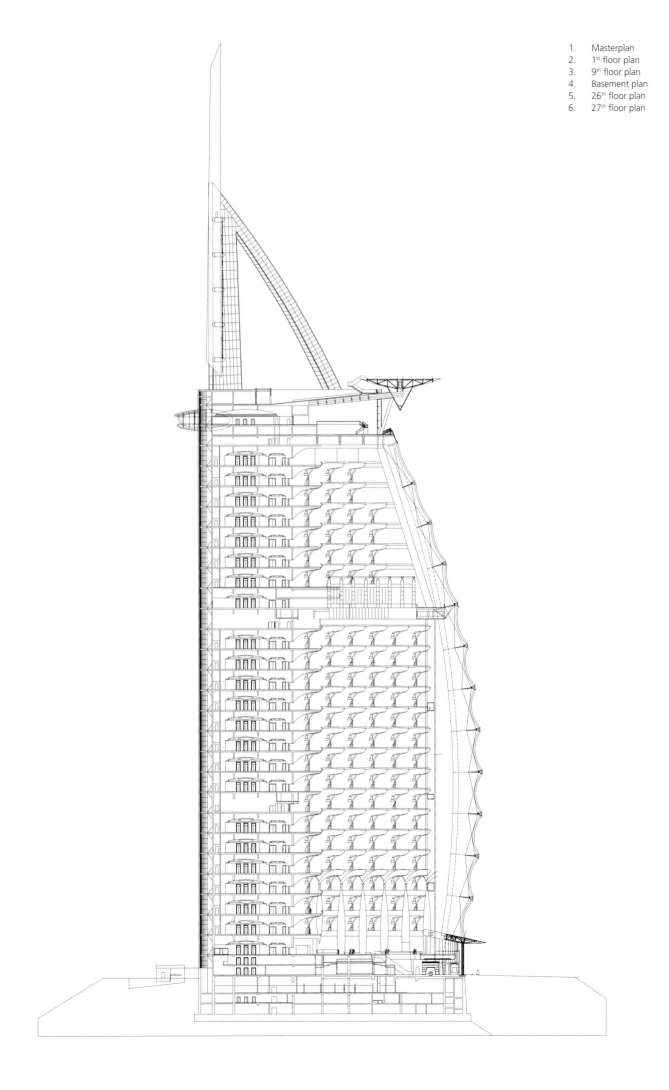

1. Masterplan
2. 1st floor plan
3. 9th floor plan
4. Basement plan
5. 26th floor plan
6. 27th floor plan

Jumeirah Beach Hotel
Dubai, UAE

HOTELS

Client
Confidential

Area
65,000 m²

Type
93 m, G+25
five-star hotel

Status
Complete

Date
1994–1997

The Jumeirah Beach Hotel was the first element of the Jumeirah Beach Resort to be completed, and it marked the beginning of Dubai's economic transformation. The 26-storey, five-star hotel opened in 1997.

Its 600 rooms, 17 bars and restaurants, 2,500 m² conference centre, sports centre and 12 ha of landscaped garden were all completed just two years after the first design proposal.

The hotel adopts the profile of a 93 m high and 275 m long cascading wave, curved in plan and elevation. Its long, layered façades compound the impression of a wave swelling

and breaking, and the double curve of the plan gives the large lobby and restaurant spaces a gentle fluidity. Single-sided corridors follow this curve along the east elevation, enabling all rooms to have sunset views over the ocean.

Embedded value such as this makes the Jumeirah Beach Hotel a classic resort hotel, which even 10 years on is consistently ranked by *Business Traveller Magazine UK* as the 'Best Resort Hotel in the World'. The hotel's appeal extends beyond the tourist sector – its restaurants, bars, beach and gardens are all well-frequented by Dubai residents.

The plan of the
Jumeirah Beach Hotel,
like its overall mass,
is designed to evoke
the sweep of a wave.

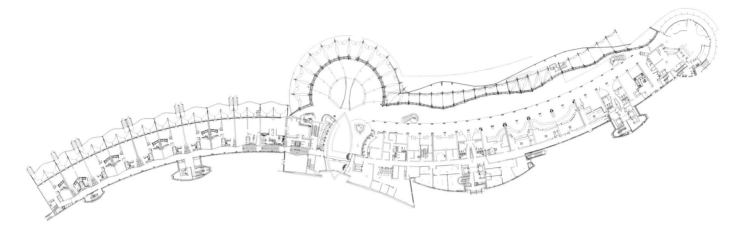

Ground floor plan

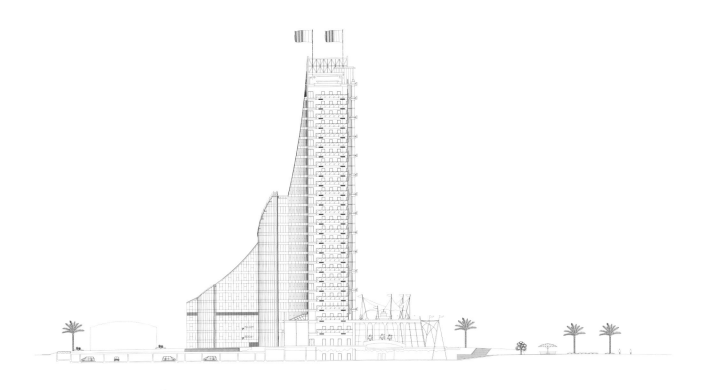

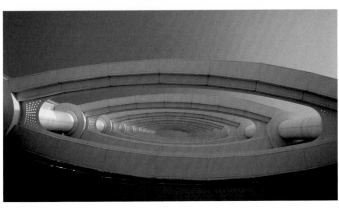

Beit Al Bahar
Dubai, UAE

HOTELS

Client
Confidential

Area
48,500 m²

Type
19 Arabian-style villas

Status
Complete

Date
1997–1999

Inspired by the vernacular architecture, these 19 Arabian-style villas are integrated into the landscape of the Jumeirah Beach Hotel and form a buffer between the noise and excitement of the Wild Wadi Aqua Park to the east and the tranquillity of the beach and the Burj Al Arab to the west.

The Arabian aspect of the villas is evident in their private and inward-looking plans, organised behind high walls around shaded courtyards and lofty main rooms. Narrow streets linking the villas converge at a central 'oasis' with a sparkling pool.

Local craftsmen were employed to recreate the details and motifs of indigenous architecture, although the technology and construction techniques used were decidedly modern. Arabian interiors are not dependent upon luxurious finishes or textures. The rooms at Beit Al Bahar need only a minimum of furniture and a few soft furnishings such as rugs, cushions and wall hangings to feel complete.

Beach Front Hotel
Dubai, UAE

The Beach Front Hotel occupies a key site at the southern tip of the Dubai Marina and is bounded on three sides by water, like the Dubai Promenade that occupies the complementary position at the north end of the marina. The high-quality hotel and serviced apartments and their related leisure and hospitality facilities align with different aspects of the site.

The 302 m tower comprises 60 levels of luxurious guest rooms, serviced apartments, royal suites, presidential suites and triplex apartments. It faces the sea to the west and the desert to the east. Balconies look north and south along the coast.

The tower half rests on a six-storey podium formed of three truncated elliptical volumes. The lowest volume houses the all-day restaurant and fronts a promenade that borders the marina entrance canal to the south.

A second space above this houses the hotel lobby, speciality restaurants and other hotel areas, and faces north towards the marina itself. A grandstand-like space overlooking the Arabian Gulf is carved out of its western end where a third elliptical volume housing a spa intersects it. The eastern end is truncated to create a drop-off zone and entrance canopy.

The external treatment of the main, framed façades is intended to suggest gently curving glazed surfaces that have been broken and the remaining pieces fused together to create a complex, textured shell. In both form and finish the Beach Front Hotel has been designed to make the most of its spectacular site.

HOTELS

Client
Confidential

Area
134,200 m²

Type
302 m, five-star hotel and serviced apartments

Status
Design

Date
2006–ongoing

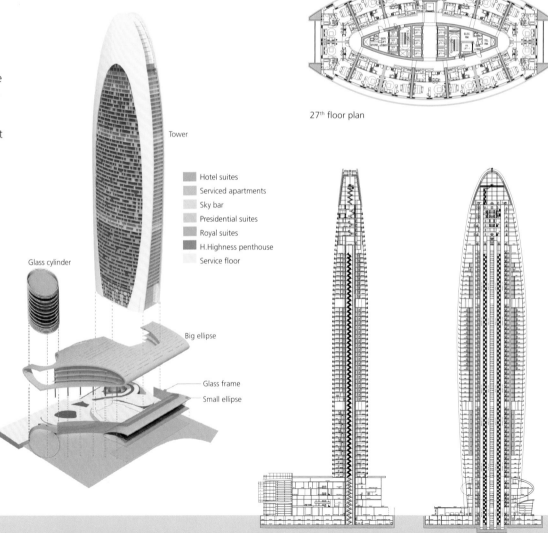

27th floor plan

Tower

Glass cylinder

Big ellipse

Glass frame

Small ellipse

Hotel suites
Serviced apartments
Sky bar
Presidential suites
Royal suites
H.Highness penthouse
Service floor

Barr Al Jissah Resort and Spa
Barr Al Jissah, Oman

HOTELS

Client
Zubair Corporation

Area
73,000 m²

Type
Three hotels, spa and
heritage centre

Status
Complete

Date
2001–2005

The Barr Al Jissah Resort and Spa is situated in an isolated cove 12 km south of Muscat on the Quriyat coast. Encircled by spectacular terrain, the development enjoys a sea-shore setting on a geologically fascinating coastline.

The site was previously inaccessible by car; now a 4 km access road (designed by Atkins) snakes along the wadi beds and cuts through the jebel before descending to a sheltered bay edged by three new hotels, a spa and a heritage centre.

The design of the hotels was developed from an initial concept produced by Wimberly Allison Tong & Goo and Derek Lovejoy Partnership, and draws heavily upon the vernacular architecture of Oman as expressed in traditional dwellings, forts and souks. Atkins embraced the concept wholeheartedly, and took the project through detailed design and construction supervision to completion, with the involvement of its engineering, marine, roads, ecology and other divisions. The project proved to be a fine example of the advantages obtained through the engagement of a single multidisciplinary consultancy.

The interior design incorporates indigenous details, colours and artefacts, and provides all the amenities demanded of five-star accommodation. The sparseness of the interiors is modern in concept, but not aggressively so. The use of colour and pattern softens the sharp edges of the design, providing a welcoming and exotic atmosphere but avoiding pastiche or parody.

Barr Al Jissah Resort and Spa nestles comfortably into the magnificent coastline of Oman, creating a feeling of security and comfort that is entirely appropriate to a hideaway resort hotel.

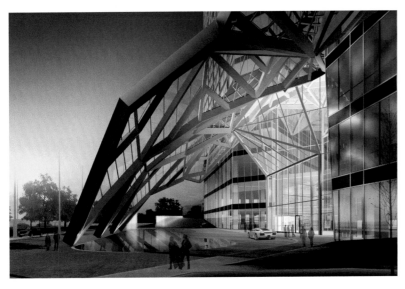

Chengdu Hilton Hotel
Chengdu, China

HOTELS

Client
Chengdu Hilton
Development Co.Ltd

Area
205,000 m²

Type
Hotel, office and
apartment tower

Status
Design

Date
2008–2011

The design treats the three independent components of hotel, office and apartments as a single sculptural composition. Three towers of equal height with triangular plan forms and chamfered top planes are arranged on the rectangular site in the new south exhibition and conference district, just outside Chengdu's third ring road.

The symmetrical hotel and serviced apartment towers face the main road to the east. The larger plan office tower sits behind, facing the apex of the space formed by the other two structures. Such symmetrical arrangements are not uncommon in China, as they project a great formality and presence to the city.

On the main street façade a dramatic crystalline canopy marks the entrance to a lobby that extends organically at ground level into the space connecting the three towers.

Above this lobby are two linear zones of landscaping that provide a peaceful garden, an area for relaxation and convivial meeting spaces shared by the occupants of the three towers.

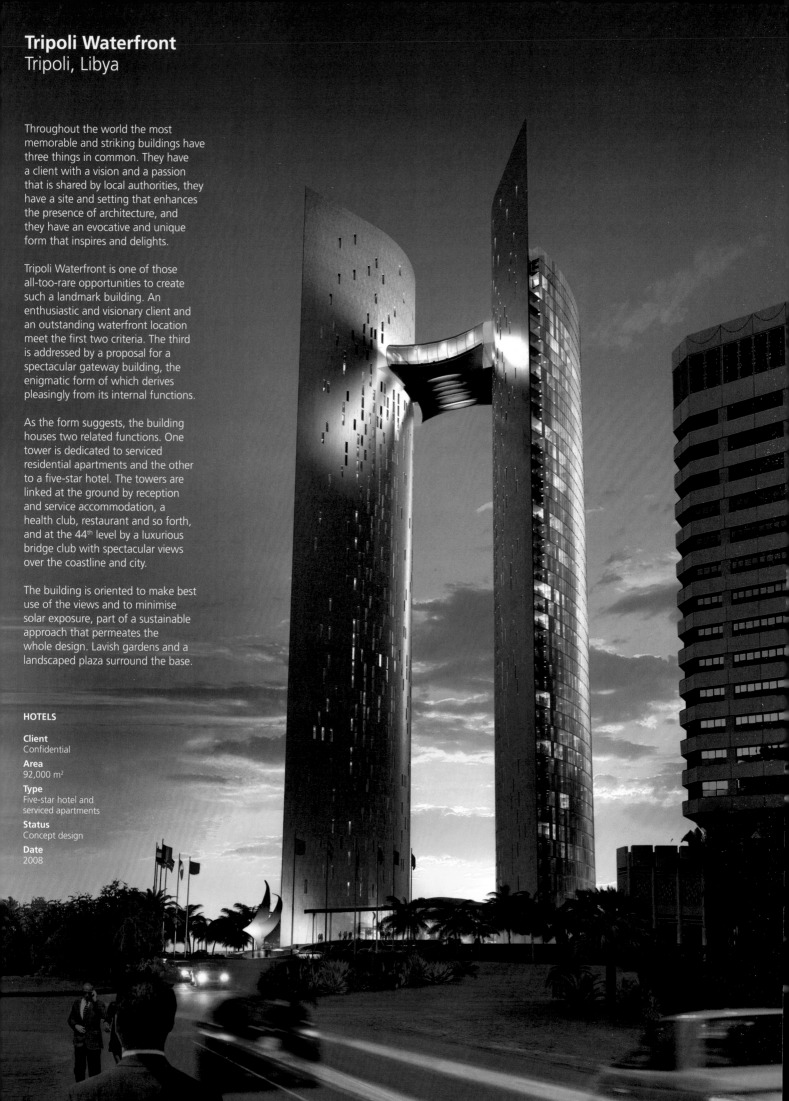

Tripoli Waterfront
Tripoli, Libya

Throughout the world the most memorable and striking buildings have three things in common. They have a client with a vision and a passion that is shared by local authorities, they have a site and setting that enhances the presence of architecture, and they have an evocative and unique form that inspires and delights.

Tripoli Waterfront is one of those all-too-rare opportunities to create such a landmark building. An enthusiastic and visionary client and an outstanding waterfront location meet the first two criteria. The third is addressed by a proposal for a spectacular gateway building, the enigmatic form of which derives pleasingly from its internal functions.

As the form suggests, the building houses two related functions. One tower is dedicated to serviced residential apartments and the other to a five-star hotel. The towers are linked at the ground by reception and service accommodation, a health club, restaurant and so forth, and at the 44th level by a luxurious bridge club with spectacular views over the coastline and city.

The building is oriented to make best use of the views and to minimise solar exposure, part of a sustainable approach that permeates the whole design. Lavish gardens and a landscaped plaza surround the base.

HOTELS

Client
Confidential

Area
92,000 m²

Type
Five-star hotel and
serviced apartments

Status
Concept design

Date
2008

Twisting Tower
Arabian Gulf

HOTELS

Client
Confidential

Area
58,200 m²

Type
53-storey hotel

Status
Concept

Date
2004

The inspiration for the Twisting Tower was the architect's observation of the dynamics of a water spiral. The concept is translated into triangular floor plates that rotate around a central, full-height circulation core that is stiffened with horizontal fins to resist torsional forces.

The floor plates shift just 2.264° at each level, exposing and creating a curving, twisting façade. The external surface of the tower is conceptualised as a fluid glass skin, and the structural curtain wall system employs a diagrid of diamond and triangular shaped glass panels to resolve these small, rigid elements into a flowing glass curtain.

The result is a sensual curved 53-storey skyscraper that rotates 120° from base to summit, catching and reflecting the changing light in myriad pinpoint highlights.

A SIMPLE START - NO TWIST IN THE TAIL

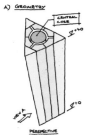

SPIRALLING IN CONTROL

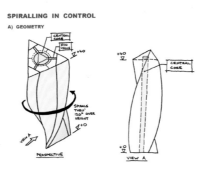

VISUAL IMPACT

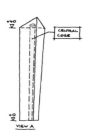
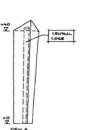

THE IMPACT OF TWIST

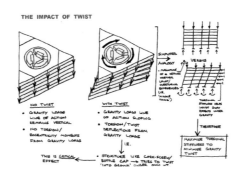

Shanghai Harbour City Crowne Plaza Hotel
Lin Gang New Town, China

HOTELS

Client
Shanghai Gang
Cheng Development
Corporation

Area
67,350 m²

Type
355-bed five-star
business and resort
hotel located on an
island

Status
Under construction

Date
2006–2011

The concept for the low-rise, 355-bed Shanghai Harbour City Crowne Plaza Hotel was developed from the award-winning masterplan that Atkins proposed for its location, Lin Gang New Town, near Shanghai. Resting on an island in a 500 ha circular lake at the centre of the new town, the design is both simple and striking, and within the 15 m height limit stipulated by the planning guidelines.

The flower-inspired plan provides a very pragmatic hotel layout in the form of a central dome connected to five petal-shaped wings containing hotel rooms, restaurants and meeting rooms. The simple geometry allows all rooms to have unobstructed views of the lake. Atriums, designed as themed gardens, efficiently illuminate and ventilate the split central corridors leading to the rooms.

The areas between the wings provide sheltered spaces for gardens, pools and sports grounds, while a low building connecting the conference and dining wings provides service and kitchen accommodation. Separate buildings house a small marina and clubhouse, while children's playgrounds, gardens and a golf course add to the attractions of this island resort.

The external walls are of natural timber, harmonising with the lush landscaping, while the many angles and gentle curves of the zinc roof serve to catch the eye with an attractive glitter when glimpsed from the shoreline.

Zhanjiang Minda Hotel
Zhanjiang, China

HOTELS

Client
Guandong Minda
Investment Group

Area
206,500 m²

Type
Hotel and offices

Status
Under construction

Date
2007–2011

Situated on the subtropical shore of the South China Seas, close to the Leizhou peninsula, this site lies between Zhanjiang's major thoroughfare and the beach. With a southeasterly outlook towards a sheltered bay lined with coastal parks and sandy beaches, the plot bisects a 50 m wide green urban axis radiating from the new civic centre.

The proposal incorporates three buildings: a hotel tower, an office tower and a dormitory unit for hotel staff. These have been carefully oriented to make the best use of the spectacular views on offer.

Tower A houses the 537-key Sheraton hotel atop a podium containing a 1,200-seat banquet hall, restaurants, bars and reception areas. Tower B accommodates high-grade office space above a podium of entertainment spaces.

The towers are splayed on plan, and the rooms within each are rotated 30° off axis, giving every room a splendid, unique view of the bay.

Slightly offsetting the floor plans up and down the towers creates a ridged, curving profile that calls seashells to mind, and the crown of sail-like tensile structures sheltering the terraced suites completes the nautical theme.

The plan reveals the splay between the two blocks designed to provide all rooms with a sea view.

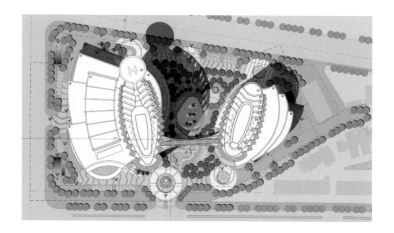

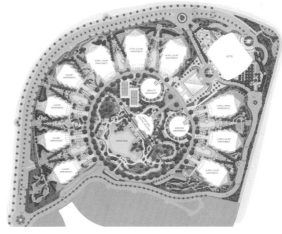

Grand royal suite plan

Regatta Arch Hotel
Jakarta, Indonesia

HOTELS

Client
Badan Kerjasama
Mutiara Buana

Area
376,550 m²

Type
Five-star hotel and
10 luxury apartment
towers

Status
Under construction

Date
2004–2010

The Pantai Mutiara development is a mixed-use residential hotel and leisure complex, destined to become a landmark development on the shores of the Java Sea. The masterplan of the 11 ha complex is based on a compass rose with the elements dispersed in radial fashion around a landscaped podium.

The focus is the Regatta Arch Hotel, which has a unique form resembling a folded tube. Clothed in a smooth, reflective skin of glass, it is topped with a 2,000 m² sky-venue at the summit. Ten fully serviced luxury apartment blocks flank the arch.

The inspiration for the design is a fleet of ships with billowing sails, evoking memories of the local vessels that once plied the Java Sea or massed at Ujung Pandang harbour in Sulawesi, the centre of the spice trade. At the heart of the development is a 2.5 ha, lushly landscaped water park.

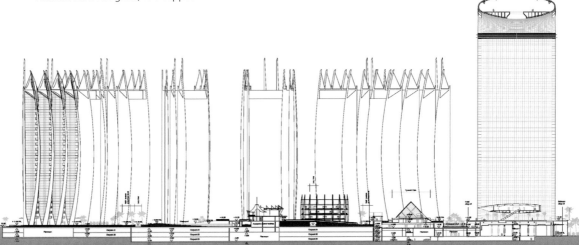

Shimao Wonderland Intercontinental
Sonjiang, China

HOTELS

Client
Shanghai Shimao
New Experience
Development

Area
49,409 m²

Type
Futuristic five-star
hotel built on the
side of an abandoned
water-filled quarry

Status
Under construction

Date
2005–2013

This competition-winning design for a 388-key five-star resort and business hotel is set within a water-filled quarry in Songjiang district, close to Shanghai.

The quarry and hotel combine to form an integrated whole where, governed by restrictions on building height, the hotel's 17 storeys only occupy two levels above ground and barely intrude upon the natural beauty for which the area is famous.

At ground level, the grass-roofed podium houses hotel and conference centre entrances that lead to a glass-clad 'river'. This eventually turns into a vertical circulation 'waterfall' that cascades down the 80 m deep quarry, giving access to the panoramic guest rooms and naturally lit internal atria contained in adjacent curved wings.

A gym centre, swimming pool and spa, restaurants and cafés, a banqueting centre and conference facilities for up to 1,000 people are located at water level. At the lowest point, two levels of rooms are submerged, offering guests a spectacular view into what is in effect a natural fresh-water aquarium.

An extreme sports centre for activities such as rock climbing and bungee jumping will be cantilevered over the quarry, with access by special lifts.

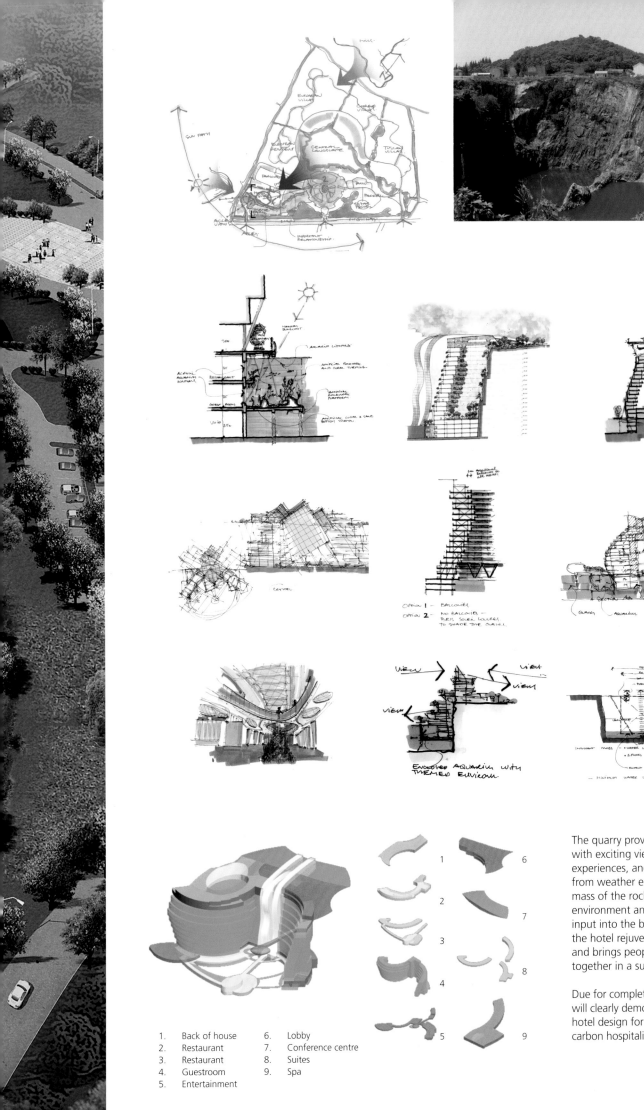

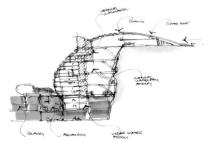

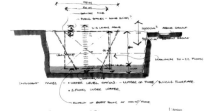

The quarry provides guests and visitors with exciting views, activities and experiences, and protects the hotel from weather extremes. The thermal mass of the rock stabilises the hotel environment and reduces energy input into the building. In return, the hotel rejuvenates the quarry and brings people and environment together in a sustainable relationship.

Due for completion in 2013, this project will clearly demonstrate sustainable hotel design for the emerging low-carbon hospitality programme in China.

1. Back of house
2. Restaurant
3. Restaurant
4. Guestroom
5. Entertainment
6. Lobby
7. Conference centre
8. Suites
9. Spa

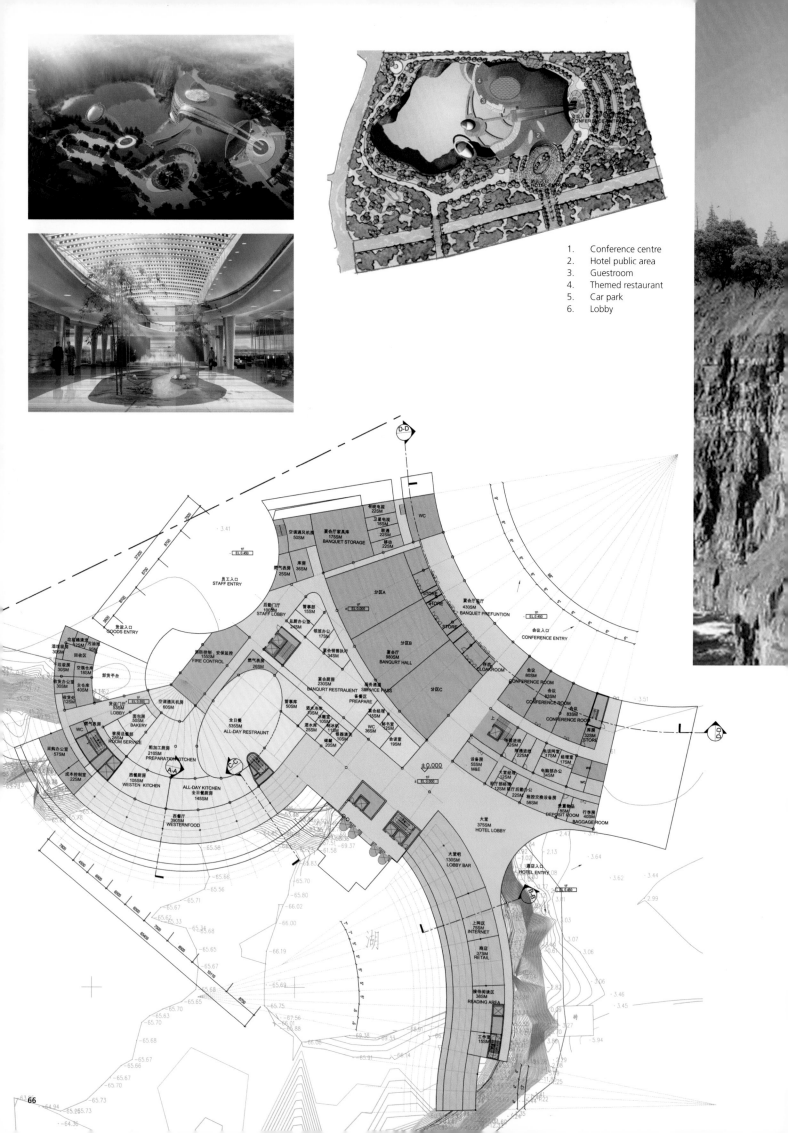

1. Conference centre
2. Hotel public area
3. Guestroom
4. Themed restaurant
5. Car park
6. Lobby

The new hotel reflects
its surroundings in
its horizontal strata,
bands of vegetation
and smooth,
curving volumes.

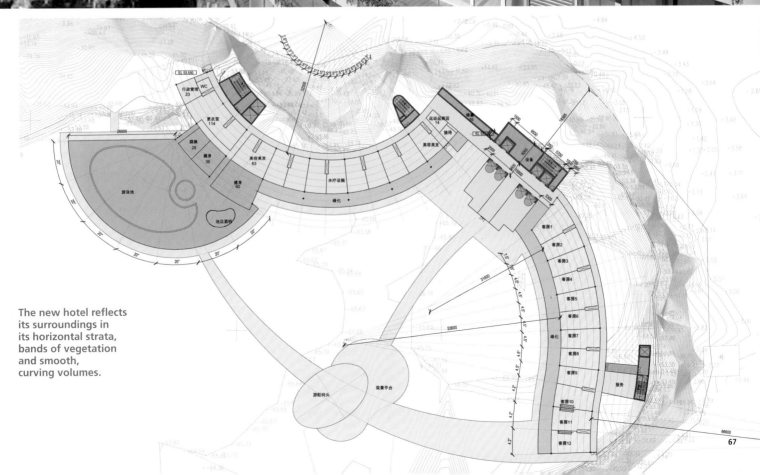

The Address, Downtown Dubai
Dubai, UAE

The Address occupies a magnificent site in Downtown Dubai, a prestigious development featuring some of the world's most outstanding buildings. It stands at the eastern tip of a central lake, flanked by the Dubai Mall and Souk Al Bahar complexes, and directly opposite the world's tallest building, the Burj Khalifa.

Despite its imposing 306 m height, The Address might have been overshadowed by its neighbours. That it more than holds its own is a result of a supremely stylish exterior. The restrained colour palette, the richly articulated plinth levels and the interaction between the volume of the tower and its dramatic crest all evoke the epitome of 1930s travel – clean, elegant, impossibly stylish.

The vertical aerofoil section of the tower rises proudly from a podium of swirling layers, calling to mind a robust seaside headland. The crisp white detailing, the exceptional landscaping of the walkways, concourses and decks, and the glint of stainless steel embellishments provide an unmistakable air of quality, which combines with its elegance to intrigue and delight. At night it positively glitters thanks to superb exterior lighting.

While it is redolent of an earlier, more elegant era, The Address is contemporary in execution, and balances between the past and present with ease and grace. Prestigious, yet lively, it's a wonderful place to be in an exciting part of the world.

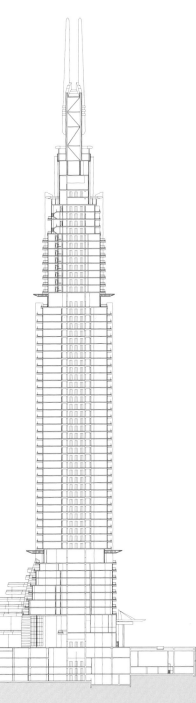

HOTELS

Client
Emaar Hospitality Group

Area
178,000 m²

Type
306 m, 63-storey five-star hotel and serviced apartments

Status
Complete

Date
2008

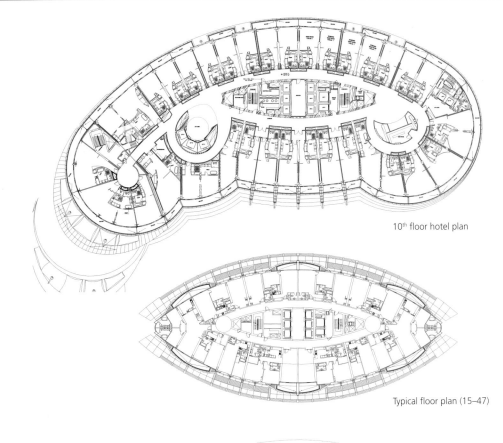

10th floor hotel plan

Typical floor plan (15–47)

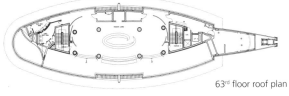

63rd floor roof plan

Tianjin Biguiyuan Phoenix Hotel
Tianjin, China

HOTELS

Client
Tianjin Biguiyuan
Phoenix Hotel Ltd

Area
300,000 m²

Type
Platinum-grade hotel
and related facilities

Status
Under construction

Date
2007–2011

Tianjin, or 'heavenly ford', is the third largest populated centre in China after Beijing and Shanghai. Its urban area is located along the 'grand canal' of the Hai He River, which connects the Yellow and Yangste rivers. The Tianjin Biguiyuan Phoenix Hotel responds to and emphasises its dramatic location at a major river bend, and succeeds in offering something special to its location as well as to its guests.

In China, water has significance beyond the visual. The river curves around the hotel, which appears to have been deposited there in a succession of curvilinear layers. Most of the hotel's 1,200 five-star guest rooms have a view over the river from its 300 m east–west frontage, stretched along the river bank.

Hidden within its layers are a 60-room conference centre, commercial facilities, a bar, a restaurant and entertainment facilities.

Beijing Yongtai Four Points Hotel
Beijing, China

HOTELS

Client
Yongtai Real Estate
Development Co.Ltd

Area
50,000 m²

Type
355-room five-star
hotel and 177 serviced
apartments

Status
Complete

Date
2005

This unconventional yet functional hotel is typical of the development of modern Beijing. The strong pattern of window openings alludes to the great traditions of Chinese masonry, and, in recognition of its potential as a wedding venue, the end elevation incorporates a pattern very similar to the 'double happiness' character always prominently displayed at Chinese wedding celebrations.

The hotel rooms are located in the building fronting the street on the south side of the site, with a courtyard separating it from the serviced apartments to the north. Banqueting facilities are provided in this inner courtyard, where curved walls provide spatial benefit from the inside and visual benefit from the outside, as do the curvilinear exteriors of the serviced apartments.

The uppermost level of the hotel is a skewed glass prism that intersects the main masonry volume of the hotel and provides interest and tension in an otherwise parallel layout. It contains an executive lounge and a corporate club for business development, and offers expansive views over Beijing.

Sports Hotel
Abu Dhabi, UAE

HOTELS

Client
Private Property
Management

Area
63,000 m²

Type
400-room hotel, to
receive LEED Gold
certification

Status
Design

Date
2009–ongoing

This five-star, 400-key hotel development is situated within the Abu Dhabi Shooting Club complex, strategically located close to the airport, central business district, industrial area and the Al Raha beach development. The design complements the spirit of the existing shooting club and is intended to evoke a dynamic form of a stretched letter 'S' rising from a field of green fabric. Its semi-rural location is recognised in its low-rise massing and sinuous plan.

A significant element of the brief was the client's determination that the hotel should meet high standards of sustainability, and a great deal of work was put into obtaining LEED Gold certification and meeting Estidama's sustainability criteria. The plan adopts an efficient double aspect layout, with a central lobby and minimised circulation space.

The basic strategy calls for the successful integration of physical and social design throughout the development, creating an architecture that is both environmentally and socially sustainable. This includes the incorporation of innovative approaches to energy conservation and environmental sustainability, with a strong emphasis on passive environmental design such as daylighting, solar shading, minimal energy consumption and careful water and waste management.

Reflecting the multiple layers of an athlete's skin and clothing, the façade is a subtle composition of layers combining a blend of aluminium composite cladding and glass curtain walling. This is enriched by a fusion of clear and tinted grey and blue-green glass, crisp white composite aluminium panels and silver aluminium fins.

The aluminium sunshade screens are brown, providing a neat transition between the clear contemporary crispness of the metal and glass elevations, and the softer tones and textures of the landscaping.

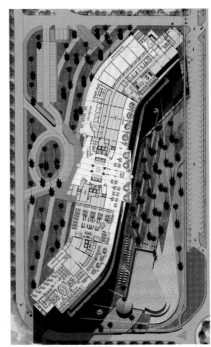

Signature Tower
Abu Dhabi, UAE

HOTELS

Client
Confidential

Area
287,000 m²

Type
Mixed-use including
five-star hotel, high-
quality office space
and apartments

Status
Design

Date
2008

Signature Tower is the first major addition to the Abu Dhabi corniche since the nearby 40-storey Abu Dhabi Investment Authority Tower was completed in 2006. Despite obvious similarities of height, curves and folding roof features, Signature Tower is differentiated from its tall neighbour by its extraordinary form.

The design is intended to meet the challenge of creating an instantly identifiable scheme among Abu Dhabi's grouping of similar masses, and produce a composition worthy of its prominent waterfront location.

Two towers are generated by extruding an angled elliptical section along an elliptical path. The towers house a 536-room five-star hotel, high-quality office space and 360 apartments, and come together at their bases to nestle into a podium containing spaces such as a ballroom and restaurants.

The podium's dune-like curves relax at the rear to present a flat sunlit area and a deep impression that forms a pool for swimming; at the front they cantilever out to define public spaces such as the main lobby, reception and hotel drop-off.

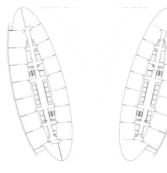

18th floor plan

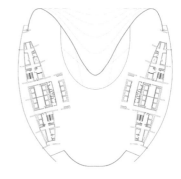

10th floor plan

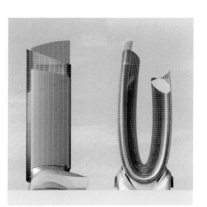

The Ibis Hotel and Offices, Al Rigga
Dubai, UAE

HOTELS

Client
Majid Al Futtaim
Hospitality LLC

Area
35,000 m²

Type
Hotel and offices

Status
Complete

Date
2010

Al Rigga Road lies in the heart of Deira, and enjoys round-the-clock liveliness. The architect's design responds by using five storeys of offices as a buffer zone between the 280 hotel bedrooms and the street.

The hotel adopts a square layout to match the site, with the main façade enlivened by a three-storey courtyard with a water wall that provides outdoor dining space. The external spaces match the interiors in terms of design and creativity, making them enjoyable interactive hubs for occupants and visitors alike.

Samuel Creations SA collaborated on the interiors, providing them with a cool, fresh and contemporary architectural identity.

Externally the simple masonry façades and regular fenestration give the building a pleasing solidity and symmetry, with a few simple elements – entrance canopies, porches and fins – used to create interesting, balanced compositions.

The results are unreservedly modern and attractive, providing the chic meeting places of choice for the design community in Dubai.

Istanbul Five-star Hotel
Istanbul, Turkey

HOTELS

Client
Tasyapi-Selcuk Ecza

Area
112,509 m²

Type
Five-star hotel and serviced apartments on the Asian side of Turkey across the Bosphorus Straits

Status
Concept design

Date
2009

The former capital of the Roman, Byzantine and Ottoman empires, Istanbul straddles the Bosphorus with one foot in Asia and the other in Europe. A mixture of past and present, it radiates a spectacle of grand splendour and simple beauty. This duality, evident in every aspect of Turkish life from social institutions to artistic expression, is synthesised in the design for this premier hotel.

The fusion of east and west is represented by the two hotel wing elements that are separated at ground level by a body of water, representing the Bosphorus, that flows through an atrium. The exquisite water feature also acts as a cooling or heating source for air as it enters the building.

Hotel access is from the west wing into the lobby, reception areas and retail outlets that are connected across the water to the ballroom and banqueting facilities.

Shops, restaurants and lounges, a business centre and other hotel functions are divided across the lower floors of the east and west wings. At higher levels, the wings connect through central core link corridors that overlook the atrium.

Above the accommodation floors, spa and serviced apartments, the two wings unify to create a sky-view restaurant and champagne lounge with breathtaking views over the surrounding hills and water.

Island Resort and Hotel
Abu Dhabi, UAE

HOTELS

Client
Confidential

Area
70,000 m²

Type
250-key hotel consisting of standard, junior, executive, diplomatic and royal suites, villas, food and beverage outlets, meeting and event facilities, leisure and recreational areas

Status
Competition entry

Date
2010

The Island Resort and Hotel shares its location with some incredibly prestigious projects by world-class architects. It responds by adopting a combination of real, unimpeachable luxury and barefoot informality as its primary aesthetic, which permeates the whole project.

The result is an intimate arrangement of hotel rooms, suites and holiday villas, all designed in a simple, clean style. They are high enough to acquire sea views over the dunes but low enough to remain domestic in scale, and are supported by the best of restaurants, cafés and bars.

Service accommodation and parking are kept hidden and largely below ground. Materials and textures have been chosen to support the informal aesthetic, and colours build on the pale greens and sands of the natural surroundings.

Boardwalks and footpaths link the outlying pavilions to the central hotel complex, which follows a simple orthogonal layout and massing. This is done with the conscious intention of providing a simple, informal structure that achieves sophistication through simplicity, control and attention to detail rather than through richness and decoration.

Namaste Hotel
Mumbai, India

HOTELS

Client
Jaguar Buildcon

Area
116,000 m²

Type
Hotel and office tower

Status
Detailed design

Date
2010–2014

The central aim of the design of this hotel and office tower was to produce a form that will be instantly recognisable on the local, regional and international architectural stage. The result is a concept based on the traditional Indian greeting of 'namaste', in which the hands are placed together in a heartfelt gesture of hospitality and welcome.

The two wings of the hotel reflect the hands, and are finished in decorative designs inspired by the hennaed patterns applied to the hands of honoured guests at Indian celebrations. In this case they enclose a vertical corridor of space, divided by access decks at each level that open into tall vertical atriums at either end and a generous quadruple-height atrium

at the summit. The atriums flood the interiors with natural daylight and provide superb views over the city. At the plant floor levels they are broken by internal gardens that bring greenery and oxygen into the space.

At ground level the towers are supported by a symmetrical podium that continues the imagery of hands and arms with fountains and cascades providing references to sleeves and clothing. Within the podium are the reception levels and a large ballroom space, along with associated services.

Above the podium is a high-quality W Hotel of 380 rooms, 5,500 m² of retail and commercial space and 9,000 m² of office accommodation.

Office

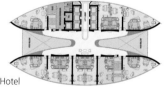
Hotel

Roof

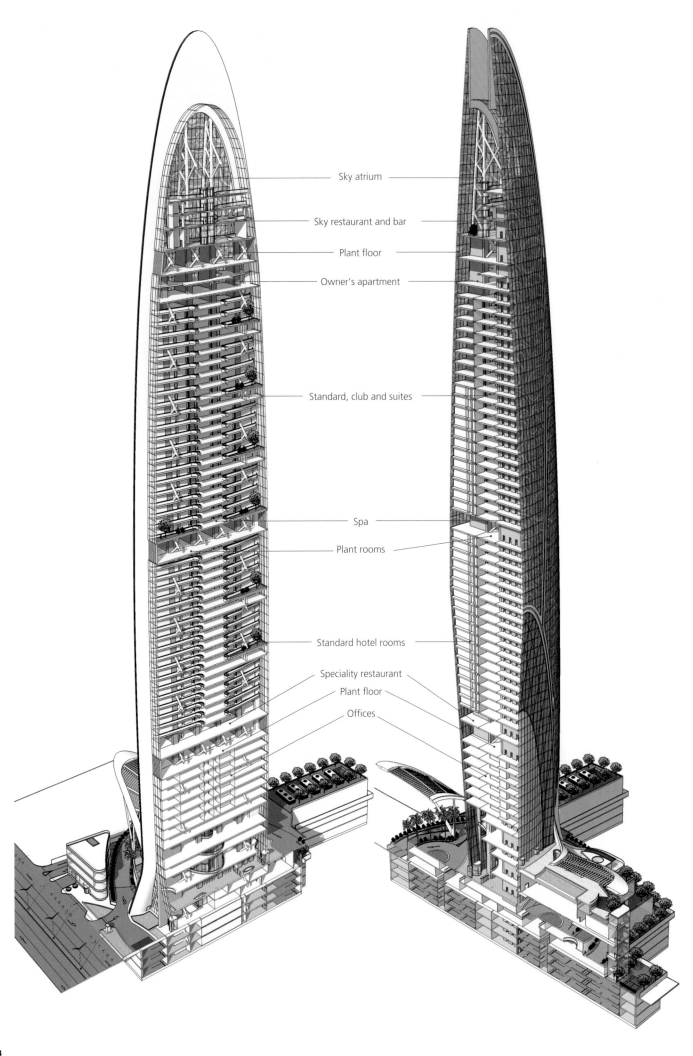

Sky atrium

Sky restaurant and bar

Plant floor

Owner's apartment

Standard, club and suites

Spa

Plant rooms

Standard hotel rooms

Speciality restaurant

Plant floor

Offices

The pattern on the external glazing is drawn from the Indian tradition of *mehndi,* which involves the application of swirling patterns of henna to the hands and feet of those involved in parties and celebrations, particularly weddings.

Palmeira Real – Residence & Resort
Barra Do Kwanza, Angola

This project involved the production of a masterplan and design proposals for a huge resort in rural Africa, combining luxury residential villas, hotels, a spa, restaurants, and sports and leisure facilities.

This is not a particularly unusual brief, but the location introduces some additional and rather unusual challenges, such as the requirements to create 1,750 sustainable jobs, to incorporate real energy efficiency and ecological awareness, and the client's instruction that the wild animal habitats on site not only be protected, but enhanced.

The response adopts two different building aesthetics in a cohesive fashion. The anchor units – the hotel, the larger villas and the restaurants, for example – have a cool contemporary style appropriate to the location, with large horizontal roof planes shading tall glazed walls, creative use of *brise soleil* to articulate the façades and pale finishes contrasted with dark accents for the many local materials and textures incorporated into the structures.

Where appropriate, though, this approach is leavened by the adoption of local building forms, subtly refined and re-proportioned to match the contemporary aesthetic. This approach has been taken for the chalets, shelters and support accommodation scattered across the site. The result is that they happily harmonise with their surroundings, sometimes to the point of invisibility – which is, of course, the idea.

The development uses the best of architecture in the creation of a resort and residential scheme that is at the top of the luxury scale in world terms. The masterplan provides the basis for exclusivity, privacy and comfort, while protecting and enhancing the unique landscape of Barra Do Kwanza.

HOTELS

Client
Tecnocarro

Area
510 ha

Type
Resort hotel and residences

Status
Concept design

Date
2009

The villas adopt a cool, contemporary approach to their architecture, *left* and *above*.

The same approach informs refinements to the indigenous architecture that is used for the open pavilions and shade structures.

Park Hotel
Rovinj, Croatia

The Urban Development Plan of the town of Rovinj prescribes the reconstruction of the existing marina to an enhanced standard, providing some 200 commercial berths for visiting yachts. The marina's existing hotel is to be redeveloped as part of this process.

The hotel is located on an inlet of the northern Adriatic, directly adjacent to the town of Rovinj, overlooking the marina and surrounded by a magnificent rural landscape. Such an outstanding site positively demands a superb development.

The proposal adopts a shapely, low-rise triangular pavilion as the basic hotel unit. The triangular form provides every bedroom with a view of both sea and land from its private balcony while internally, bedroom access decks are arranged around a daylit central atrium above a court space at ground level. Four of these triangular units are linked together to provide the majority of the accommodation, with the spaces between given over to pools, decks, landscaped courtyards and in the central space, the main entrance.

Particular attention has been paid to the interiors, with finishes and colours chosen to reflect the nautical location and focus on natural, ecologically sound materials. Following Atkins' basic design principles, the hotel naturally adopts a strongly sustainable approach to its services systems.

HOTELS

Client
Maistra

Area
34,000 m²

Type
240 high-end luxury guest suites and apartments

Status
Concept complete

Date
2009

Projects such as this will see Croatia consolidate its emerging position as a major holiday destination.

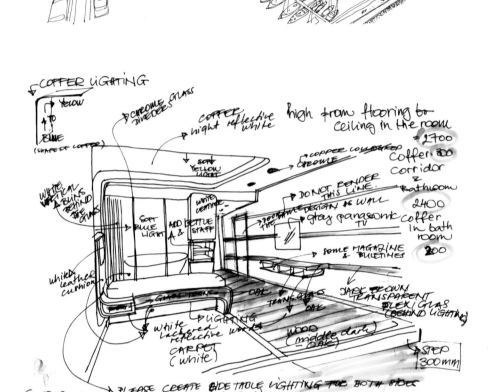

The nautical theme is continued into the interiors, as detailed in the design development sktech, *left.*

The triangular plan may have been developed for sea views, but it also provides a beautiful reference to the prows of the yachts at anchor in the marina.

RESIDENTIAL

9GG-9HH
Dubai, UAE

The Tower of Babylon, the world's first truly tall building, was constructed in Arabia – in what is now Iraq – some 5,000 years ago. Medieval images interpret it as a spiral structure rising towards the heavens, and it is these images that provided the inspiration for 9GG-9HH.

In this case the spiral form is generated by stacking identical floor plans, which are then gently rotated (by 1.8° per floor) as they rise over 50 floors, creating the spiral. The plans take their form from interlocking squares around a circular core, inspired by aspects of femininity and masculinity in the culture of Arabia, and also from the double helix of DNA, a subtle allusion to the heredity of the tower form. The appearance is of two interlocking towers spiralling towards the sky, the square white tower extending a little higher than the black, adding to the dynamism and elegance of the composition.

The tower is supported on a podium inspired by the shallow wave forms of the Gulf seas and the desert dunes, and their intersection at the Dubai Marina, the site for the development. The podium houses a spa and health club, a swimming pool and retail space. The first 39 floors of the tower each house two 475 m² apartments, and the higher floors consist of luxurious 870 m² duplex units. The interlocking form gives apartments on the lower floors an unobstructed view over a sweep of 270°, while the more exclusive duplex apartments above enjoy 360° panoramas over modern Dubai.

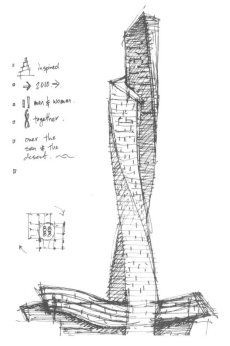

RESIDENTIAL

Client
Emaar Properties PJSC

Area
53,552 m²

Type
50-storey tower on a six-level podium with a spa, health centre, pool and retail space

Status
Concept design

Date
2007

30th floor plan

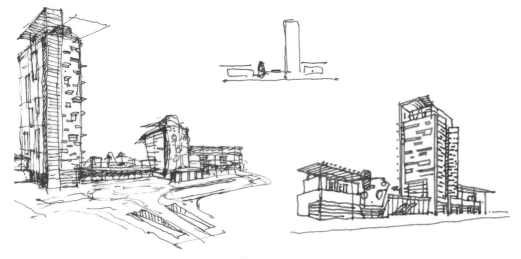

Typical floor plan

2CDE Residential Development
Dubai, UAE

RESIDENTIAL

Client
Ahmed Ramadhan
Juma Establishment

Area
33,642 m²

Type
116 m, 27-storey
residential tower

Status
Under construction

Date
2005–2010

Dubai Marina is the world's largest created marina and 2CDE is the plot number for this residential development. At 116 m in height, the tower is typical of many of the mixed-use residential and retail developments that skirt the periphery of the marina complex, and provides a mix of serviced apartments, penthouses and townhouses over 27 floors.

2CDE differs from the norm in presenting an environmentally conscious building at no additional cost. A number of sustainable features are incorporated into the design, and these served as a springboard for Atkins' sustainable building design processes for hot climates.

The exterior of the building has electro-coated clear glazing that can withstand the thermal impact of high summer temperatures without diminishing light transmission, thereby reducing power consumption.

The new technology of Integrated Foil Photovoltaic (IFPV) panels will be installed on the top of the horizontal car park shading structures and will generate power sufficient to light all of 2CDE's public spaces including corridors, the shopping arcade and car park. More conventional shading techniques are used to reduce solar gain elsewhere, for example, on the south façade, where the window openings are significantly smaller than those on the north.

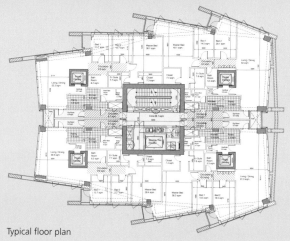

Typical floor plan

Regatta Luxury Apartments
Jakarta, Indonesia

RESIDENTIAL

Client
Badan Kerjasama
Mutiara Buana

Area
376,550 m²

Type
10 luxury apartment
towers and a five-star
hotel

Status
Complete

Date
2004–2009

This project occupies 11 ha of the Pantai Mutiara canal estate, and comprises a five-star tower hotel, 10 luxury apartment towers, two serviced apartment towers, a water park and basement parking.

The estate is one of the most luxurious housing complexes in Jakarta, and the brief was to target the top level of the high-class apartment market. In architectural terms, the development is expected to become the landmark feature of the Jakarta waterfront.

Atkins' design approach in this case was to combine its strengths in architecture and engineering to deliver an exceptionally pleasing form, exceeding the client's expectations.

The composition was structured to suit the required phased completion strategy, and adopts a nautical theme, orienting the buildings on the major points of the compass to create the best possible views of the waterfront for each phase.

The cluster of apartment buildings represents elegant yachts sailing for distant destinations, with the sail-shaped architectural fins on the apartment façades emphasising their nautical character. The concept is simple, dynamic and elegant.

Business Bay
Executive Towers
Dubai, UAE

RESIDENTIAL

Client
Dubai Properties

Area
300,000 m²

Type
Five residential towers
varying in height from
27 to 47 storeys

Status
Complete

Date
2005–2009

The Business Bay Executive Towers
project is located in the prestigious
Business Bay precinct of Dubai, a short
distance away from the tallest building
in the world. Five individually sculpted,
contemporary towers that vary in
height from 27 to 47 storeys rise from
a two-storey podium, providing a total
of 1,041 apartments ranging from
spacious studios to luxury penthouses.

Abundant restaurants and shopping
opportunities are offered within
6,186 m² of commercial space
provided by the continuous curvilinear
double-height podium arcade.
Further apartments and duplexes are
arranged at plaza level, set within a
landscaped area at the heart of which
is a swimming pool and health spa.

The multi-layered façades of the
towers blend with the semi-detatched
townhouses and retail podium edge
to create a sophisticated urban living
environment. At the eastern edge
of the site the towers face the New
Creek, a series of interconnecting
waterways that lead to the sea, while
the western boundary skirts an area of
parkland. The blues, greys and greens
of these surroundings are reflected
in the cool, translucent palette of
materials adopted for the towers.

The layered elevations and complex podiums create a sophisticated urban environment. The diagonal orientation of the towers is in deliberate contrast to the orthogonal podium layouts, creating interesting spaces and visual intrigue.

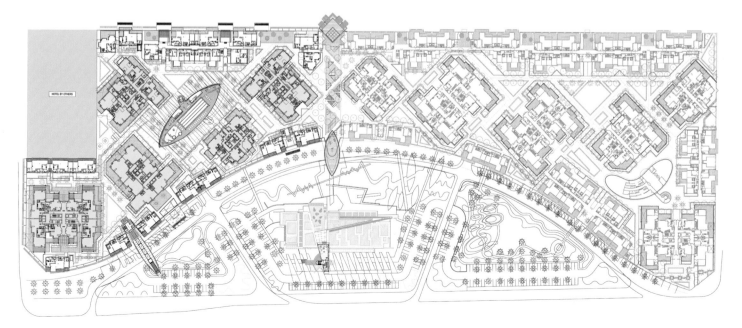

Pier 8 Residences
Dubai, UAE

RESIDENTIAL

Client
Abyaar Real Estate
Investment

Area
48,000 m²

Type
170 m, 40-storey
residential tower

Status
Under construction

Date
2005–2011

Dubai's burgeoning and vibrant Marina community is home to several Atkins-designed buildings. Pier 8 occupies a promontory in the Marina, providing commanding views up and down the waterfront from its 40 storeys of luxury serviced apartments.

The studio, one- and two-bedroom apartments enjoy leisure and recreational facilities provided in the four-storey podium, including restaurants, swimming pools and a health club. Retail shops and townhouses along the waterfront increase the sense of community living.

The breezy design embodies a waterside mentality. Materials are crisp and clean with the simple white form of the tower wrapped by clear and grey-tinted glass and white composite aluminium *brise soleil* cladding panels.

Apartments are planned around a rectilinear core to maximise views, and these are protected by a further variety of shading elements such as deep projecting balconies and movable aluminium screens that serve to reduce solar gain and animate the façade. The result is a clean, contemporary building entirely at home in its marine environment.

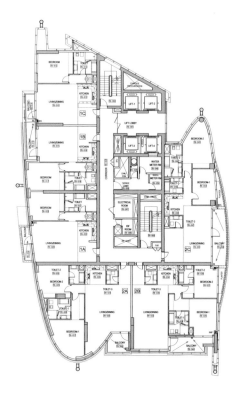

Typical floor plan (4–37)

Durrat Al Bahrain
Residential Villas
Bahrain

RESIDENTIAL

Client
Durrat Khaleej Al
Bahrain

Area
20 km²

Type
Residential,
commercial and
leisure resort

Status
Under construction

Date
2004–2011

Durrat Al Bahrain is a world-class residential leisure and tourist destination offering an urban lifestyle experience equalling that of anywhere else in the Middle East. It has an international atmosphere, but focuses on the requirements of the Gulf market, and will eventually be home to 60,000 people.

These stylish and practical villas and apartments offer luxury accommodation in a very contemporary manner, avoiding the clichéd themes of many resort developments. Tailored to the unique setting and qualities of the Durrat site, every villa will have uninterrupted views to the sea or, in the case of the golf course, the fairways. In all villas, boundary walls are short, and views of the sea and sky are enhanced by the open layouts and the careful design of glazing.

Phases 1 and 2 consist of 1,042 luxury villas on four atolls and three petals. Phase 3 of the island development is in the design stage, and will add an estimated further 600 villas on the last two atolls and two petals.

The total ground floor area of villas under construction in Phases 1 and 2 is 382,292 m² with a further 2,934 m² being used to build a community facilities building, prayer halls, grand mosque, shops and public conveniences.

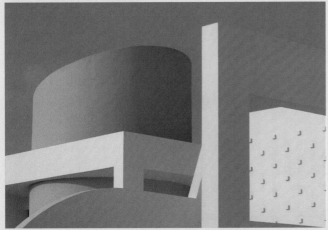

Mahboula Towers
Kuwait City, Kuwait

Mahboula Towers is an imposing 312-unit, sea-facing, high-end residential development providing owner-operated rental accommodation for the expatriate market. As a five-star tenanted complex it will offer hotel facilities within a secure residential environment.

Typical of similar developments in Kuwait City, the site benefits from a singular uniform sea view to the east, and all habitable rooms naturally face this. To mitigate the effects of the harsh desert climate with its hot summer and cold winter extremes and periodic sandstorms, the building is protected to the west by an active wall that encloses a void space that acts as a solar buffer to reduce energy loads.

To the east the building's façade has been modelled in response to the sun. All residences open onto wide balconies that shade the façade from overhead sun, and provide sheltered outdoor seating areas and opportunities for natural ventilation during the cooler months.

The development offers a range of apartment sizes, many accessible directly through private lifts, thus reducing the traffic within the shared corridors. All apartment services are completely separated and located on the western side of these corridors.

Triple-floor penthouses with their own pools and gardens provide additional exclusivity, but at the podium level, and accessible to all residents, is a resort-like sequence of pools, palms and planting that provide spaces for individual or group leisure.

RESIDENTIAL

Client
Al Tijaria (Commercial Real Estate Company K.S.C.C)

Area
140,000 m²

Type
312-unit high-end residential tower

Status
Design complete

Date
2008

The Iconia
Hyderabad, India

RESIDENTIAL

Client
Kondapur Towers
Pvt Ltd

Area
55,225 m²

Type
18 20-storey buildings
on a 21.35 ha site

Status
Under construction

Date
2007–2010 (Phase 1)

Typical four-unit floor plan

Located in Hyderabad on a 21.35 ha site in Banjara Hills, The Iconia was conceived as a city within a city. Eighteen 20-storey buildings are arranged to create external spaces that foster the social interaction required to sustain a community.

Pedestrian-only ground level space that is extensively landscaped for residents' use is maximised by containing vehicles at the perimeters where there is easy access to three levels of basement parking. The formation of a sustainable community is furthered by the range of apartments on offer, catering to households of many different sizes and compositions.

Clubhouses and leisure zones provide gymnasiums, swimming pools and indoor game areas for badminton, squash, table tennis and snooker.

The buildings incorporate daylight, ventilation and thermal strategies in their orientation, layout and services specifications. The restraint exercised in external treatment is ameliorated by the simple pairing of towers to create unique relationships within the greater development.

MBZC Tower
Abu Dhabi, UAE

RESIDENTIAL

Client
Confidential

Area
22,000 m²

Type
23-storey building
with two levels of
underground parking

Status
Competition entry

Date
2009

The MBZC Tower is a distinctive response to the masterplan principles and specific requirements for a tall, slender 21–23 storey building with a minimum of two levels of underground parking and a single-storey transparent lobby, without a podium. It provides a total of 106 apartments over 22 storeys, the majority being two-bedroom units, but with 21 single bedroom apartments,16 three-bedroom and five four-bedroom units.

Externally the building is vigorously modelled to suggest the idea of stacked accommodation units. The clear demarcation between floors and the recessed and projected façades enable balconies and terraces to be recessed or projected. In both cases privacy is enhanced and external space can be combined with internal

space more successfully, extending usable floor area and enhancing the architectural quality of each unit. Plants and furnishings on the balconies will add to the atmosphere of the building, enhancing the notion of the tower becoming a 'vertical village'.

At ground level the lobby walls are fully glazed and recessed, giving the upper levels the appearance of floating above broad pavements. These serve to integrate the nearby plaza with the building, extending it below the overhanging upper floors and deep into the lobby.

With a site of only 2,500 m², MBZC may be compact, but it presents a richly detailed, robust and inviting place to live.

Typical floor plan

Sama Tower
Dubai, UAE

Challenged by the perpetual debate between form and function, Atkins developed this spirited design in response to the client's aspirations for a unique, landmark residential tower in the Trade Center area of Dubai.

The design of the Sama Tower strives to create the illusion of continuous movement in a static object. This is achieved by the slight twist imparted to the façades that catch the light and reflect it in a dynamic fashion. In effect, the tower dances for the moving viewer, so that from every angle the building changes its appearance. It's a building designed for Dubai.

More than 700 residential units are offered in a mix of one-, two- and three-bedroom apartments, all served by full amenities including a rooftop health club, spa and panoramic gym. At 50 storeys and 193.6 m in height, the tower is poised and stylish, not adjectives that one normally applies to modern skyscrapers, which all too often achieve height at the expense of elegance. By seemingly responding to the shifting position of the viewer, the tower creates a special relationship with the city and its inhabitants.

RESIDENTIAL

Client
Al Hamid Group

Area
93,980 m²

Type
50-storey, 193.6 m
residential tower

Status
Complete

Date
2005–2010

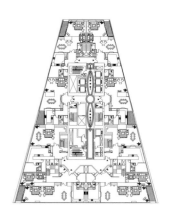

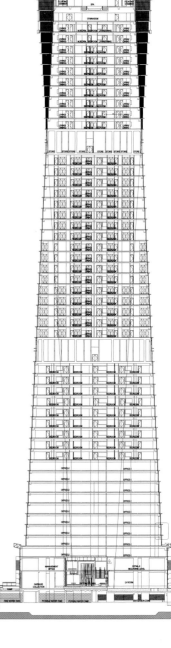

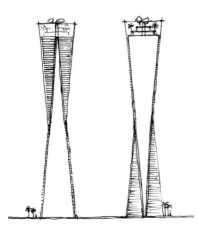

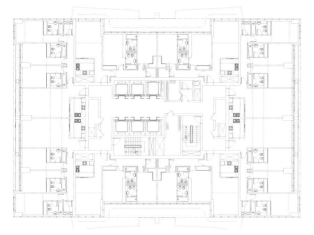

Typical floor plan

Millennium Tower
Dubai, UAE

RESIDENTIAL

Client
Confidential

Area
99,800 m²

Type
285 m, G+59-storey
residential tower

Status
Complete

Date
2003–2006

On the edge of Dubai's main highway, the 60-storey Millennium Tower combines a series of visual elements into a symmetrical composition that evokes tradition with an entirely modern edge.

Articulated in a stylish, contemporary visual language, the tower meets the client's aspiration to create a modern interpretation of the art deco skyscrapers of the 1930s. The clean, elegant interlocking 'slipping' volumes suggest the appearance

of movement towards the sky, and create the classic stepped skyline that diminishes to a sharp apex.

A solid frame visibly anchors the building to the ground, expressed on either side and encompassing a lighter, more transparent glazed wall behind its diagonal bracing. Contained between the frames is a composition of contrasting solid masses, which resolve themselves into a single fin at the peak, which in turn incorporates a needle-like pinnacle pointing

skywards. At the base deep recesses impart a sense of lightness to the main body of the tower. The result is a skyscraper of sophisticated simplicity.

A total of 407 residential apartments are served by a swimming pool, gymnasium and squash courts housed in the separate 471-bay multi-storey car park. The project was tailored to the needs of the client, to accommodate 1,400 of its staff, in what is currently, at 285 m, the second tallest residential building in the world.

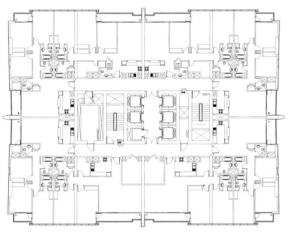

11th floor plan

Global Lake View
Dubai, UAE

RESIDENTIAL

Client
Venus International
(Best Homes Emirates)

Area
38,000 m²

Type
136 m, G+34-storey
residential tower

Status
Complete

Date
2004–2007

Located at the entrance to the Jumeirah Lakes Towers Development, the simple rectangular plan of the Global Lake View tower belies its striking form. The longer façades of the building bow outwards as they ascend, providing the 136 m, 35-storey tower with a gently swelling 'waistline' that tapers towards the roofline.

The roof profile is relatively underplayed, which enables the overall form of the tower to dominate. The external façade is clad in silver-coated aluminium and bronze reflective glass, providing an air of understated elegance.

The curved façade has the practical advantage of permitting a variety of floor plate sizes, with two-bedroom apartments occupying the lower and upper parts of the tower, while the central part is devoted to three-bedroom apartments. All apartments enjoy a lake view.

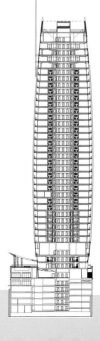

21st Century Tower
Dubai, UAE

RESIDENTIAL

Client
Al Rostamani Group
of Companies

Area
86,000 m²

Type
269 m residential
tower on 56 floors

Status
Complete

Date
2000–2003

In the period between 2003 and 2005, the 269 m 21st Century Tower was the tallest residential building in the world. With 400 two- and three-bedroom apartments on 56 floors, the building is occupied by Emirates Airlines, whose cabin crew can make full use of the 24-hour availability of the rooftop swimming pool, gym and leisure facilities, and the ground level shopping mall.

The building occupies a prestigious corner plot adjacent to the city's main highway, to which it responds with simple, clean lines, gentle curves and refined elegance.

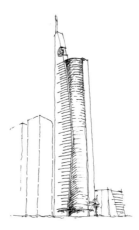

The dynamic, curved silver aluminium and glass elements represent graceful flight, while to the rear of the tower a simple, symmetrical structural spine provides stability and strength, elegantly terminating with a simple needle spire pointing skywards.

The design makes use of robust materials, capable of maintaining their appearance for the lifetime of the building. The result is a clean, elegant composition that fulfils the client's desire for a modern signature building that complements Dubai's contemporary urban landscape.

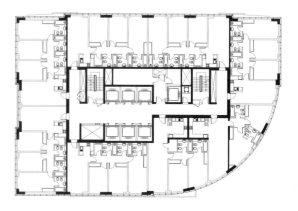

Typical floor plan

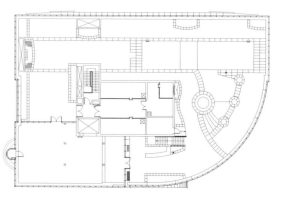

Lower roof plan

Chelsea Tower
Dubai, UAE

One of the most visually arresting towers in Dubai is the 51-storey Chelsea Tower. It accommodates 282 serviced apartments, with a swimming pool and leisure facilities on the roof of the separate nine-storey car park.

Its plan form is essentially a square with two corners linked via the central core to form a diagonal structural spine. This spine is the main support for the floor plates, allowing the remaining corners and the intervening walls to be lighter and their gently curved external surfaces to express movement.

The corner elements of the structural spine extend above the roof and bridge across to support a majestic, 40 m tall suspended needle above the central core, taking the building height to 251 m.

The lighter elements of the tower are clad in grey/blue glass and white aluminium panels divided vertically into three sections at the service floors. The tripartite division creates a tower of truly elegant proportions while the unique roof form is a landmark feature amid a profusion of mediocre high-rise buildings along Dubai's main highway.

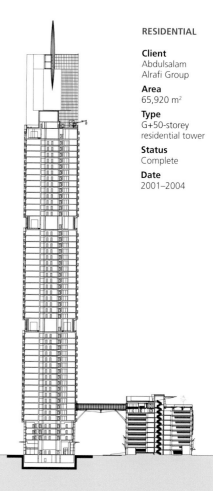

RESIDENTIAL

Client
Abdulsalam Alrafi Group

Area
65,920 m²

Type
G+50-storey residential tower

Status
Complete

Date
2001–2004

Manazel
Dubai, UAE

RESIDENTIAL

Client
Confidential

Area
35,145 m²

Type
Two towers of
22 and 26 storeys

Status
Complete

Date
2001–2004

This competition-winning design provides prestigious apartment accommodation combined with efficient spatial layouts. A pair of elliptical towers, of 22- and 26-storeys, are clad in glass and aluminium and placed at a 90° angle to each other. They are connected by a curved glazed bridge, punctuated by a circular elevator shaft.

The towers stand on a three-storey podium accommodating car parks and retail outlets. The leading edge of each tower has an inclined splay and the elevations are enlivened by balconies that strike off at a tangent to the curved façades, so that they appear to be angular metal shards.

The result is a refined, modern aesthetic form that provides a striking landmark in a predominantly low-rise area of Dubai city. Residents of the

124 apartments enjoy a host of leisure facilities, including two swimming pools, a gymnasium and squash courts.

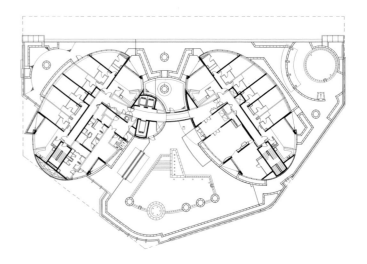

3rd floor plan and pool layout

Goldcrest Views
Dubai, UAE

RESIDENTIAL

Client
Confidential

Area
57,231 m²

Type
159 m, 40-storey
residential tower

Status
Complete

Date
2005–2007

The strength of the design concept for the striking 159 m Goldcrest Views emanates from the two tapering fins that dominate the long façades of the simple rectangular form.

The fins enhance the tower's distinctly slender and elegant proportions, and form the boundary of the building at the lower level. They provide support and strength for the residential apartments both visually and structurally.

Complementing its lakeside location, the interplay of colour (predominantly blue and white), shadow, texture and materials results in a rich but clean, balanced composition enhanced by the sharp horizontal lines of the residential balconies.

The 376 luxury apartments are arrayed around a rectangular inner core, and enjoy panoramic views of the lake from the spacious external balconies and the roof-level pool deck.

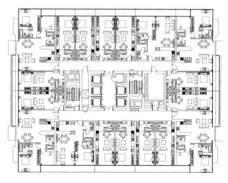

Typical floor plan (2–14)

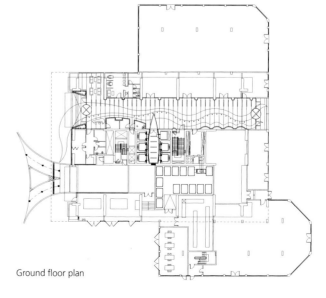

Ground floor plan

Downtown Al Areen
Al Areen, Bahrain

RESIDENTIAL

Client
Gulf Holding
Company

Area
390,000 m²

Type
Mixed-use township
featuring low-
rise residential
townhouses and villas,
some retail, bridges
and public realm

Status
Detailed design

Date
2008–ongoing

Located among some of Bahrain's key tourist spots, including the Lost Paradise of Dilmun, the Al Areen Wildlife Sanctuary and Sakhir International Race Circuit, Downtown Al Areen is ideally located to become a world-class tourism destination. The development will be subdivided into three distinct areas, namely The Boulevard, The High Street and The Old Town. Each will have a unique character and ambience, yet in combination with its neighbours will form a coherent 'whole', the relationship established by means of harmonious architecture and landscaping.

The site is traversed by a main boulevard, framed by abundant greenery. This broad walkway will pass between a series of complexes, incorporating residential and office space as well as restaurants, cafés and retail outlets. Extending from the boulevard is the main promenade, which will lead visitors to The Old Town. Inspired by historical Arabian architecture, it captures the charm of randomly placed homes flanking the narrow, winding streets of the past.

Bordering The Old Town are traditional townhouses, constructed in strict accordance with environmentally-friendly techniques and using sustainable materials. Further residential accommodation will be provided by spacious terraced apartments, each of which will have a commanding view of the Al Areen Wildlife Park and Reserve.

The development is predominantly low-rise, and will provide a balance of contemporary and traditional architecture as well as further advances in sustainable design in Bahrain. By emphasising the importance of good urban design and enjoyable public spaces, Downtown Al Areen is pioneering techniques that will increase tourism and boost the economy of the region.

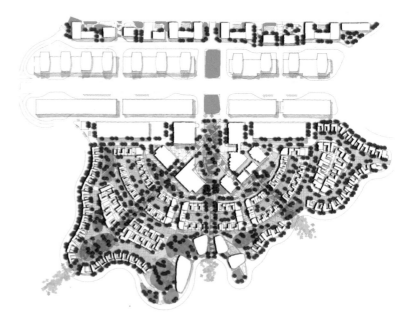

Villa Royale
Tangiers, Morocco

Traditional Moroccan architecture is well known for its strict formality and rich traditions of decoration, colour and texture, and the incorporation of charming and useful architectural devices such as *mashrabiya* screens and pergolas. The new proposals reinterpret all of these elements in a contemporary way, keeping the colour palette restrained while simplified screens are used to shade and define space.

A key element of the design is the importance of pedestrian connectivity, with much of the landscape given over to areas for community entertainment and small 'pocket' parks. This approach has also allowed the rising and falling ground levels, a feature of the site, to be turned into an advantage – they are embraced by the architecture and planning, and profoundly influence the character of the development. They are used to create small vistas, intimate concealed parks and to enhance privacy.

RESIDENTIAL

Client
Gulf Holding Company

Area
66.21 ha

Type
High-end, low-rise residential development featuring 330 villa plots and 60 townhouse sites

Status
Concept design

Date
2009–ongoing

Pedestrian paths follow the contours of the site and provide privacy between adjacent terraces of houses.

The architectural forms are a cool, contemporary reworking of traditional masses and decorative elements.

113

Aypara Residence
Baku, Azerbaijan

RESIDENTIAL

Client
Baku White City

Area
24,000 m²

Type
G+8 residential building with 62 duplex apartments

Status
Design

Date
2009–ongoing

Within Aypara Residence's arresting sculptural form is a surprisingly straightforward, high-quality residential building. Offering 62 apartments, ranging from single-storey single bedroom to five-bedroom duplex penthouses, it provides all the discerning resident could expect from the best of residential developments.

The design evolved in accordance with current best practice, and incorporates a number of initiatives to minimise energy consumption. Each apartment enjoys a deep south-facing balcony to provide shading from the high summer sun, but is enhanced by large areas of high-performance glazing, affording good sunlight penetration in the winter months.

The building's power requirements are met in part by an array of photovoltaic panels that shade the top floor, and are mitigated by a greywater recycling system, naturally cooling cross-ventilation and high levels of passive insulation of the opaque surfaces. The building is elevated to provide every level with enhanced security and clear views over the Caspian Sea. With access via four stone-clad podium supports, each lift serves only two apartments per floor on average, enhancing the exclusive nature of the project.

This high-quality but somewhat conservative approach is invigorated by a striking enclosure in a direct response to a brief that called for a building with a "unique form, distinct from the average residential development in the city". The apartments are set around an arc and clad in a toroidal section of perforated aluminium cladding on the 'outer', northern face, which curves around to cover the roof and underside of the raised block.

Aypara Residence is a spectacular creation, and is set to become the developer's signature building, charged with setting a standard for all following developments in White City.

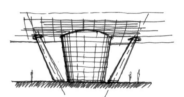

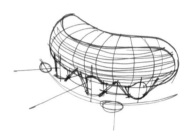

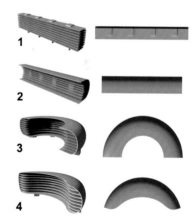

Form generation: these sketches indicate the sequence followed in the development of Aypara Residence's structure.

1
2
3
4

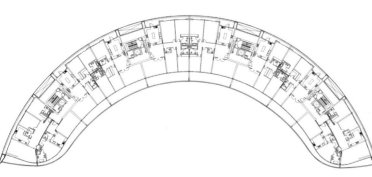

Typical floor plan

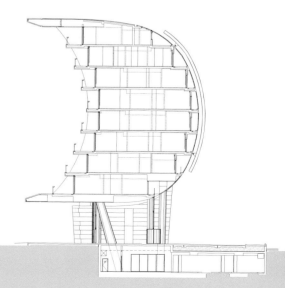

Marina City Development
Abu Dhabi, UAE

RESIDENTIAL

Client
National Investment
Corporation

Area
11,530,000 m² plot
area with total built
area of 240,000 m²

Type
Mixed-use including
residential villas, office
and retail

Status
Detailed design

Date
2010–ongoing

Marina City actually comprises two different developments on two separate sites, but both spring from the same root – architectural quality through refinement and simplicity.

An architectural language of materials, colours and forms has been established and applied to masses based on an area module of 45 m², which is used singly or in multiples of up to four to create studio, single, double and triple bedroom apartments. The regularity of the module and the careful application of the architectural language gives the finished scheme a beautiful spatial rhythm and cohesion, with curved plan forms, differences in mass and size and the sparse use of layers and vertical elements on the elevations providing a remarkable range of variations.

The main plot is given over to apartments stacked above a ground-floor level of retail units. The plan adopts a sweeping S-form, defining two separate bays. The seaward bay accommodates a mixture of public access and retail use at ground level, with private accommodation above; the landward bay is entirely private, and is rather more densely developed with gardens and courts used to maximise privacy and provide good sound control.

Similar apartment blocks have been used to provide a buffer to the rear of the second site, separating it from the main body of the island. This new private enclosure, bounded by the sea on three sides, has been devoted to high-quality private villas, each sitting in its own garden.

The villas are remarkable for their simplicity in terms of contemporary Gulf design. That simplicity is produced by rigorous control and refinement, and the result is a continuation of the calm, high-quality aesthetic established by the apartment blocks, and an architecture that will prove durable and timeless.

The villas for the Abu Dhabi Marina City Development take the contemporary reworking of the traditional Gulf house to a new level.

Naseel Corniche Tower
Jeddah, Saudi Arabia

RESIDENTIAL

Client
Naseel Holding

Area
116,250 m²

Type
High-end exclusive
77-storey, 340 m
residential tower

Status
Concept design
complete

Date
2009–ongoing

Naseel Corniche Tower is a 77-storey, high-end exclusive residential tower located on Jeddah's north corniche. The client requested a landmark to distinguish it from other buildings in Jeddah, and, at 340 m in height, it will be the fourth tallest building in the Middle East and the tallest in the Kingdom of Saudi Arabia.

The tower follows a simple rectangular plan. At the low- and mid-levels there are two spacious apartments per floor, while single penthouses fill the next 20 levels. The top three floors form a single, stunning, penthouse.

Visitors approach beneath a floating canopy, entering a triple-height lobby incorporating a waterfall plunging from the ceiling into a central reflecting pool with a floating lounge at the edge. A second entrance from the street leads into the car park podium, which also contains a dedicated children's pool and play area and a pair of health clubs, each with an internal green patio and an open swimming pool.

The sculptural form of the tower comes from a desire to transform the formality and solidity of the rectangular skyscraper by introducing

the ephemeral effects of translucency and the organic nature of a tower sculpted by wind and gravity. This is achieved by introducing sinuous, curved surfaces. These contrast with the simple rectangular volumes of the tower and podium that they serve to link, and derive from a dynamic, fluid form – a wind-filled sail.

The forms have practical as well as aesthetic value. They incorporate solar shading devices that are a highly efficient means of reducing the summer cooling load and thus reducing energy consumption.

Before   After

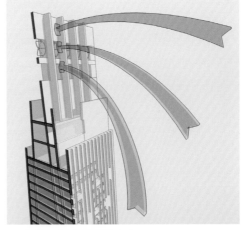

Shading devices have been introduced in order to reduce solar heat gain and thus mitigate summer cooling loads.

Due to the location of the tower and its significant height, there is potential for integrating wind turbines as a means of generating on-site renewable energy.

OFFICES AND COMMERCIAL

The Riyadh Tower
Riyadh, Saudi Arabia

OFFICES AND COMMERCIAL

Client
Al Ajlan Allied Group

Area
66,000 m²

Type
220 m, 42-storey
office development

Status
Tender

Date
2009–ongoing

The Riyadh Tower, located on King Fahd Road in downtown Riyadh, will be the city's third tallest building after Kingdom Tower and the nearby Al Faisaliah Tower. As such, it will be highly visible and will contribute to Riyadh's evolving architectural character.

The office tower has 42 floors of high-quality office space and four levels of underground car parking. Its complex double-curvature envelope effortlessly accommodates the subtle geometries of the *mashrabiya* that extends over its full façade.

This geometric theme, strongly related to the region, continues on the generous canopies arching over both the drop-off zone and the souk on either side of the tower. From the street, the architecture is one of texture and pattern.

Shading, screening and water are provided for traditional, functional and aesthetic reasons. Integrated shading is oriented to maximise its effect, while the souk is an outdoor space laid out in a time-honoured manner, channelling the prevailing breezes between and over the two-storey pavilions.

This souk is a new place for old activities and provides a welcome home for the social interaction between modern financial structures and bygone traditions that have been largely lost in the dysfunctional marketplace of the contemporary mall.

For people from the western world, these buildings will be little more than a progressive piece of contemporary architecture, embodying familiar urban values in a somewhat distant land. However, The Riyadh Tower's significance is found in the way it makes a contemporary place for the city's significant cultural traditions.

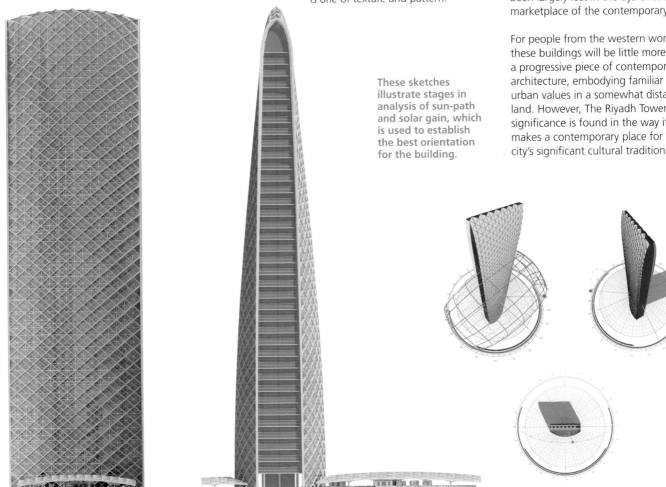

These sketches illustrate stages in analysis of sun-path and solar gain, which is used to establish the best orientation for the building.

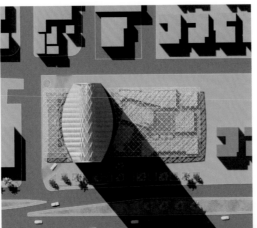

Al Sharq Office Complex
Kuwait City, Kuwait

OFFICES AND COMMERCIAL

Client
Al-Mar and Aqar

Area
28,000 m²

Type
180 m office complex
with related facilities

Status
Concept design

Date
2005

This competition-winning office complex combines work and leisure, internal and outside spaces, and offers a variety of scenarios for business within a sustainable and environmentally responsible design.

The building takes its distinctive linear form from two parallel 210 m blades, from which the office spaces are suspended. These spaces are vertically zoned, and change function and appearance depending upon the level they occupy in the building.

The blades are topped at roof level with an executive gym, health club, spa and an open-air pool deck with a panoramic restaurant suspended above. The podium is transmuted into a lower accommodation block, which hovers above a glass-fronted entrance with shaded shop-fronts and is topped by a landscaped food court.

Additional foliage is used in sky gardens to shade the end elevations on the office levels and provide space for office workers to step outside and recharge. The long elevations have vertical tinted glass fins that further reduce heat gain while their integrated photovoltaic panels make a significant contribution to the building's power requirement.

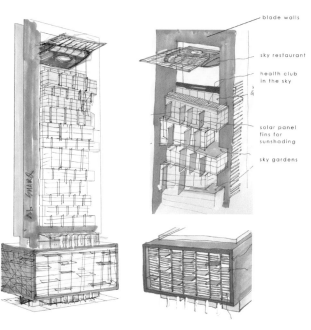

blade walls

sky restaurant

health club
in the sky

solar panel
fins for
sunshading

sky gardens

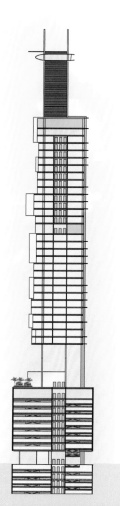

sky restaurant

pool/services
gym

offices

services

offices

retail

podium
carpark

retail

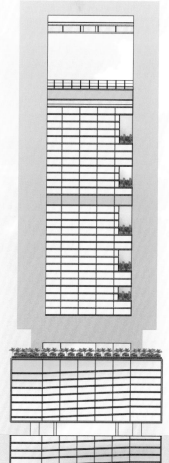

Almas Tower
Dubai, UAE

The home of the Dubai Diamond Exchange, Almas Tower is the distinctive centrepiece of the city's Jumeirah Lakes development. The two gracefully interlocking elliptical towers of commercial accommodation gently taper as they ascend, the taller 66-storey tower rising 360 m to the tip of the mast at the summit, making it the second tallest building in Dubai and the 18th tallest in the world.

The towers respond respectively to their solar aspects; high-performance externally treated insulated panels protect the south-facing tower, while the north-facing tower is more transparent, allowing the occupants to benefit from the cooler ambient light.

At the base of this elegant superstructure is a three-storey podium in the form of eight interlocking triangles, inspired by the glittering facets of a cut diamond. Radiating from the central core and corresponding to the principal points of the compass, the triangles are visible from all sides of the tower, reflecting the surrounding water while animating the façade.

The diamond exchange centre is located in the largest of the triangular spaces, which is cantilevered 35 m out above the lake and has glass flooring to the trading lounge. This is matched by a generous roof lantern, allowing daylight to illuminate the trading floor and facilitate expert diamond inspection and trading.

OFFICES AND COMMERCIAL

Client
DMCC (Dubai Multi Commodities Centre)

Area
183,000 m²

Type
Commercial, retail and a diamond exchange centre

Status
Complete

Date
2005–2008

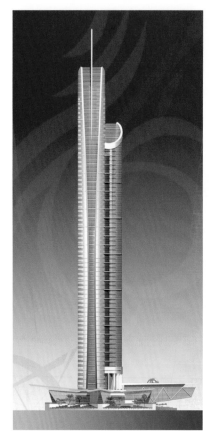
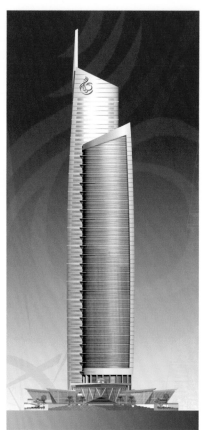

Ground floor plan

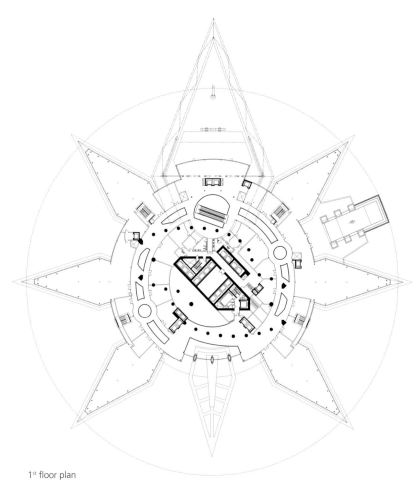

1st floor plan

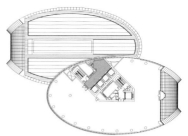

60th and 61st floor plan

47th floor plan – sky lobby

Typical floor plan

The subtle curves of
Almas tend to minimise
its bulk from close
up, but do nothing to
undermine its landmark
status. It is visible
from miles around.

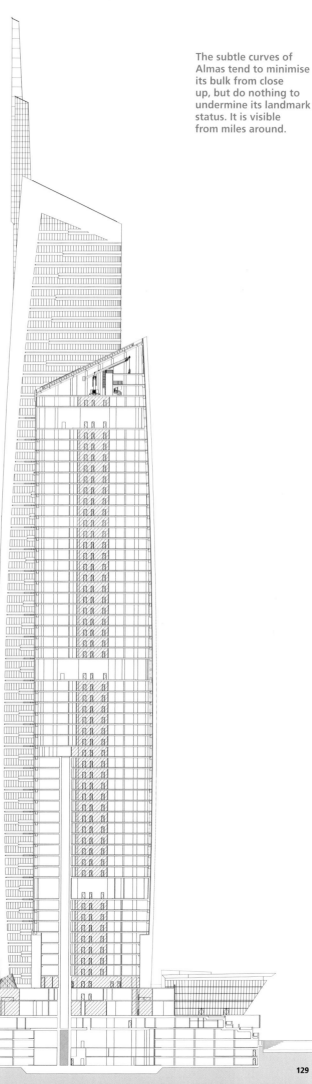

Bahrain World Trade Center
Manama, Bahrain

OFFICES AND COMMERCIAL

Client
Confidential

Area
120,000 m²

Type
240 m twin
office towers
and shopping mall

Status
Complete

Date
2003–2008

The brief called for the regeneration of a mid-1980s commercial development and an under-used park on a superb seafront site in Manama. Consideration of the context of the existing mall, and extending its major axes, suggested a framework for the introduction of twin commercial towers on a podium incorporating both existing and new shopping centres, restaurants, hotels and car parking.

During the site analysis a constant northwesterly onshore breeze was noted, and further investigation revealed this to be consistent and surprisingly strong. To harness it, three aerodynamic bridges were introduced, spanning the space between the towers and each bearing a 29 m diameter wind turbine – the first such installation in the world. The relatively standard

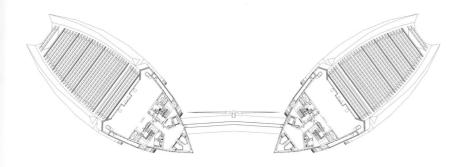

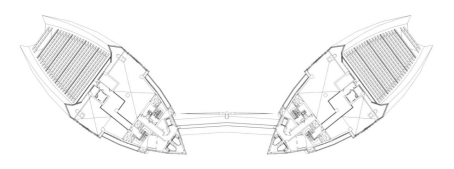

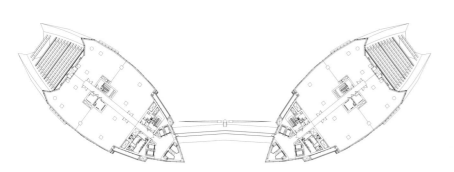

The World Trade Center is a flagship development for Bahrain, creating the world's first example of large-scale integrated wind turbines on a commercial building.

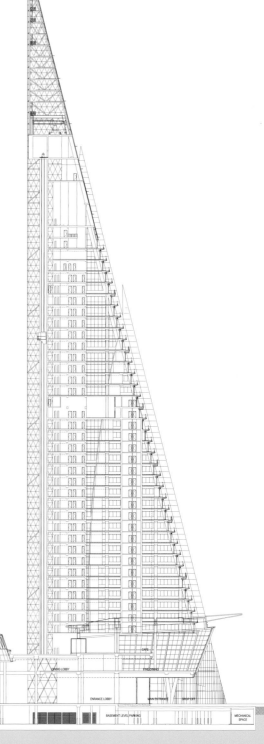

design brief for the initial stages had metamorphosed into a groundbreaking development on the world stage.

The towers rise to a height of 240 m, and together provide 50,000 m² of office space over 41 storeys, with a viewing deck on the 42nd level. They stand on a large podium that incorporates much of the original shopping mall, which has been extended and reworked into an extremely high-end retail centre, offering the world's foremost brands through compact, luxurious shops with the intimacy of a traditional Arabian souk.

The towers' elliptical plan forms and sail-like profiles act as aerofoils, funnelling the onshore breeze and creating a negative pressure downstream, thus accelerating the wind velocity between them. Vertically, the sculpting of the towers also influences airflow dynamics, in that as they taper upwards, their aerofoil sections reduce. This counteracts increasing wind speed with height, and creates an equal regime of wind velocity on each of the three turbines, a critical factor in the successful design of the system. Wind tunnel testing reveals the way in which the shapes

and spatial relationship of the towers sculpts the airflow, creating an 'S'-curve to the airstream whereby the centre of the stream remains nearly perpendicular to the turbine within a 60° wind azimuth to either side of the central axis. This increases the turbines' potential to generate power and reduces fatigue on the blades.

Together the three turbines generate over 700 kW, more than 20% of the building's total power requirement, and they are supported by an extensive suite of sustainability measures to reduce energy and water consumption. The financial premium for this aspect of the development was less than 3% of the project value, which is more than outweighed by the rental premiums attracted by such a world-leading initiative.

The result is a modern reinterpretation of the Arabian wind tower that harnesses the wind's power to serve the built environment, and is a prototype for the next generation of office towers around the world. It has raised the profile of Bahrain, establishing it among the more progressive of the Middle Eastern countries, and in the process provided both a source and a focus for the pride of the Bahraini community. These social benefits bring economic benefits in their wake, as commercial clients actively seek to be identified with the project. The Bahrain World Trade Center addresses the essence of truly sustainable design by making a positive contribution in the areas of economy, environment and social cohesion – the three elements that combine to underpin sustainability.

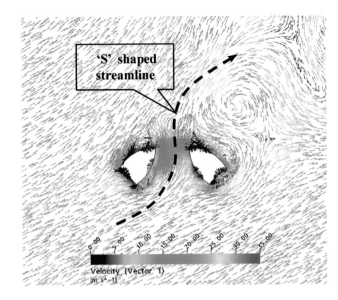

'S' shaped streamline

Velocity (Vector 1) [m s^-1]

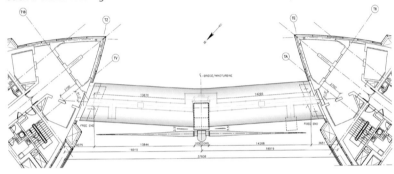

A feature of the design is the way the towers modify the wind flow, ensuring that it is always perpendicular to the turbine over a broad range of general incident angles. This has a significant effect on efficiency.

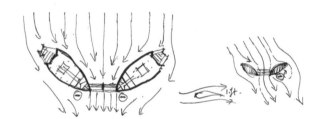

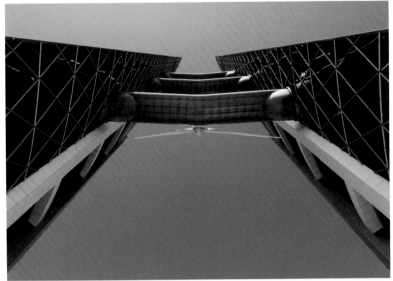

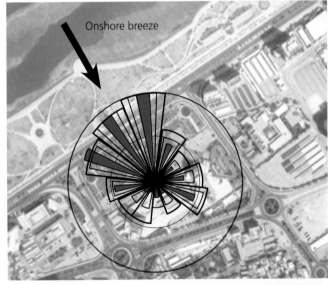

Onshore breeze

Business Bay Sales Centre
Dubai, UAE

OFFICES AND COMMERCIAL

Client
Dubai Properties

Area
3,400 m²

Type
Administrative
office for sales of
commercial and
residential property
in Business Bay

Status
Complete

Date
2005–2006

The Sales Centre is the first and only point of contact for prospective purchasers of commercial or residential property in the Business Bay development. Intended to serve as an indicator of the design quality of the development, the 80 m long, 20 m wide and 8 m high building is an attention-grabbing piece of modern architecture in clear glass, white aluminium panels, sandstone-faced blade walls and stainless steel. The building is designed as a progression from the entrance rotunda through to the main areas, with important entrances and thoroughfares defined by variety in materials and spatial layout.

The main reception area is finished in a combination of rainbow-coloured sandstone and slate. The cavernous sales centre, divided by timber-clad, inverted-cone-shaped columns, contains a show apartment and an auditorium for audio-visual presentations, as well as a café, ten individual sales booths and a scale model of the development.

Raised above the landscape and sitting above a reflecting pool, the building's horizontal emphasis is counter-balanced by a vertical element in the form of a 13 m diameter double-height rotunda at the main entrance. This in turn supports a stainless steel-clad rooftop VIP viewing pod, access to which is obtained by means of glass passenger lifts. From the pod, visitors experience uninterrupted views of the Executive Towers and the soaring structures of Business Bay that provide their backdrop.

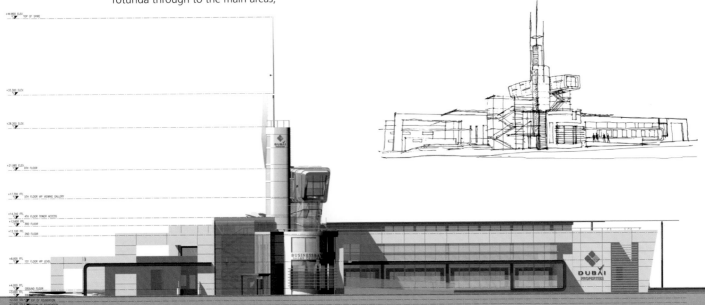

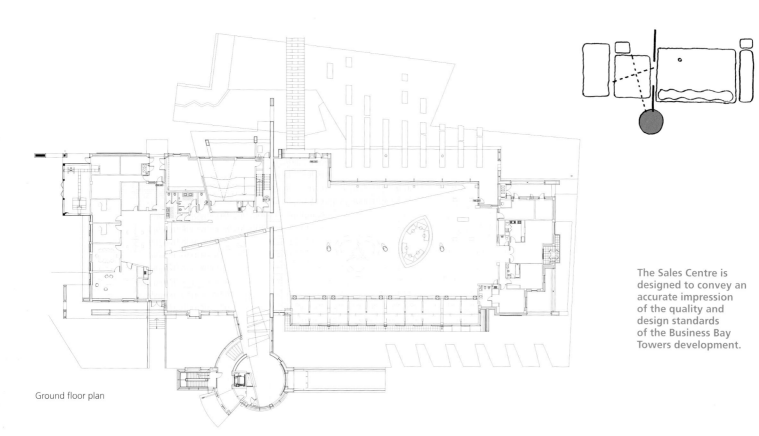

Ground floor plan

The Sales Centre is designed to convey an accurate impression of the quality and design standards of the Business Bay Towers development.

DIFC Lighthouse Tower
Dubai, UAE

OFFICES AND COMMERCIAL

Client
Dubai International
Financial Centre

Area
172,600 m²

Type
Low-carbon,
sustainable
development
comprising a 402 m
office tower

Status
Design

Date
2007–2011

The 402 m high Dubai International Financial Centre Lighthouse Tower. provides 90,000 m² of A-grade office space in Dubai's financial heart for the organisation that serves the region between Western Europe and East Asia. The tower's extraordinary design has produced a building that not only extends the architectural context of the existing precinct, but also expresses DIFC's new prominence in the form of a tall and progressive building on Dubai's skyline.

DIFC Lighthouse Tower slots into the rectilinear cityscape of the DIFC precinct, balancing and complementing the Emirates Towers that sit on the opposite side of the district's centrepiece, The Gate building. The tower's structural bracing, which connects the two cores, reinvents The Gate's diagonal motif as a combination of both *mashrabiya* and the DIFC logo, illuminated by over 6,000 LEDs in a filigree of light against the night sky.

The 64-floor tower accommodates prestigious offices over a two-storey podium and leisure deck with health club, swimming pool, an executive lounge and cultural event spaces. Atkins expanded the brief for the commercial tower to deliver all this in a low-carbon, sustainable and environmentally responsive building, identifying more than 150 techniques to achieve an optimum solution.

The narrow plan of DIFC Lighthouse Tower provides high levels of daylight throughout. When sunlight strikes the façade, blinds are automatically lowered to maintain comfort. In corridors, restrooms and the car park, motion sensors raise local lighting levels from 20% to the normal 11 W/m². In all, a 58% saving in lighting energy has been predicted, which represents 13% of the total energy saved.

The façade system was chosen from 27 different energy models and the

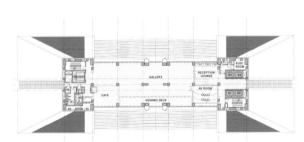

64th floor plan – visitors centre

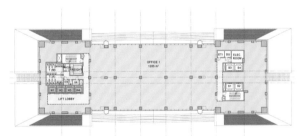

32nd floor plan

9th floor plan

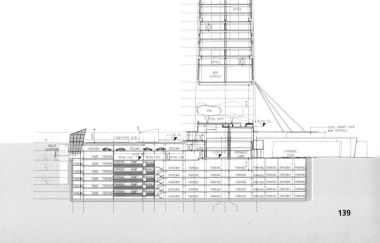

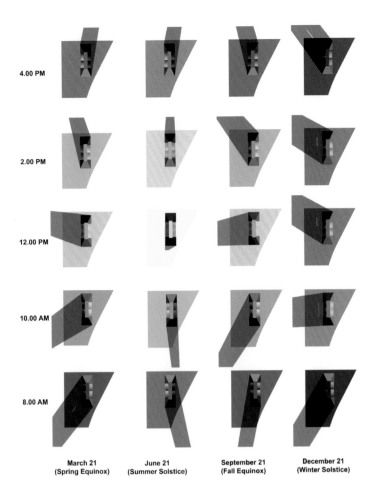

4.00 PM			
2.00 PM			
12.00 PM			
10.00 AM			
8.00 AM			
March 21 (Spring Equinox)	June 21 (Summer Solstice)	September 21 (Fall Equinox)	December 21 (Winter Solstice)

Sun path analysis (*left*) and thermal gain investigations are used to refine building orientation and develop initiatives such as shading, PV cell integration, the introduction of opaque or reflective surfaces and insulation standards.

North elevation

Wh/m2
1100000+
1030000
960000
890000
828000
760000
688000
610000
540000
470000
400000

South elevation

resulting 57% reduction in energy accounts for 3% of all energy saved. Vertically mounted spandrel photovoltaic panels were selected after monitoring the energy output of seven different technologies over different seasons, angles, orientations and cleaning regimes. Reductions of 21% in air conditioning requirements and 69% in ventilation energy use account for a further 6% and 2% savings on total energy consumption.

The synergetic effect of all the applied techniques was analysed in multiple combinations to select the option that resulted in the single most efficient and sustainable outcome, which was then adopted for the building. Intelligent building control synchronises all the systems and reduces the total building energy requirement by another 5%. The final designed solution is estimated to provide a 55% reduction in electrical energy, a 36% reduction in water use and a 55% reduction in district cooling energy compared to business-as-usual for other tall towers.

The project is subject to continual refinement in the quest for efficiency, without allowing for additional

renewable energy investment or rent increases. The payback period for the capital cost of the sustainable initiatives to convert to profit is 3.6 years. Factoring in a rental premium conservatively estimated at 20% brings this down to 1.6 years.

Visitors and regular occupants are unlikely to notice the regenerative braking or increased efficiency of the double-deck elevators, the solar-heated hot water, the lack of draughts or glare or any of the other benefits passive solar architecture brings. They may notice the solar switched lighting and blinds, waterless urinals and cold-water-only staff restrooms as evidence of a low-carbon, high-rise tower, but in time they will come to think of all of this as normal. The most enduring, far-reaching and immeasurable benefit of the DIFC Lighthouse Tower is that it has explored and found the way towards a more sustainable future for high-rise buildings.

DIFC Lighthouse Tower also happens to be an extremely elegant building, beautifully demonstrating that sustainable architecture need not result in dull or bizarre compromises.

The viewing level in the resource centre for sustainable architecture and the built envirnoment.

Energy consumption analyses for different zones, times of day and seasons provide invaluable data for use in developing the building and services design.

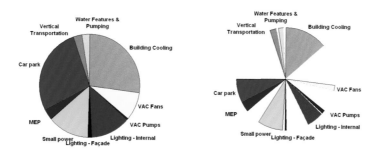

Electrical energy (-55%)

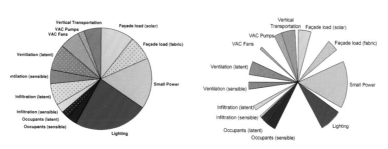

District cooling (-55%)

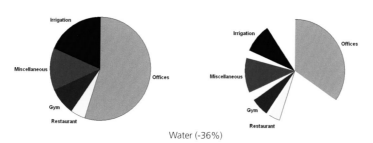

Water (-36%)

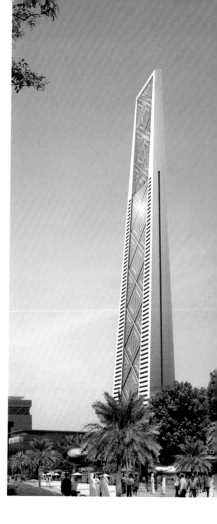

China Resources Power Administration Centre
Changshu, China

Commissioned to design the administrative headquarters of China Resources Power, Atkins produced a 21,000 m² masterplan integrating three components, namely an administration building, a residential complex and a sports centre.

The project is located close to one of the company's coal-fired plants on the banks of the Yangtze River. The three separate elements are symmetrically disposed about a north–south axis terminating in a four-storey atrium that overlooks a body of water at the southern boundary of the site.

The layout is invested with excellent *feng shui,* with the sports centre providing a firm barrier to the north while the façade of the administration building explores the metaphor of a billowing sail as an expression of good luck and prosperity. The sail is transformed into a curved curtain wall that employs high-quality materials.

OFFICES AND COMMERCIAL

Client
China Resources Power

Area
21,000 m²

Type
Administrative centre

Status
Complete

Date
2003–2005

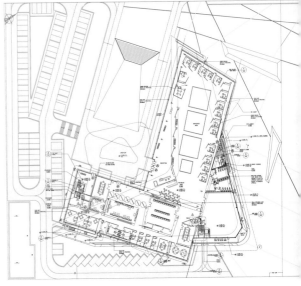

JGC Sales Centre
Dubai, UAE

OFFICES AND COMMERCIAL

Client
Confidential

Area
14,716 m²

Type
Sales centre
and offices

Status
Design

Date
2008

This sales centre will be the first structure designed and delivered for a planned redevelopment of the Al Satwa and Al Wasl areas of Dubai into a mixed-use zone. As well as its functional purpose, the sales centre is designed to indicate to developers the benchmark design standard for the entire project, and represent the project to prospective purchasers.

The building's boomerang shape – a response to limiting boundary conditions – presents a dynamic and energetic profile. A bridge connecting the sales and office areas has at its mid-section a water tank wrapped in a lightweight transparent material, presenting a backdrop onto which the developer projects images and videos. A tower leads to a viewing platform from which prospective buyers can survey the site.

The sales centre is integrated into carefully landscaped surrounds. The various water features emphasise the centre's bold design and colours, particularly at night when 1.7 km of LED lights unite the building and landscape in subtle moving patterns of light and colour.

Crystal Oasis
Dubai, UAE

Dubai Silicon Oasis Authority wanted to develop a planned community that would be the Middle East's leading centre of advanced electronic innovation and development. Crystal Oasis is the design response to that desire, and is planned for a central location to the south of the Authority's present headquarters.

The concept calls for the development of a campus integrating the main office buildings, support services and a large, landscaped site. The site is notionally subdivided into four plots, each of which has a cluster of three office buildings, their cores connected by lobbies and each providing access to a café and restaurant expressed as pavilions within the landscape.

The main buildings take their inspiration from the crystals in the title, with their connotations of natural beauty, sparkling surfaces and electrical properties. The metaphor is extended by the adoption of a diagonal grid support structure in which the floors are supported by an exoskeleton. In this exoskeleton, the voids are glazed with reflective facets of high-performance glass and perforated metal shading.

The buildings were carefully oriented to minimise solar heat gain, a feature further enhanced by the use of cambered, self-shading walls. They are generally similar in size, with local adjustments for different plot sizes, building locations and solar orientation.

An important feature of the plan is the landscaping, which is envisaged as an integrated part of the development. Cooling water, the shade of trees and the crystal offices create a true oasis for occupants.

OFFICES AND COMMERCIAL

Client
Dubai Silicon Oasis Authority (DSOA)

Area
223,000 m²

Type
Business park comprising office complexes including retail, and food and beverage outlets

Status
Design

Date
2008–2011

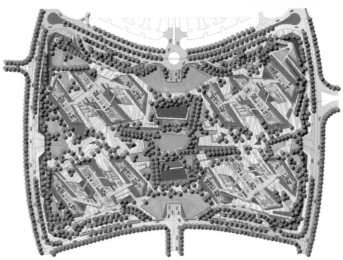

The strongly directional diagonal orientation is a direct result of sun-path studies, and is designed to significantly reduce cooling loads in the summer months.

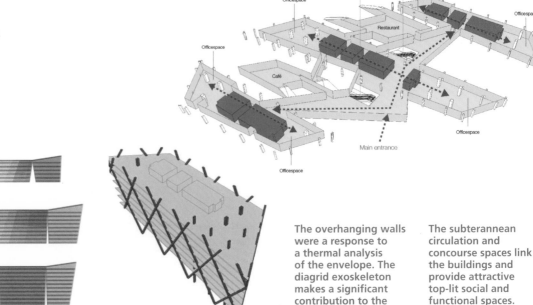

The overhanging walls were a response to a thermal analysis of the envelope. The diagrid exoskeleton makes a significant contribution to the shading of the façade.

The subterannean circulation and concourse spaces link the buildings and provide attractive top-lit social and functional spaces.

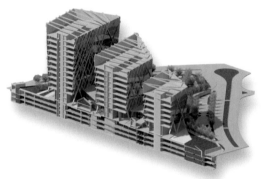

The buried concourses
are intriguing and
attractive spaces,
carefully lit and
landscaped.

Harbour City
Dubai, UAE

This 142 m tower development provides a landmark indicating the seaward entrance to Dubai Maritime City, a large-scale development to be built on reclaimed land off Port Rashid. Here it marks the symbolic point where the sea engages Dubai, and the entry to the shipping lane along which cargo and passenger vessels enter Port Rashid.

From afar, the curves of the tower allude to wind or water, but at closer range the tower is seen to emerge from a podium, the proportions and timber cladding of which are suggestive of traditional boats. This podium has a health club and a generous landscaped deck incorporating seating areas, water features and a swimming pool.

The main entrance to the building is through a four-storey glazed atrium that flows from a deep, naturally illuminated canopy. At ground level there is close to 900 m² of retail space. Nine high-speed lifts provide access to the office floors.

Atkins aims to make energy conservation mainstream in all its projects, and Harbour City has been designed to achieve LEED Silver certification.

OFFICES AND
COMMERCIAL

Client
MENA Capital
Investments (Amwaj)

Area
39,300 m²

Type
142 m
office tower

Status
Design

Date
2008

Bloom Office Tower
Abu Dhabi, UAE

Client
Bloom Properties LLC

Area
44,600 m²

Type
Office and commercial
development

Status
Concept design

Date
2010–ongoing

Bloom Office Tower was commissioned to make a powerful statement in accordance with its prestigious corner site overlooking Abu Dhabi's southern waterway. Selected from a pair of competing proposals, it uses a simple but carefully developed device to create its arresting appearance.

The tower form is straightforward, achieved by wrapping core and floor plates in a vertical curtain of silvered glass and metal, which flows in a smooth curvilinear sheet around the irregular curves of the façade. The façade is additionally articulated by the use of perforated metal sunshades, glittering, semi-transparent veils that partially cover the glass below. The projection and angle of each veil varies, producing a rhythmic pattern of waves and ripples, reflecting its waterfront location.

The veils only hint at the comprehensive system of energy efficient devices adopted to reduce energy and water consumption.

Shading, good insulation, low-transmission multi-layer glass, solar power generation and water conservation and harvesting systems are all integrated into the design.

Restrained landscaping and a simple site road plan provide a clean, rational backdrop in perfect keeping with the project's urban, waterside location.

Tianjin TEDA Centre
Tianjin, China

OFFICES AND COMMERCIAL

Client
TEDA

Area
486,236 m²

Type
25 medium-rise blocks along a 1.5 km site

Status
Under construction

Date
2008–2011

The centre is part of the central government's plan for the regeneration of Tianjin, formerly a foreign 'concession port' in northern China. The Tianjing Economic Development Area (TEDA) is approximately 45 km from downtown Tianjing, which is the port city for Beijing and northeast China.

This competition-winning urban design is for the central zone of TEDA. It creates an important urban gateway and connects the government, cultural and retail buildings that line the main route into the development zone.

Some 25 new buildings will provide over 400,000 m² of office and retail space. They will be arranged around new civic spaces along a strip of land that is 1.5 km long but only 140 m wide.

The winning concept creates a folded surface in which a series of green civic spaces connect the various office buildings. These green surfaces are 'folded' horizontally and vertically to simulate smaller urban squares, and to enable the introduction of hotel and office buildings.

The medium-rise office buildings, none more than 80 m high, all serve the technology and service companies in the development zone. Vertical green walls of vegetation ameliorate the impact of both the high density and the cold climate.

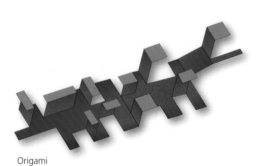

Origami

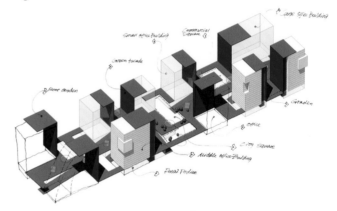

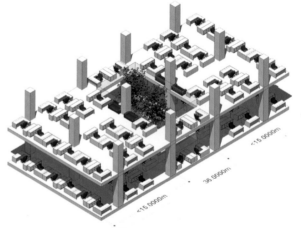

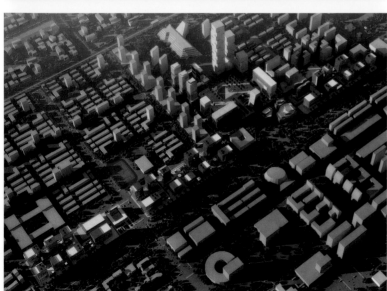

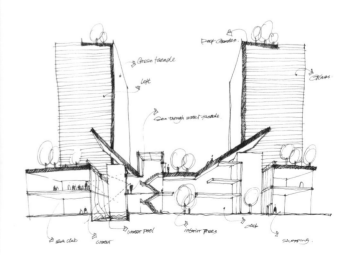

The 25 'building blocks' at Tianjin are used to articulate pedestrian walkways, courtyards and plazas along the 1.5 km spine of the development.

Photovoltaic mesh is integrated into the luminated glass panel to harness the suns energy and provide shade to the facade

Perforated facade allows assisted natural ventilation

Plant room and services are located in the middle of the tower for a more efficient distribution of services

Minimized windows in side facade for lesser heat absorption

Natural ventilation through building facade helps the cooling of the tower

Green environment enhance both micro climate and total aesthetic

Suspended and grade level water features improve micro climate

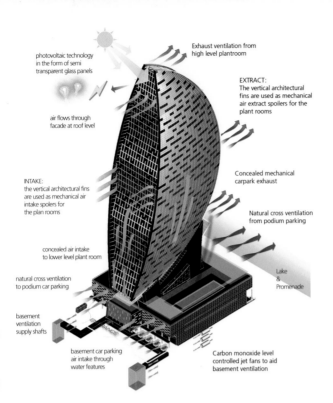

photovoltaic technology in the form of semi transparent glass panels

air flows through facade at roof level

INTAKE:
the vertical architectural fins are used as mechanical air intake spoilers for the plan rooms

concealed air intake to lower level plant room

natural cross ventilation to podium car parking

basement ventilation supply shafts

basement car parking air intake through water features

Exhaust ventilation from high level plantroom

EXTRACT:
The vertical architectural fins are used as mechanical air extract spoilers for the plant rooms

Concealed mechanical carpark exhaust

Natural cross ventilation from podium parking

Lake & Promenade

Carbon monoxide level controlled jet fans to aid basement ventilation

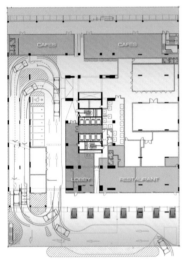

Ground floor plan

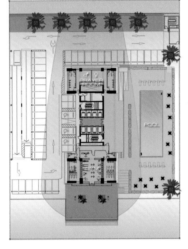

Podium roof plan

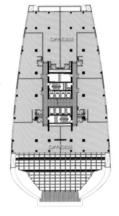

20th floor plan

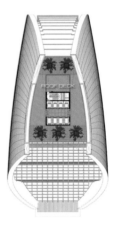

Roof deck plan

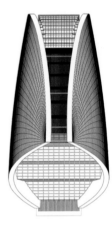

Roof plan

Iris Bay
Dubai, UAE

OFFICES AND COMMERCIAL

Client
Sheth Estate (International) Ltd

Area
36,000 m²

Type
170 m, 32-storey tower located in the Business Bay area

Status
Under construction

Date
2006–2010

Iris Bay is located at the southwest corner of the burgeoning Business Bay district of Dubai, and sits adjacent to the main Sheikh Zayed highway. The 170 m high, 32-storey tower rests on a four-storey podium containing the entrance, retail facilities, a restaurant and café, a gymnasium, a swimming pool and shaded relaxation spaces on the podium roof. Beneath are three levels of basement parking for 920 cars.

The project was an early opportunity for Atkins to explore the challenges of sustainable design in a hot climate, and incorporate both passive and active environmental features to arrive at a holistic solution.

Cantilevered and rotated over the podium are a pair of identical, pixellated, spherical shell segments. These are separated at the rear by a continuous vertical curve punctuated by balconies, while the front elevation is made up of seven angled zones of glazing.

The tower has a low window-to-wall ratio where appropriate, with glazed areas that are shaded by balconies with openings to facilitate natural ventilation or incorporate photovoltaic panels.

The distinctive ovoid shape creates areas of negative pressure that draw air through the building and reduce dependence on mechanical ventilation, particularly for the underground car park. The arrangement satisfies many requirements, not least of which is an immediately recognisable identity.

Wind flow analysis shows that Iris Bay will be able to use ventilation to make a major reduction in the length of its cooling season, including basement levels.

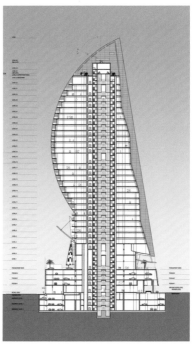

TEDA Buildings
Tianjin, China

OFFICES AND COMMERCIAL

Client
TEDA

Area
400,000 m²

Type
Three mixed-use towers on a podium comprising commerical areas

Status
Design

Date
2005

Understanding historical and cultural complexities is important when designing in China. There is always a search for some deeper symbolic meaning, and contrary to western thinking, clients like this symbolism to be manifested quite literally in the architecture. The challenge is to create a building that satisfies this important requirement and also 'travels well'.

Here, the proposal was to design three towers ranging from 100 m to 300 m tall, incorporating retail space, apartments, offices and, at the highest level of the tallest tower, a hotel. There is no podium as such, but a linking structure provides common services at ground level and sits within the space defined by the towers.

The stacked cubes of the TEDA Towers have been likened to a stack of gold bars, representing wealth and economic success. They also resemble a stack of containers, in reference to the nearby container terminal at Tang Sin – one of China's key commercial world gateways.

Comprehension of the design worldwide however, seems to rely more on the universally recognised symbol of the box, whether that box be a container or a treasure chest.

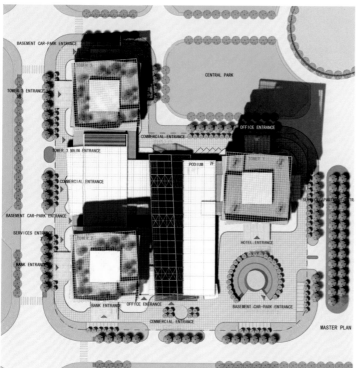

MASTER PLAN

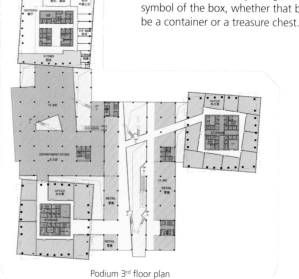

Podium 3rd floor plan

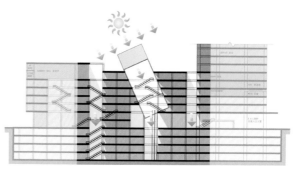

The creation of distinct identities for the towers' occupants is also important, especially in such large buildings at the centre of a business district. The separate blocks each have their own corner atria and each one possesses a unique view of the city, providing originality as well as a sense of belonging within the development.

TEDA Towers benefits from geothermal energy sourcing and solar heating from the double-glazed walls of the atria, and the top cube at the summit of the tallest tower houses vertical-axis wind turbines that are the subject of continuing design development.

These energy conservation measures enhance the status of the buildings in Chinese culture and improve their credibility in world terms.

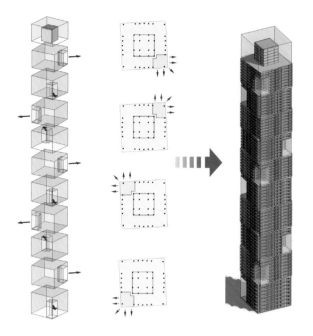

A corner atrium in each cube creates a green social space with a variety of views and an individual identity.

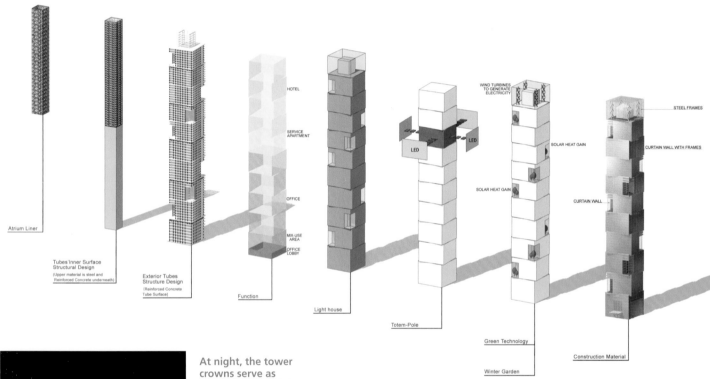

Atrium Liner

Tubes' Inner Surface Structural Design
(Upper material is steel and Reinforced Concrete underneath)

Exterior Tubes Structure Design
(Reinforced Concrete Tube Surface)

Function

HOTEL

SERVICE APARTMENT

OFFICE

MIX-USE AREA

OFFICE LOBBY

Light house

Totem-Pole

WIND TURBINES TO GENERATE ELECTRICITY

LED

LED

SOLAR HEAT GAIN

SOLAR HEAT GAIN

Green Technology

Winter Garden

STEEL FRAMES

CURTAIN WALL WITH FRAMES

CURTAIN WALL

Construction Material

At night, the tower crowns serve as beacons, highlighting TEDA and adding a spectacular element to the nightscape of the city.

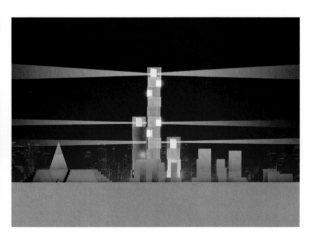

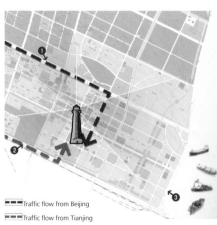

--- Traffic flow from Beijing

--- Traffic flow from Tianjing

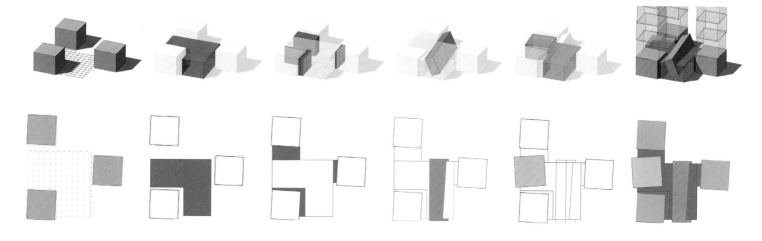

The sketches above are used to explore the devlopment of the massing of the buildings; three towers rotated by 3°, a separate linking structure inserted, the strange tension of the trapped spaces between towers and the link, a grand atrium introduced, the 'golden' ballroom defined and ultimately the whole concept integrated and revealed.

The TEDA Towers employ two categories of sustainable energy:
1. External – harnessing wind, geothermal and solar power.
2. Internal – recovering waste heat.

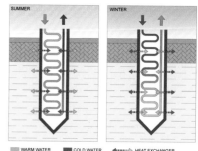

SUMMER   WINTER

WARM WATER   COLD WATER   HEAT EXCHANGER

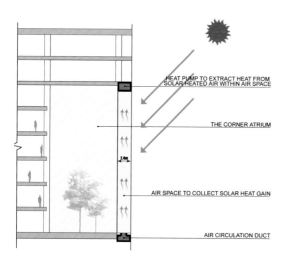

HEAT PUMP TO EXTRACT HEAT FROM SOLAR HEATED AIR WITHIN AIR SPACE

THE CORNER ATRIUM

AIR SPACE TO COLLECT SOLAR HEAT GAIN

AIR CIRCULATION DUCT

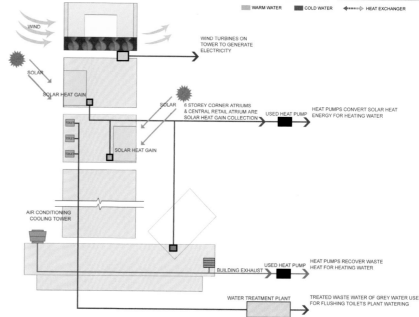

WIND

WIND TURBINES ON TOWER TO GENERATE ELECTRICITY

SOLAR

SOLAR HEAT GAIN

SOLAR

6 STOREY CORNER ATRIUMS & CENTRAL RETAIL ATRIUM ARE SOLAR HEAT GAIN COLLECTION

USED HEAT PUMP

HEAT PUMPS CONVERT SOLAR HEAT ENERGY FOR HEATING WATER

SOLAR HEAT GAIN

AIR CONDITIONING COOLING TOWER

BUILDING EXHAUST

USED HEAT PUMP

HEAT PUMPS RECOVER WASTE HEAT FOR HEATING WATER

WATER TREATMENT PLANT

TREATED WASTE WATER OF GREY WATER USED FOR FLUSHING TOILETS PLANT WATERING

TEDA's vertical landscape design maximises green areas by utilising the podium roof as well as the corner and internal atria, thus enabling the provision of more trees on a constrained site area.

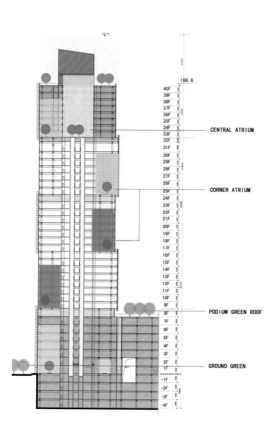

169.6

40F
39F
38F
37F
36F
35F
34F   CENTRAL ATRIUM
33F
32F
31F
30F
29F
28F
27F
26F   CORNER ATRIUM
25F
24F
23F
22F
21F
20F
19F
18F
17F
16F
15F
14F
13F
12F
11F
10F
9F
8F   PODIUM GREEN ROOF
7F
6F
5F
4F
3F
2F
1F   GROUND GREEN
-1F
-2F
-3F
-4F

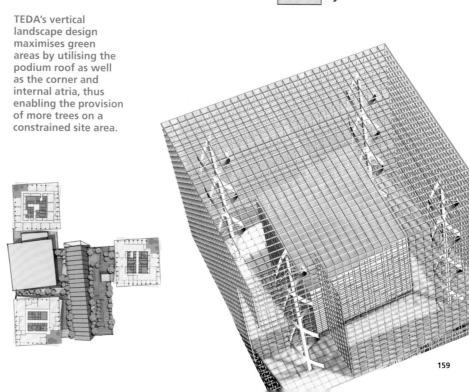

Zero Carbon Office Campus
Abu Dhabi, UAE

**OFFICES AND
COMMERCIAL**

Client
Confidential

Area
92,400 m²

Type
Headquarters office
building

Status
Concept design

Date
2007–2008

This suite of offices was designed as the headquarters for a zero-carbon campus. Its design had to be a paragon of sustainability.

In preparing its proposals, the design team considered every aspect of the project from the site climate and orientation to the configuration of table and chair in the smallest of offices.

The design inevitably addresses the 'standard' techniques of sustainability;

minimising cooling loads through shading, maximising daylighting through shallow plan forms, capturing and recycling water, employing natural ventilation for comfort and cooling, and so forth. In this case, though, they were applied to an exceptional degree, making the best use of the client's open-mindedness and 'pushing the envelope' to a significant extent.

Unusual roof forms and building massing were developed to capture

even the lightest of breezes, with raking, overhanging walls providing deep shade and funnelling air from the roof level down to the ground, eight floors below.

The result of this radical and open-minded approach was fascinating. The completed, resolved and refined design turns out to be a contemporary take on the traditional Arabian desert village, neatly validating both traditional and modern approaches.

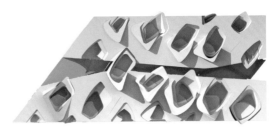

The fascinating roof shapes were developed to funnel moving air down to provide cooling breezes for occupants right down to the ground floor level.

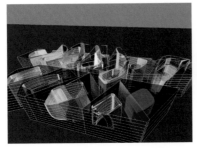

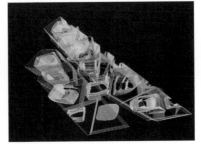

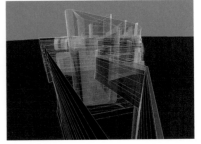

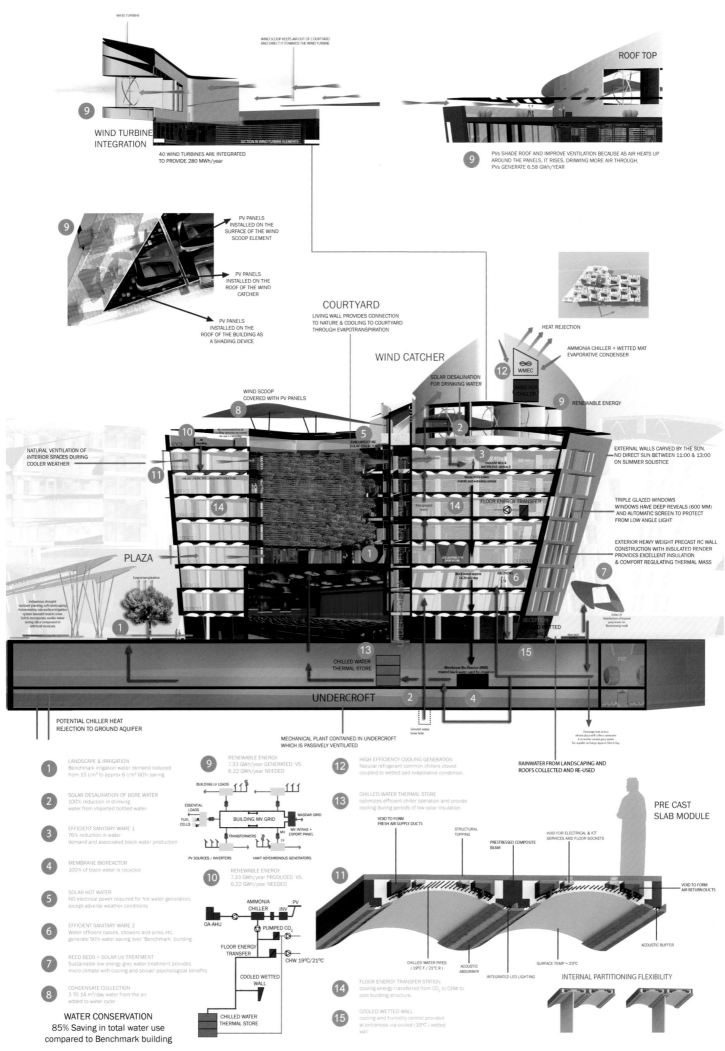

Translucent, transparent and reflective materials are carefully combined to achieve particular control over daylight, infra-red and UV penetration.

The shady streets and enclosed courtyards were developed from first principles, but replicate traditional desert architecture to a remarkable degree.

The Hub
Bristol, UK

This 9,500 m² spectacular office building at Aztec West, Bristol started off as an Atkins-designed project, and is now home to the firm's consolidated Bristol-based businesses. Although housing only one tenant, the design required a flexible floor plate arrangement for future versatility.

From the outside, the building appears to be a considered glass and galvanised steel box. The façade design was deliberately kept simple to contain costs, but visual interest is provided by solar shading that

wraps sections of the elevations in anodised aluminium blades, while protruding at first-floor level from the north and west elevations are the faces of a second, smaller box, inserted at an oblique angle into the volume of the main building.

Cutting deep into the whole is the large atrium, animated by two glass-and-steel staircases, bridge links and an imposing curved core. Three levels of office space overlook the atrium from three sides; the fourth side is a full-height, recessed entrance screen

that is flanked by tall fire-escape staircases with zinc rain-screens.

The BREEAM rating of 'excellent' makes The Hub an exemplar of sustainability. Fundamental to this was ensuring the building orientation and form were correct, but contributions were also made by a variety of initiatives including the use of chilled beams, ground source heat pumps, solar shading, rain harvesting and low water-use installations.

OFFICES AND COMMERCIAL

Client
Rok Development

Area
9,500 m²

Type
Office development

Status
Complete

Date
2007–2009

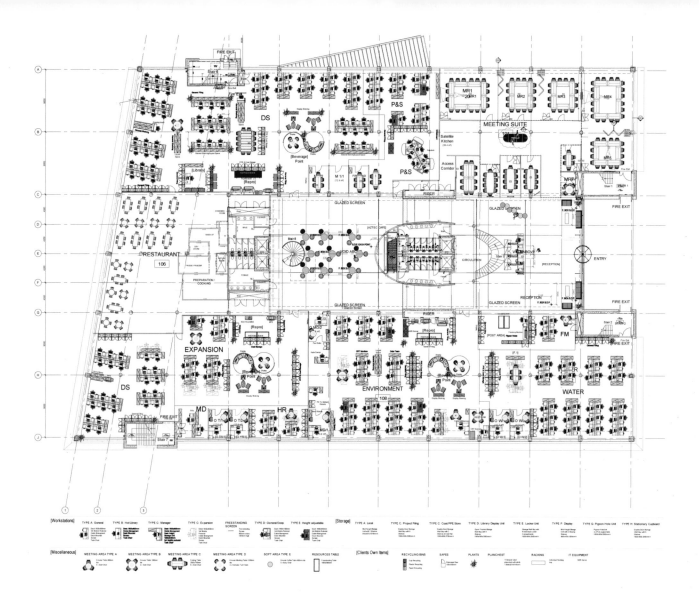

An exploded diagram of The Hub shows the central atrium and the long side wings flanking the large entrance screen.

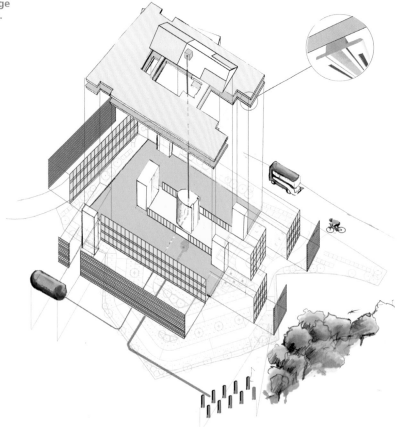

Qingping Highway Management Centre
Shenzhen, China

OFFICES AND
COMMERCIAL

Client
Shenzhen Huayu
Highway Investment
Co. Ltd.

Area
50,000 m²

Type
Highway control
centre

Status
Competition entry

Date
2004

The 50,000 m² Shenzhen Qingping Highway Management Centre is significant for its explicit sustainable-design agenda. The project comprises a management office block as well as recreational and support buildings, all incorporating green roofs, sun shading and passive cooling.

The design evolved from a study of the microclimate in this subtropical city. Solar gain in the management centre is minimised by its orientation, its tapered oval form and the detailed design of its skin. Other buildings were similarly positioned to take advantage of the cooling effect of winds blowing over the nearby lake.

The management centre fronts the access road, but the support and recreational buildings are shielded by a barrier that encloses them in a landscaped, leaf-shaped compound – an appropriate form for a design based on ecological principles.

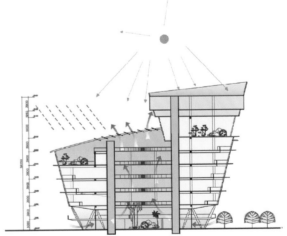

Green roofs, solar shading, stack-effect ventilation, controlled daylighting – the full range of sustainable technologies has been applied.

A waterside location provides a number of sustainable options when it comes to environmental control, and is always desirable.

Overhanging walls provide significant shade benefits in warmer climates, and are a form that seems destined to become increasingly common.

Baku Tower
Baku, Azerbaijan

**OFFICES AND
COMMERCIAL**

Client
Confidential

Area
80,000 m²

Type
32-storey office
component

Status
Design

Date
2008

Baku Tower is a 32-storey mixed-use
commercial and retail development
occupying a prominent site close
to downtown Baku. The tower
design follows the architect's
tradition of shallow floor plates
to provide egalitarian access to
views and natural light throughout
the office environment, while
supporting a highly efficient structure
and space planning regime.

Two medium-rise towers
provide separate, A-grade office
accommodation within the park
setting. A low-rise retail building
functionally connects the office
buildings and unifies the composition.

The south façades of the office
towers are shaded by an outer skin
of architectural louvres that filter
glare and minimise heat gain, and are
entirely recessed within a structural
frame. On the north side, this element
becomes a picture frame with glazing
set within it to form a simple and
effective architectural device.

Al Rostamani Office and Residential Building
Dubai, UAE

OFFICES AND
COMMERCIAL

Client
Al Rostamani Real
Estate

Area
30,800 m²

Type
Offices and residential

Status
Complete

Date
2002–2005

Located in the city's banking district, the Al Rostamani Building is a bold sculptural structure in the form of a triangular shaped block with gently curved sides that appears to float above a glazed podium. The building responds to its corner site and urban context by being stepped back from the pavement edge to create space for landscaping and open views.

The curved form is clad in reflective dark-blue glass that contrasts sharply with the vertical shaft of the elevator and stair tower that is formed of white composite aluminium panels. The service element seemingly pierces the main block to reappear on the opposite elevation as a sharp arris supporting four balconies.

Access to the banking hall at ground level and the four commercial floors is separated from the apartments housed on the upper nine residential floors. The building is home to the Dubai office and regional headquarters of Atkins, the sole occupant of the commercial floors.

Tiffany Tower
Dubai, UAE

OFFICES AND COMMERCIAL

Client
IFFCO

Area
49,000 m²

Type
183 m, 42-storey
office tower

Status
Complete

Date
2005–2010

Tiffany Tower occupies a prime location in the Jumeirah Lakes Towers (JLT) development in 'New Dubai', some 20 km south of the old city centre. JLT features 78 towers set in groups of three around a series of created lakes and the centrepiece Almas tower. In such a concentrated group of towers, all similar in terms of height and mass, the client's determination that Tiffany Tower would stand out from the crowd was understandable, but challenging.

The response was to use two simple aesthetic devices – tapering forms and curves. The building is rectangular in plan form, with the longer side walls flaring out in a gentle curve as they rise, gradually becoming vertical at mid-level and then converging to meet at roof level. The graceful curved planes they follow are divided into four bays of textured blue glass, delineated by fine aluminium ribs.

The shorter end elevations are vertical planes, articulated by horizontal balconies and a pair of vertical ribs placed on either side of the central axis, which take an angled turn towards the top and base to form canopies above the ground levels and below the roof vault.

This curvaceous shape readily differentiates the building from its neighbours during daylight hours. At night the glass vault at roof level is gently illuminated to provide a beacon visible from all around the site.

Within the elegant 183 m high envelope are 38 floors of offices, with guest suites on the upper levels, retail and restaurant outlets at ground level and also a mosque that serves the whole development.

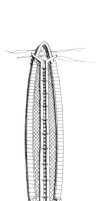

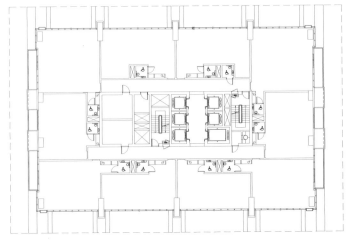

Typical floor plan (3–19)

DSEC Commercial Tower
Dubai, UAE

OFFICES AND COMMERCIAL

Client
DSEC Corporation FZC

Area
47,968 m²

Type
19-storey office and commercial tower

Status
Under construction

Date
2006–2010

This is a commercial building located in the heart of Dubai's Business Bay district. The development has basement parking for 650 cars and a three-storey podium comprising entrance and ground floor retail outlets, with health, restaurant and other leisure facilities on its rooftop deck. Above this are 19 floors of office space.

The entrance to the building is landscaped with water features, and leads to the reception area where five high-speed lifts serve the office floors. The office volume is suspended two storeys above the podium and is configured as a rectangular, glazed block mostly contained within but just penetrating the sides of an extended ovoid cylinder. Office space has been designed to facilitate either an open plan layout or partitioning into smaller spaces if required.

The roof of the podium doubles as a leisure deck, enjoying excellent views of the city from its landscaped gardens, reflection pool, relaxation decks and fully equipped gym.

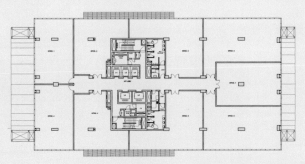

Typical floor plan

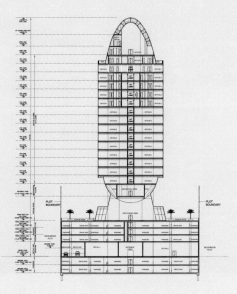

Supreme Education Council Headquarters
Doha, Qatar

**OFFICES AND
COMMERCIAL**

Client
Qatar Petroleum and
Supreme Education
Council

Area
86,000 m²

Type
Five two-storey office
buildings linked by a
'wall of knowledge'

Status
Design complete

Date
2008

This 86,000 m² campus integrates five office buildings for the Supreme Education Council Headquarters in Doha. The five units occupy lower ground, ground and first floor levels and are connected via a double-height internal street termed the 'Wall of Knowledge'. This corridor links the buildings to a central courtyard but preserves their functional autonomy,

clearly expressed in their architectural form. Its gallery allows drop-off access from the landscaped deck, while the lower-ground level responds to climatic realities by enabling direct pedestrian access from the car park. The buildings and a central fountain rise through openings in this landscaped deck that also serves to direct light and fresh air down to lower levels.

The individual buildings mimic this organisation with central courtyards acting as social spaces, surrounded by office accommodation.

Externally, the buildings are wrapped in delicate, stainless steel *mashrabiya* screens. These filter the harsh light and moderate the environment above ground.

Beautiful graphical patterns of Islamic origin are used to create the delicate shade screens that are used to provide solar control.

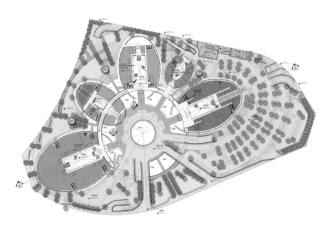

Office Tower
Kuwait City, Kuwait

**OFFICES AND
COMMERCIAL**

Client
Confidential

Area
77,800 m²

Type
Commercial
headquarters tower

Status
Concept design
complete

Date
2006

Kuwait City has an unusual microclimate, with frequent sandstorms driven by strong winds out of the harsh sunlight to the south contrasting with attractive coastal views to the sheltered north. This long, narrow site amplifies these conflicting elements, and makes them particularly influential in the architectural form of the new building.

The tower follows the proportions of the site, with the form articulated as a stack of light with open glazed spaces overlooking the coastline and sea views, sheltered by a shield wall facing the stormy south. The shield adopts the form of a vast, billowing sail, falling to the deck in folds that contain the retail podium accommodation. The wall is pierced by the traditionally defensive form of horizontal slit windows.

The northwestern façade enjoys a more tranquil outlook and views over water. The elevation employs a regular colonnade of metal fins as a vertical *brise soleil*, shading the glazing from low morning and evening sun, allowing this elevation to become a tall, transparent box from which the occupants can look out in comfort, and which provides a welcoming location for the building's main entrance.

ITC Campus & Towers
Bangalore, India

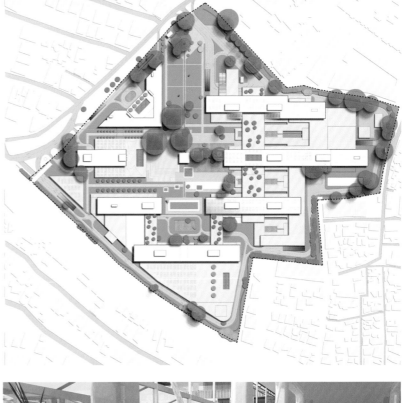

ITC recognised that its existing horizontal campus facility within converted industrial warehouses had a number of advantages, in particular the way in which the green spaces between buildings created a strong sense of working community. However, owing to the need to greatly increase the campus population from around 3,000 to 12,000 staff, ITC decided to adopt a vertical mid-rise tower arrangement for its new offices, but was reluctant to lose the benefits of the horizontal, landscaped campus.

Atkins' response was to first look at optimising the arrangement of buildings on the site by orienting them with the long axis running east to west. This has the dual advantage of minimising solar gain while maximising natural daylight in the office spaces. This orientation also takes advantage of the prevailing east–west winds that provide thermal comfort in the courtyard spaces that lie between the office tower buildings.

The arrangement of the buildings was also governed by the desire to retain a large number of existing trees on the site, some of which are more than 100 years old. These trees provide extensive canopy shading and support inner-city habitats for birds and wildlife.

Architecturally, Atkins sought to create a 'vertical campus' by including elevated green spaces throughout the buildings in the form of landscaped atria and triple-volume sky gardens.

The façade design has been considered to mitigate solar gain and encourage wind movement through the building structures. This analytical concern with sustainable design has led to an architectural language and provides a fine example of how good sustainable practice can provide benefits at every level.

The project aims to achieve the highest possible LEED Platinum Green Building rating, enabling us to push the envelope of best practice in sustainable design.

OFFICES AND COMMERCIAL

Client
ITC

Area
147,521 m²

Type
Commercial office tower

Status
Concept design

Date
2011

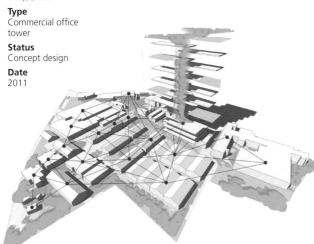

MIXED-USE

Dubai Promenade
Dubai, UAE

MIXED-USE

Client
Nakheel LLC

Area
42 ha

Type
High-end, mixed-use,
integrated community

Status
Design complete

Date
2008–2012

The Dubai Promenade is formed on approximately 420,000 m² of reclaimed land extending from the southern corner of the Mina Seyahi entrance to the Dubai Marina – the largest created marina in the world and home to many residential, commercial and hotel developments. It meshes with established water, road, pedestrian and urban networks and is the gateway to the entire Dubai Marina development, extending southwards along the Dubai shoreline from the Burj Al Arab and The Palm Jumeirah.

The Dubai Promenade is a simple, linear extension of the land deep into the sea, which develops into a sheltered, circular lagoon at its tip. The length of the promenade is punctuated by tower developments – residential, commercial and hotel – all broadly similar in scale and mass, brought to a full stop by the extraordinary Dubai Promenade Hotel. There is no through traffic; landscaping in the generous spacing between those buildings and along the shoreline makes it a place to be appreciated on foot.

The simple form of the promenade site belies its potential effect. While it will be a pleasure to experience on foot, either from the promenade itself or across the water, it is those entering and leaving the marina who will find it most engaging. Instead of passing below a set of functional road bridges and past a shallow beach, their route will be transformed into a procession lined with buildings, trees and spectators.

DUBAI PROMENADE HOTEL

Modernists believe that form should follow function, and accordingly expect hotels to be simple towers. However, that approach depends on the definition of 'function'. In the case of the Dubai Promenade Hotel, the function is to be a hotel and to be iconic: to act as a spectacular attraction, to provide a single unique response to a superb location and act as a defining architectural punctuation point on Dubai's waterfront. In that regard it has some pretty stiff competition – it is located at the entrance to the world's largest created marina, looks straight out onto The Palm Jumeirah and is just down the coast from the Burj Al Arab.

The dramatic torus form is at heart a straightforward pair of towers connected at the top by a bridge. The latter element houses presidential and standard suites, restaurants and bars, all with spectacular panoramic views, and all connected directly to the lobby by a transparent lift shaft rising externally through the centre of the torus. The lower podium and the two shapely wings house the entrance lobby, lounges and retail areas, function suites, restaurants and cafés, a major conference suite,

car parking and so forth. In all of this, the polished architectural forms involve surprisingly few compromises and a great many benefits, not least the creation of some fascinating architectural spaces – while remaining fully functional, the larger public spaces become inherently dramatic through their unusual geometry and transparent materials. The spaces around the hotel are truly spectacular, and travelling within the transparent lift or looking out of the conference suite will provide genuinely unique visual experiences.

Externally, the landscaping and layout of the site match the standards of creativity and style set by the architecture. The hotel stands at the end of the Dubai Promenade and as such is a terminal rather than a gateway. Pedestrians are given priority over a minimal and largely concealed road layout, an approach that the landscaping supports by providing shaded walks down to the beach or towards the Marina. The external environment is carried into the hotel lobby, which is treated as a series of islands floating in mirror pools, an appropriate entrance to a unique and thoroughly stylish composition.

The Dubai Promenade will extend out into the sea at the entrance to the Dubai Marina, with the Dubai Promenade Hotel occupying the prime site at the seaward end.

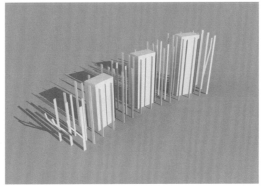

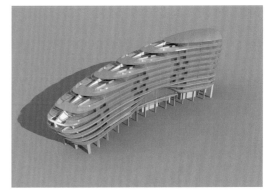

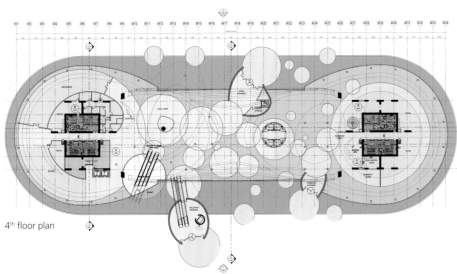

4th floor plan

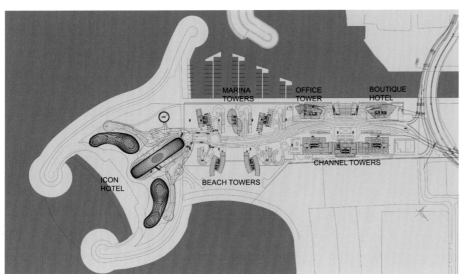

MARINA TOWERS

OFFICE TOWER

BOUTIQUE HOTEL

CHANNEL TOWERS

ICON HOTEL

BEACH TOWERS

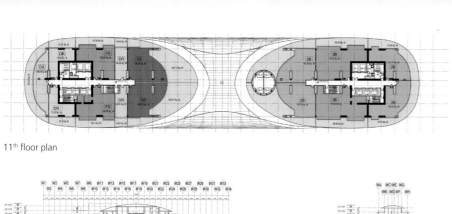

11th floor plan

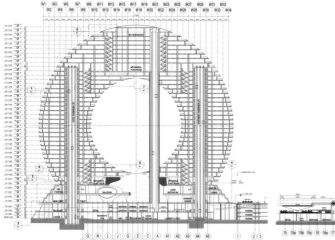

The Dubai Promenade Hotel has a distinctive form worthy of an iconic building. The shape actually proves to be surprisingly efficient and creates some truly spectacular spaces.

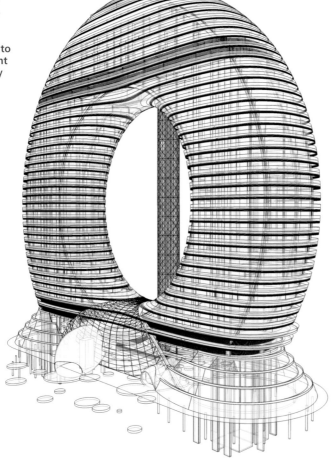

Specific functional
spaces are enclosed
in shiny metal pods
that penetrate the
hotel's skin and create
fascinating internal
and external spaces.

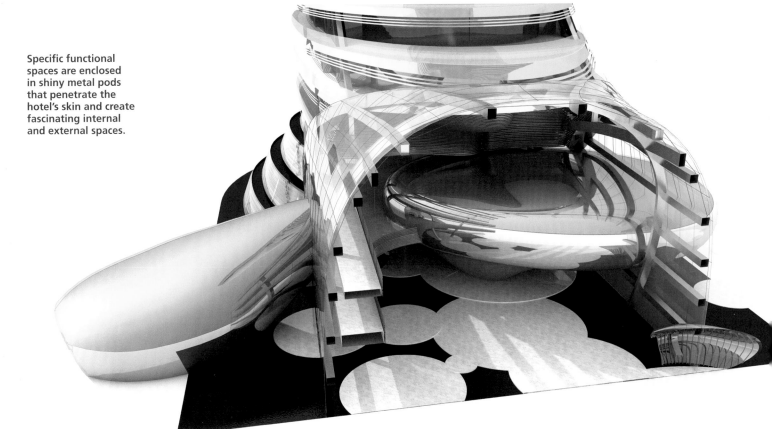

DUBAI PROMENADE
BOUTIQUE HOTEL

The 48,000 m² five-star Boutique Hotel rises 14 floors above a three-storey podium. Its façade is articulated as a series of ripples, a catspaw of wind-whipped water on an otherwise placid sea.

In its quest for reduced energy consumption it is set 30° off the north–south axis to give the best overall energy performance.

The design of the balconies has been given special attention in terms of both amenity and comfort. This dictated the use of materials with low heat-retention, enabling the balconies to be used for longer and further into the summer months.

The entrance lobby has expansive views over the water and features a sculptured staircase leading up to an infinity pool, a pool bar and an open landscaped deck.

DUBAI PROMENADE
OFFICE TOWER

Together with the Boutique Hotel, this 45,000 m², 15-storey Office Tower sits as a balance to the Channel Tower on the other side of the Dubai Promenade. The tower stands on a four-storey podium that forms a spine for the promenade development and accommodates car parking and a retail strip on the marina side. The ground floor has a café and health spa, and a lobby that overlooks the water.

Designed to cater to the premium office space market, the building has a gently curvilinear exterior, fronting an efficient, flexible internal arrangement. Like the Boutique Hotel, this is achieved by passive energy-saving measures including rotating the building 30° off the north–south axis to minimise solar gain. This allows maximum use of natural daylighting and enables the building control system to reduce the level of artificial lighting accordingly.

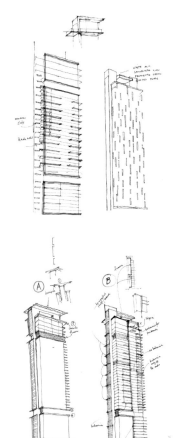

DUBAI PROMENADE
CHANNEL TOWERS

The Channel Towers complex is an important part of the Dubai Promenade. These are relaxed buildings that resist the urge to be statement towers – instead they form a pleasingly calm, simple composition that provides a foil to the vibrancy of the Dubai Promenade Hotel.

The central 45-storey tower and two flanking 40-storey towers have a total of 959 apartments sitting above a common, single-storey podium. The podium incorporates the ubiquitous leisure deck, swimming pool and other shared facilities, as well as a supermarket and convenience store.

The layout and orientation of the Channel Towers is determined by site constraints and the path of the sun. Sheer walls, deep balconies and vertical louvres create passive shading to the east and west without sacrificing views.

As part of a sensible design for the Middle East residential market, the Channel Towers incorporate a number of water-saving and energy efficiency systems. Unusually for such a development, however, they have also been designed with some flexibility in the internal layout, with the space between the shell and the cores left open so that they may be offered as open-plan units or divided at will into more traditional apartments.

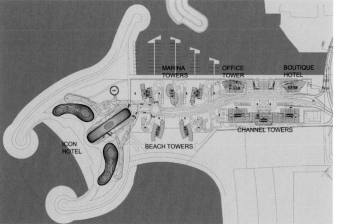

The three developments extend along the length of the promenade and overlook the marina entrance.

189

Al Rajhi Tower
Riyadh, Saudi Arabia

MIXED-USE

Client
Business Management
Board of Al Sheikh
Al Rajhi

Area
300,000 m²

Type
Mixed-use commercial
tower

Status
Design

Date
2006

From the outset, Al Rajhi Tower was destined to become a landmark in the centre of Riyadh. Planned as the tallest tower in the city, it aspires to be distinct from and more prominent than either the Kingdom Tower or Al Fasaliah Tower. It was also conceived as having a mixture of uses to ensure that it became a lively, active place for the people of Riyadh and their visitors.

Pyramidal in form, the over 400 m tower uses a geometric mesh façade structure at its base. This frames a cavernous volume that lifts the building and draws the eye to its lofty apex, complete with helipad. Set in water gardens, the development

incorporates high-quality commercial units, conference facilities and a business centre, all supported by coffee shops, a gymnasium, a viewing gallery and a high-level restaurant offering diners breathtaking city panoramas.

Adjacent to the tower is a mall complex that further diversifies Al Rajhi's range of facilities, offering a mix of shop units and a substantial food court. Above this are another four storeys of high-quality office accommodation. Balancing out this commercial activity is a mosque, with separate entrances for men and women accessible directly from the offices and the mall.

Anara Tower
Dubai, UAE

MIXED-USE

Client
Tameer Holdings
Investments

Area
470,000 m²

Type
650 m, 125-storey
mixed-use tower

Status
Design complete

Date
2008

Anara Tower will be one of the world's tallest buildings when it is complete, and that height is a major driver for its distinctive architectural form. It will offer 125 storeys of mixed-use development, and a series of stacked communities in a distinctive architectural statement.

The shape of the shaft is a synthesis of economic and structural requirements: the V-shaped plan allows for the maximum possible building width, but when this is extruded into a super-high-rise elevation, consideration of wind dynamics generates features such as the balcony-like bracing, without which the building would simply collapse. One of the outstanding features of the V-form plan is that it is remarkably resistant to oscillation. Whereas other tall structures are designed to bend in the wind, Anara Tower simply stands stationary while the wind moves around it.

Architecturally and functionally, the V-form works extremely well. The structural braces are developed into external sky terraces, accessible from the community levels of 27-storey 'villages'. Each community enjoys discrete restaurant, retail, leisure and health facilities at the sky terrace level, with apartments above. The building is a stack of three of these communities above 12 storeys of branded apartments, eight floors of offices, seven hotel floors and a large car park at podium level, all capped by penthouses, a palace apartment, and an amazing skypod restaurant, the highest restaurant in the world.

The tower is unusual for an edifice of its height in that it doesn't taper. It rises as a single column, and in doing so, provides 39% more floor area than say, a 10% taller but tapered building. It's this unusual form, as much as the sheer scale of the building, that will ensure that Anara Tower will become a landmark for southern Dubai.

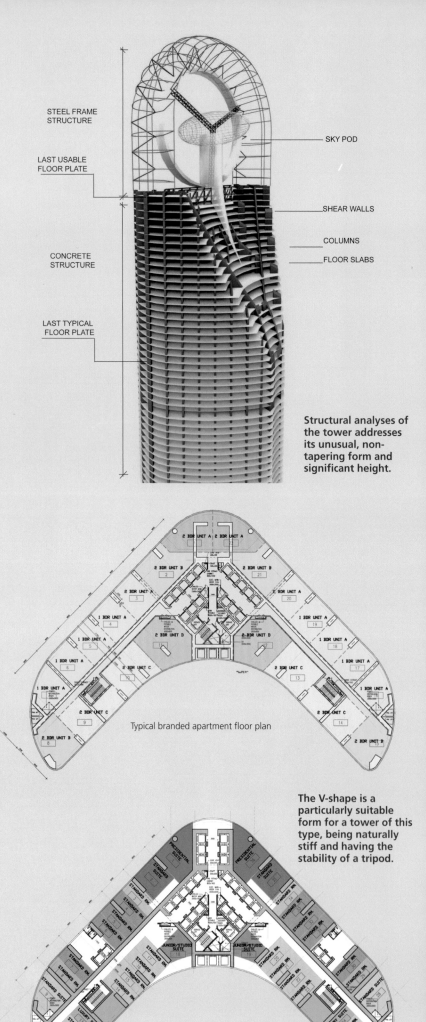

STEEL FRAME
STRUCTURE

LAST USABLE
FLOOR PLATE

CONCRETE
STRUCTURE

LAST TYPICAL
FLOOR PLATE

SKY POD

SHEAR WALLS

COLUMNS

FLOOR SLABS

Structural analyses of
the tower addresses
its unusual, non-
tapering form and
significant height.

Typical branded apartment floor plan

The V-shape is a
particularly suitable
form for a tower of this
type, being naturally
stiff and having the
stability of a tripod.

Typical hotel floor plan

194

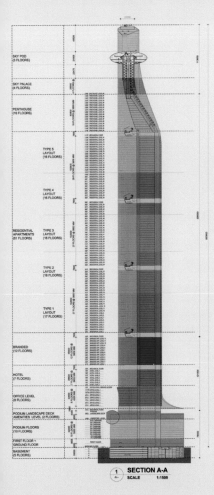

SECTION A-A
SCALE 1:1500

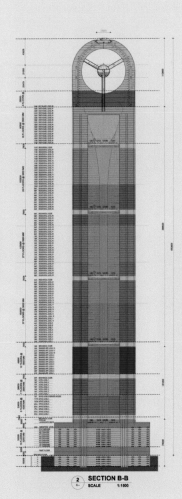

SECTION B-B
SCALE 1:1500

195

TB Simatupang Development
Jakarta, Indonesia

MIXED-USE

Client
PT Intiland
Development tbk

Area
13.66 ha

Type
Mixed-use
development (office,
retail and serviced
apartments)

Status
Concept design
complete

Date
2010

Indonesia's cities are in a constant state of evolution, in which dense populations, advancing technology and construction are combined in a rich urban environment. Jakarta is the country's economic, cultural and political centre, and the project site is a prime target for multinational corporations setting up business ventures in Indonesia.

The concept for TB Simatupang Development draws on the dynamic philosophy that opposing forces are interconnected in the natural world. Taking inspiration from the natural environment of Indonesia, architectural elements are reduced to minimalist geometric shapes. One of the key aims of the design is to create harmony between the buildings, the landscape and the natural environment.

The magnificent ETFE dome above the retail hub and multifunctional deck forms a key focal point for the whole development. Carefully designed landscape elements, *al fresco* dining areas on waterborne timber pads and varying outdoor spaces create an alluring experience for the visitor.

Sustainability is central to the design approach. Analysing the balance of light and shade, canopies and louvres are tuned according to the orientation of the buildings, complemented by an innovative balustrade overlay inspired by the ubiquitous hand-woven Indonesian basket. This innovative organic façade design contributes to an overall reduction in energy demand of 35%.

The use of canopies with deep overhangs for rain harvesting and greywater recovery systems provide an integrated water conservation strategy with a 25% reduction in fresh water demand for the project. These two features make this development one of the most sustainable in Jakarta and put it at the forefront of the Indonesian Greenship rating system.

The overall composition of the TB Simatupang Development is understated and elegant. The built form and landscape features provide a pleasant environment for visitors and residents, and serve to differentiate this development from others – it is a composition that is both beautiful and sustainable.

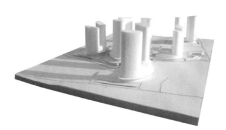

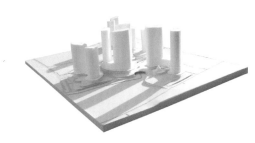

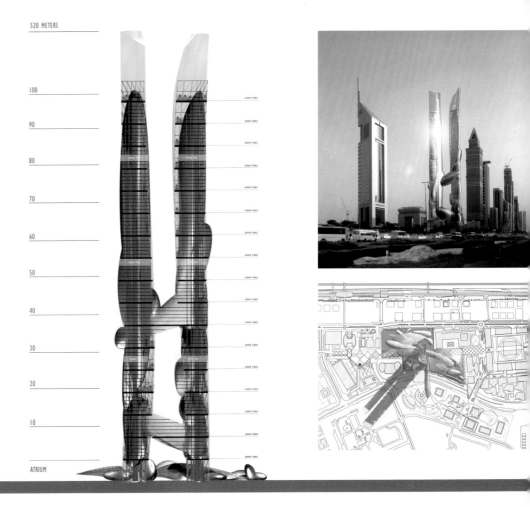

Central Tower 1
Dubai, UAE

MIXED-USE

Client
Confidential

Area
350,000 m²

Type
Mixed-use
development

Status
Competition entry

Date
2006

Architectural competitions are often fraught with difficulty, but they do have one significant benefit – they allow a firm to stretch its creative legs a little and go exploring.

Central Tower 1 is a classic mixed-use development that shows off its contents by means of an innovative structural system. A central core is surrounded by a ring of columns that support the various functions – office, retail, commercial, residential

– in shapely but amorphous linked volumes. These are clad in leaves of reflective, mirrored metal, speckled with an occasional coloured sheet.

Surrounding this stack is a network of slender tensile steel members that both brace the structure and support a crystalline skin of glittering glass leaves. The intended appearance is that of shiny, liquid forms inhabiting a frozen column of ice.

X-Change Gateway
Dubai, UAE

MIXED-USE

Client
Confidential

Area
350,000 m²

Type
Mixed-use
development

Status
Competition entry

Date
2006

X-Change Gateway is a response to a competition to create a zero-energy supertower. Two raking towers intersect at midpoint to create a startling dynamic composition, and define three levels of occupancy; disparate below the intersection, combined at mid-levels and power-generation above.

Six 50 m diameter wind turbines are located in the steel pinnacles of the towers, and combine with photovoltaic panels used to shade southern exposure to provide a generative capacity of 6 Mw, against a total power requirement for the site of 4.5 Mw – a comfortable surplus allowance for low wind conditions. The towers are supported by a random exoskeleton of slender concrete (to 350 m) and steel elements, rising to 500 m in height.

The towers are supported by a random exoskeleton of slender concrete and steel elements.

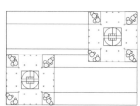

Upper level

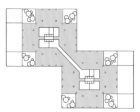

Mid level

Lower level

Centaurus Development
Islamabad, Pakistan

Centaurus is a mixed-use development in the Blue Area of central Islamabad. It efficiently combines four different uses in a single building. Articulating each use with a separate building element enables the potential building mass to be broken down into a more acceptable composition.

On one side of the site is a five-storey shopping mall with an undulating roof, upon which two 20-storey apartment buildings and a 21-storey office tower appear to rest. At the other end of the site, in the prime corner position, is a five-star deluxe hotel tower. The undulating roof of the shopping mall spans the covered public plaza that connects the hotel and the mall, sheltering the entrances to both buildings, which are surrounded by restaurants and airy meeting places. The roof runs up one side of the hotel, narrowing to a point 246.5 m high; that point makes this the tallest building in Pakistan, and is a reference to the Himalayas that provide a distant backdrop to the building.

MIXED-USE

Client
Pak Gulf Construction Ltd

Area
3,300,000 m²

Type
Five connected mixed-use buildings

Status
Under construction

Date
2005–2010

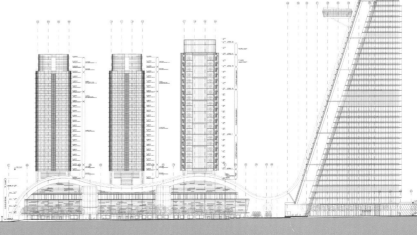

Zero Carbon Urban Plaza and Convention Centre
Abu Dhabi, UAE

The 'trees' in the plaza are set out on the regular grid so characteristic of a real Arabian palm grove.

The concept is simple: an urban oasis in the city where the undulating desert plain extends into an urban plaza that sprouts a grouping of palm trees, whose fronds interlock to create a canopy sheltering the inhabitants below from the harsh desert environment.

The realisation of the concept uses a canopy of photovoltaic panels, supported on a grid of steel 'trees', that are actually ingenious downdraught towers bleeding cool air into the plaza, while solar chimneys ventilate the undercroft. The plaza floor is paved with locally sourced sandstone blocks – the rough-hewn finishes provide a natural grip when wet as well as diffusing sunlight to avoid glare. The plaza is at once subtle, ingenious and beautiful.

The convention centre located within the plaza combines three volumes containing the main functions, disposed around a large, central, climate-conditioned public space. The unique building form is achieved with mirror finish stainless steel in a rain screen cladding configuration that ensures easy maintenance of the metal panels without the need to interfere with the function of the building itself. The connection between the inside and outside is created through 'peeling' away the metal panels, exposing the rain screen structure and glazing beneath.

The other technologies incorporated in the development include green roofs, greywater recycling, the use of wadi stones to attenuate flooding and ensure efficient recharging of aquifers, and solar and wind powered pumps powering re-circulating water-based cooling systems that avoid the use of chemicals.

MIXED-USE

Client
Confidential

Area
60,000 m²

Type
Mixed-use commercial plaza and conference centre

Status
Concept design

Date
2008

Guangzhou East Tower
Guangzhou, China

What is universally defining about towers, and tall ones in particular, is their shape. A satisfactory balance has to be found between distinctiveness, familiarity and representation. To Chinese eyes, the shape of Guangzhou East Tower is suggestive of the emblematic bamboo and thus it satisfies all three counts. If we add to this the suggestion of future growth and prosperity, then this is a building that sits comfortably within the Chinese psyche.

Western viewers may be unaware of these associations, and for this group they do not have the same resonance. For them, the restrained curves speak only of the new era of refined tower design that, if anything, might appear understated.

Inside, there is a 580-room five-star hotel and a banqueting hall, which at 3,000 m² is Guangzhou's largest. Offices and serviced apartments occupy the lower floors. The low-rise podium sympathetically connects the building elements and houses commercial facilities that form an integral part of Guangzhou Zhujiang New Town's rail and metro traffic hub.

MIXED-USE

Client
Evergrande Real Estate Group

Area
410,000 m²

Type
Five-star hotel above serviced apartments and offices

Status
Competition entry

Date
2008

Noida Mixed-use Development
Noida, India

MIXED-USE

Client
Madhvilata Granite
(India) Ltd.

Area
413,000 m²

Type
Mixed-use
development
including a hotel,
offices and retail

Status
Pre-concept

Date
2010

The river Yamuna is revered as the divine mother in Hindu mythology, and is considered the cradle of Indian civilisation and a lifeline for the northern Indian heartland. The river originates in Yamunotri, the glacier located in the Garhwal Himalayas, 4,421 m above sea level. Mythology holds this locale sacred as the seat of the Goddess Yamuna.

This project draws inspiration from the mystic charm of Yamunotri, in tribute to the Yamuna river that borders the site. The architectural language comprises free forms and fluid lines, metaphorically reminiscent of the nascent Yamuna gushing through the snow-capped river boulders.

The accommodation incorporates two hotels – a 550-room hotel with 60 serviced apartments, a ballroom, a spa and 12 restaurants, and a smaller, high-quality hotel, with 230 spacious bedrooms, restaurants and leisure facilities. The hotels and 66,000 m² of offices occupy the tall, slender elements of the building, while the 'boulders' accommodate elements such as the multiplex cinema, atrium, auditorium, health club and ballroom. The retail mall (38,000 m²) emulates the river, 'flowing' through the space and providing a connection between the various elements.

The project embraces sustainability as symbolising the aspirations of the city towards a greener future. Yamunotri evokes memories of a cleaner Yamuna of previous times, conveying a strong message of sustainable design through low-carbon strategies and in partnering with the Noida Authority in its vision: Green Noida, Clean Noida.

Ground floor plan

2nd podium plan

3rd podium plan

4th podium plan

Atrium City Competition
Dubai, UAE

MIXED-USE

Client
Confidential

Area
600,000 m²

Type
Mixed-use commercial
development

Status
Competition entry

Date
2007

The brief for this international competition called for two 600 m towers, designed to frame the Burj Khalifa from a coastal viewpoint. In terms of habitable storeys, the towers exceed even the Burj Khalifa in height, both gracefully extruded from an interconnecting podium. The podium contains a transport hub, linking an important road junction with monorail and metro stations, an abra station for a new system of waterways, and pedestrian access into the new development.

The response developed the theme of the 'essence of Dubai', where the desert meets the sea in a vertical city. The towers emerge from the sand

on one side and the water on the other, almost as though the materials have been swept up in a wave. The flowing form that results incorporates towers and podium in a single entity rather than as a composition of vertical and horizontal forms.

The two towers differ slightly in their height and composition, emphasising the natural amorphous nature of both sand and water and the layered forms they adopt when they come together in nature. The façades are treated in accordance with their orientation, with the northwest being transparent (water) and the southeast largely opaque (sand), with tiny windows shaded by photovoltaic panels.

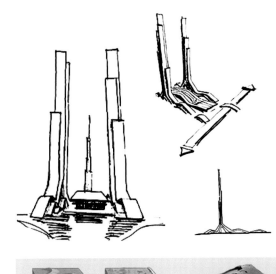

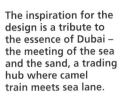

The inspiration for the design is a tribute to the essence of Dubai – the meeting of the sea and the sand, a trading hub where camel train meets sea lane.

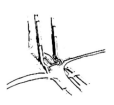

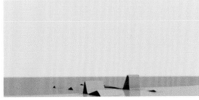

Nomas Towers
Juffair, Bahrain

The Nomas Towers development, located in Juffair, Bahrain's new eastern city centre, has been designed to be economically, socially and environmentally sustainable. It combines premium residential apartments and townhouses, three floors of retail space and entertainment, a five-star hotel and a boutique waterfront office facility.

The development features an imposing 11-storey podium that hints at the diversity of activities within, giving social and visual meaning to the four towers it supports and bringing a welcome addition to the Bahrain corniche. Peppered with cafés and restaurants and lined with public attractions and amenities, it is a true mixed-use facility that relieves the pressure on the road network by offering the potential for localised living, work and leisure.

Its innovations include the podium sky villas aimed at attracting young families into the development, and extensive rooftop gardens and pools that create microclimates suitable for year-round use. Insertion of flexible office facilities within the development in proximity to homes and restaurants ensures that the site will be efficiently utilised throughout the day.

MIXED-USE

Client
Nomas Enterprises
WLL

Area
400,000 m²

Type
Residential apartments
and townhouses,
retail, entertainment,
a five-star hotel
and boutique
waterfront office

Status
Design

Date
2008

Typical apartment floor plan

Typical hotel floor plan

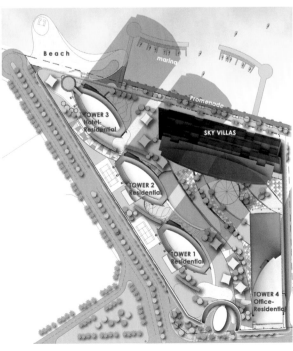

Mixed-use Development
Kuwait City, Kuwait

MIXED-USE

Client
Confidential

Area
50,000 m²

Type
Mixed-use hotel, residential, commercial and retail complex

Status
Concept design

Date
2006

This development is a vital part of the urban regeneration programme for Kuwait City, and its three towers form an instantly recognisable landmark on this important waterfront site. The tallest, northern tower is a hotel, and a second, western tower contains serviced apartments. Guest facilities, including banqueting for up to 1,000 guests, are contained within the podium.

The relatively low-rise office tower is operated independently and its entrance is separated from the hotel and residential components.

The 20,000 m² of retail space is spread over the ground and first floors, but all of it relates to a landscaped square that forms a street-level public space shaded with distinctive glazed canopies in the spirit of Kuwait's tradition of landmark towers.

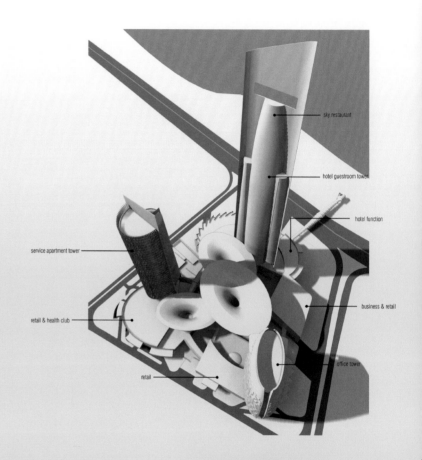

sky restaurant

hotel guestroom tower

hotel function

service apartment tower

business & retail

retail & health club

office tower

retail

Trump International Hotel & Tower
Dubai, UAE

MIXED-USE

Client
Nakheel Hotel
and Resorts

Area
120,000 m²

Type
Luxury 'condominium'
hotel, apartments and
other related facilities

Status
Design complete

Date
2008

Located at the very centre of Nakheel's Palm Jumeirah, a created island off the west coast of Dubai, the Trump International Hotel & Tower will stand as a powerful landmark on what is one of the most ambitious projects in the world. As the centrepiece of The Palm, it occupies a prime position halfway along its trunk and, at 61 storeys, will be the tallest building on the island.

The striking building, with its stainless steel, glass and stone façades, climbs to over 250 m in height and houses a luxury 'condominium hotel', a Trump concept that will be a first for the Middle East. The tower also incorporates a three-storey entrance lobby, exclusive residential apartments, boutique offices, a high-end resort spa, a swimming pool and health club, restaurants, a business centre and the Trump Beach & Yacht Club that serves a 200-berth marina, all with spectacular views of the Dubai coastline.

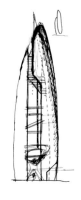
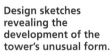
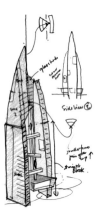
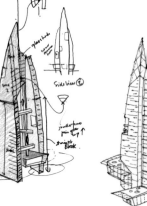
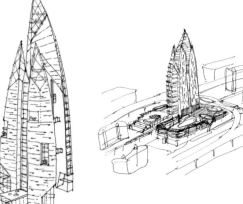
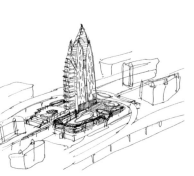

Design sketches revealing the development of the tower's unusual form.

The Trump International Hotel & Tower is really a blend of two asymmetric towers that join at the 40th floor to straddle the island's monorail. The split edifice creates a symbolic gateway to the heart of this major development, which all Palm visitors must approach or pass. The towers themselves stand on a four-storey bisected podium that contains the main car parking provision for over 1,200 cars, and extensive services and retail outlets.

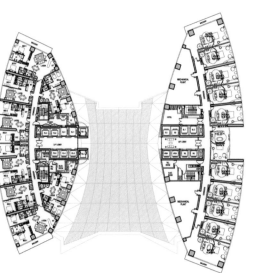

14th floor plan

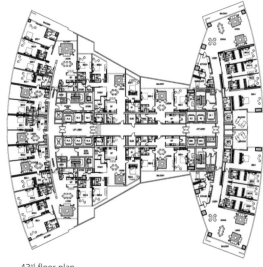

43rd floor plan

The taller tower houses 394 apartments and townhouses and two high-profile penthouses, while the smaller, wider tower contains the Trump International Hotel. At the tips of the two towers sit glazed, diamond-shaped structures that incorporate restaurants, bars and viewing galleries for guests, residents and the visiting public. These are conjoined with machine-like precision, creating a spectacular facetted pinnacle of great grandeur and complexity.

- Restaurant and dining
- Kitchen
- Offices
- Conference
- Spa and gym
- Plant room
- Lift and stairs

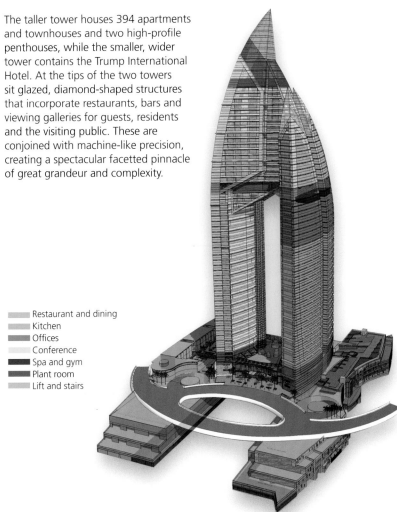

Aeron
Tehran, Iran

MIXED-USE

Client
Pars Ibn Battuta

Area
434,079 m²

Type
500 m long, two-storey shopping mall with twin towers containing a hotel and office/residential

Status
Concept complete

Date
2008–2009

Aeron will be the first major retail mall in Iran. Based on the sculptural elements of an aircraft, the mall represents a fuselage, the roof an elegant, sweeping wing, and the twin towers tail fins. The composition is intended to evoke concepts of travel, tourism and a gathering of world trade.

The towers – one a hotel, the other a mixture of office and residential spaces – sit on raked columns that rise through the mall into a full-height atrium, linking their 23 floors and creating dramatic internal spaces with views over the Alborz mountains. The raking walls are intended to draw the eye upward to the sky-pods that house dining and conference suites.

Back on the ground, the retail mall accommodates shops, a water park, a multiplex cinema, a kid's play zone and an ice rink. The building is intended to become a focus for a range of activities: facilities for travel, family leisure, business and social events will all be provided under one amazing roof.

Century City
Doha, Qatar

MIXED-USE

Client
Retaj Developments

Area
285,000 m²

Type
10 ha urban
regeneration project

Status
Design

Date
2008

Century City is an impressively sized complex occupying some 285,000 m² in the centre of downtown Doha. It has a five-star hotel with 350 rooms, 30 serviced apartments, 38,000 m² of office space and retail facilities, and 10,500 m² of conference facilities. There are also 700 apartments, a mosque for 700 worshippers and a total of 3,400 car parking spaces.

The retail and café areas sit below a landscaped podium roof that wraps around and links the various elements. Sharing the space is a summer garden with a climatically-controlled zone that recreates a tropical rainforest. Joined towers mark the gateway to the development for visitors, as well as providing a landmark for the development itself from a distance.

Shi Liu Pu Development
Shanghai, China

MIXED-USE

Client
Hong Kong
Construction
Investment

Area
410,000 m²

Type
Hotel, office and
commercial space

Status
Competition entry

Date
2008

This project places office, retail and hotel towers on a site between the old walled city and the Huang Pu River in central Shanghai. The riverfront site enjoys great potential and prestige, serving as a gateway to both the historic city and the new Pudong financial district across the river to the east.

Six slender towers of varying heights fragment the site, carefully oriented to maximise shared views of the Shanghai skyline. The office towers are grouped at the southern end of the site and feature restaurant and bar spaces with panoramic outlooks over the river. To the north a hotel overlooks the public park, which interlocks with the urban environment at ground level. A retail podium, interspersed with a series of public squares and green spaces at lower levels, returns life and activity to the waterfront.

Connection is a recurring theme of the design. The project restores the links between the park, the buildings and the existing riverfront gardens, while planted terraces at upper levels connect the buildings throughout the length of the site.

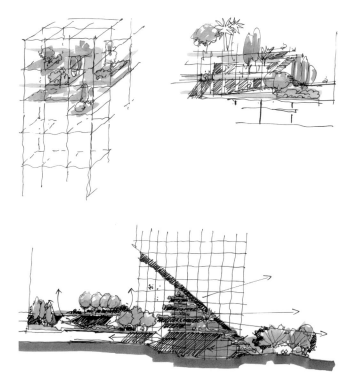

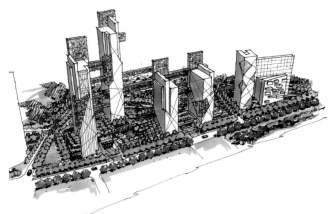

The green spaces and gardens are an integral part of the scheme and form linking pathways traversing the site.

Al Salam Tecom Tower
Dubai, UAE

MIXED-USE

Client
Abdulsalam Alrafi
Group

Area
94,500 m²

Type
46-storey mixed-use
tower

Status
Complete

Date
2004–2008

The Al Salam Tecom Tower is typical of many mixed-use developments in the Middle East. It adopts what has become the basic layout for such developments, employing a retail and parking podium supporting a residential and office tower above.

Located within Dubai's energetic Technology, Electronic, Commerce and Media zone – Tecom – the 195 m building is divided into three distinct vertical zones. Within the six-storey podium are the community facilities, including the entrance lobby, a retail mall, a food court, meeting rooms, a health club with a lap pool and associated car parks. The next 14 storeys house 225 serviced apartments, and open-plan offices occupy the remaining 23 floors, terminating at the 46th floor's inclined roof.

Although only really practical for winter use in Dubai's climate, the potential for balconies to provide shade and surface interest to a building makes them justifiable in terms of energy efficiency and aesthetics. Unusually, the cladding for the residential floors is the same curtain walling that is used for the office levels. It is given added interest by the strong diagonal elements that call to mind the sails of the nearby marina, imagery reinforced by the wave pattern incorporated into the solar shading of the car park levels.

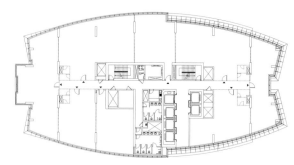

Office floor plan (23–36)

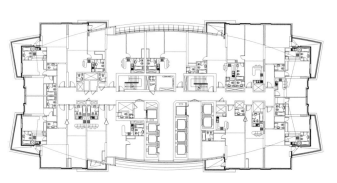

Typical residential floor plan (7–11)

Limassol Landmark
Limassol, Cyprus

Limassol Landmark is intended to be just that – a new landmark for the capital of Cyprus. In addition to a major building with a distinctive form, it also brings some welcome green space into the city.

The tower comprises 30 floors on top of four basement levels, configured into a Y-shaped plan rising to a height of 122 m. The upper storeys are residential, with a mixture of two- and three-bedroom apartments with duplex units and penthouses at the top. The tripartite arrangement provides every unit with views of both the island and the Mediterranean Sea.

Below this is a two-storey podium of double-height retail units, each fronted by full-height glazed walls and with the option of an internal mezzanine floor. The shops open off a showpiece entrance foyer, a lively space with the atmosphere of a luxury hotel lobby. It is enveloped in a dramatic, 7 m high glass wall that fills the lounge and front desk area with natural light and provides a link to the new landscaped plaza.

The plaza is a generous response to the brief, which emphasised the need to focus on social interaction. It is almost double the statutory requirement in size and provides restful but inviting green spaces and gardens for both residents and the public.

The raking roof lines provide an attractive terminal to the towers and serve a functional purpose in providing stepped terraces for the penthouse apartments.

The new public plaza will provide a venue for social interaction and ensure a lively buzz at the main entrance.

MIXED-USE

Client
PAFILIA

Area
48,000 m²

Type
Mixed-use commercial tower

Status
Design stage

Date
2008–2009

The new terraced gardens around the tower are welcomed as a valuable contribution to the city environment.

SSFI Tripoli
Tripoli, Libya

MIXED-USE

Client
SSFI

Area
72,000 m²

Type
Mixed-use tower including offices, serviced apartments, a hotel and an exclusive club

Status
Design

Date
2009–2011

Libya's history is as rich as any on the Mediterranean coast, with Phoenician, Roman and Muslim Arab styles and systems contributing to its rich architectural heritage. Tripoli Tower is designed to build upon that tradition, engaging Phoenician simplicity, Roman columns and the Muslim arch as its prime references.

The tower is a classical mixed-use confection. The 45-storey, 210 m main volume incorporates 25 floors of offices and five floors of serviced apartments, with the balance made over to hotel suites and an exclusive club for the petroleum industry.

The building initially takes the form of a circular column that is progressively cut away as it rises to become a pair of linked arches, creating an intriguing composition of curves. The skin is a mixture of glass curtain walling and aluminium louvres that can be varied in angle to provide the optimum shading from the sun as it circles the building (and for ease of cleaning). The shading forms part of a sophisticated system for reducing energy consumption that also incorporates reflection, insulation and orientation measures.

At its peak is a diagrid glazed with ETFE, a highly durable translucent skin that will play host to a colourful display of low-energy LED lighting at night. At ground level the building opens onto an expansive entrance plaza, with a carefully graduated pattern of rectilinear paving forms creating a sense of place and contributing to the public realm of Tripoli.

Raptis Gold Coast
Brisbane, Australia

A spectacular site on a land spit off Australia's Gold Coast provides the location for Raptis, a mixed-use development incorporating a 250-key five-star hotel, 300 one- and two-bedroom luxury apartments and shared service facilities. The site is the subject of tight planning regulations that limited the overall height to eight storeys.

The brief called for a piece of innovative and timeless design incorporating quality, luxury and clear 'street' presence, but at the same time respecting and enhancing the outstanding tropical marine environment. Given that these requirements were entirely in accord with the design team's natural wishes, the design process became a pleasurable exercise in creativity, innovation and attention to detail.

The resulting concept, strongly influenced by the beauty of the surroundings, is a building inspired by the stimulating seaside spirit of the place. The forms created by the double-curvature roofs evoke images of giant dolphins jumping the spit, a tarpon fighting the line, or a great seabird taking flight. The intention is that Raptis will become a recognisable landmark for the Gold Coast.

MIXED-USE

Client
The Raptis Group

Area
40,000 m²

Type
Mixed-use hotel and
luxury apartments

Status
Concept design

Date
2006

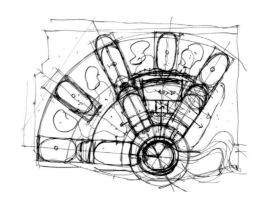

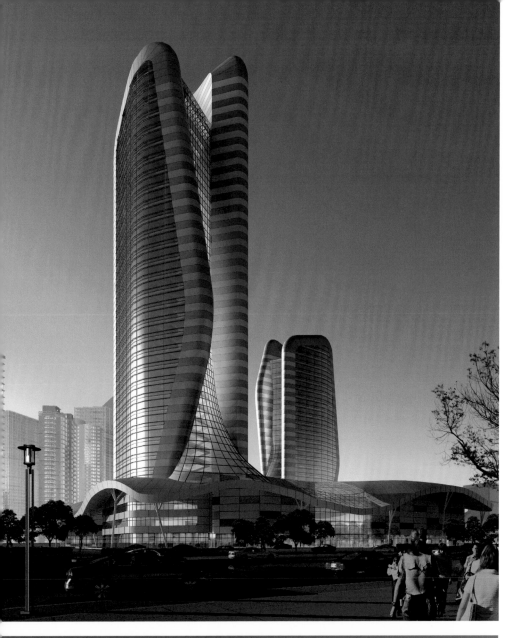

Wuhan Jiayu Landmark Hotel & Mixed Development
Wuhan, China

Wuhan is one of the largest Chinese industrial cities, located at the confluence of the Yangtze and Han rivers in central China. As a consequence of its strategic location on an important crossroad for rail and river transportation, this city of over six million has a rich culture and history.

These landmark buildings are part of the masterplan for a new central business district that faces the main approach to the city from both the airport and the major railway station. At 160 m in height, the taller tower houses a five-star hotel and is complemented by a 100 m high apartment building. Both rise from a four-storey podium containing commercial and leisure facilities that include retail and banqueting spaces, a conference centre for 2,000 people and an eight-screen cinema complex.

The rounded and polished towers stand proudly upon the gently undulating roofscape, and call to mind the vertical rock outcroppings so often seen in Chinese landscape painting.

MIXED-USE

Client
Jiayu Group

Area
140,000 m²

Type
Mixed-use tower
with retail and leisure
podium

Status
Design

Date
2008–2012

The twin towers are deliberately offset to one end of the site to provide a broad, unobstructed deck for landscaping and terracing on top of the podium.

Al Waha Complex
Tripoli, Libya

MIXED-USE

Client
ALMAABAR

Area
154,000 m²

Type
Four-star hotel, offices
and commercial

Status
Design

Date
2010

Situated on the communication spine connecting the Tripoli town centre to its airport, the Al Waha Complex serves an area of primarily low-rise houses and apartment buildings. It comprises three main architectural elements: a 34-storey, 200-room Rotana Hotel tower, a 33-storey office tower of 54,000 m² and a retail mall of 14,000 m² of lettable floor area. Its location and character make it a landmark expression of Tripoli's new cultural, political and economic aspirations.

The buildings make reference to three aspects of Libyan history and culture to reflect these cultural changes, and to link the past to the future. The first is the ancient town of Ghadames, a pre-Saharan Tuareg village around 2,500 years old, and now a UNESCO World Heritage site. Its layered levels and mosaic plans provided inspiration for the form and surface textures of the horizontal elements of the project.

The second element is that of mosaic, in particular the outstanding mosaic floors from Libya's early Roman period. These further inspired the external form of the mall's outer skin, through which the towers burst and thrust skywards. The skin is lifted in this fashion to create vertical as well as horizontal mosaic patterns of masonry and timber. The other elevations of the new towers continue the metaphor through glittering mosaic curtain walls of coloured glass.

Finally, there is the concept of the oasis. Tripoli is the oasis of North Africa, and the rooftop landscaping of the mall makes reference to this concept. The towers are located at the far corner of the mall, leaving the roof a wide-open space punctuated by trees, green spaces and pools.

Gateway Building
Baku, Azerbaijan

MIXED-USE

Client
Baku White City

Area
28,000 m²

Type
Retail facilities on
the ground and first
floors,16 boutique
apartments on floors
four to seven and
office space from the
third to the 12th floor

Status
Design

Date
2010–ongoing

The clue is in the name. This is a
building designed to punctuate the
entrance to White City, a new urban
renewal site on a formerly polluted
and redundant area of land in Baku.
Here is a building designed from the
outset to stand out, to contrast with its
neighbours and to act as a marker for
those entering and leaving the new city.

The Gateway is actually more of a
gatepost, and complements a similar
form on the opposite side of the
main access road. Apparently a self-
contained, moulded form that has been
carefully and delicately placed in an
urban setting, it uses colour and shape
to impress. The building is actually a
large mixed-use structure, rising from
seven storeys at its lowest end to 14
at its highest. The levels are expressed
on the exterior as bands of silvered

glass set deep behind balconies and
terraces faced with bright, colourless
cladding in metal or acrylic polymer.
The arrangement of decks and
promenades, and the gleaming silver
and white of the façades, are clearly
inspired by the cruise ships that ply
the Caspian Sea, lapping against the
shoreline just a couple of blocks away.

Within that curvaceous, almost freeform exterior is a rational, controlled
layout of residential, commercial
and office accommodation. The
internal arrangement follows
sound design principles, with no
compromises on usability required
by the dramatic external form.

The structure is a simple system of
slabs and columns, braced by the
three vertical service cores that are

required by a building of this length.
It employs raking columns where the
deep overhangs on the building façade
occur, but is otherwise a simple and
straightforward technical exercise.

The landscaping is simple, and is limited
to definition of the site and circulation
systems through groundscape and
low planting. This is to avoid softening
the contrast between the dominant
building, its counterpart and the road
between them. Passing through the
gateway should be an experience, an
action of note, and a heavier, more
lush planting scheme would screen the
buildings and reduce their impact.

Despite its seemingly
amorphous shape,
the Gateway
Building is actually
based on a regular
layout of standard
repetitive modules.

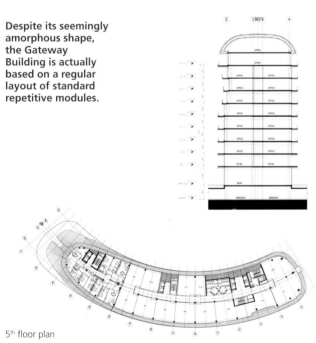

5th floor plan

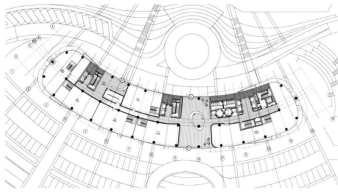

Ground floor plan

MIXED-USE

Client
Confidential

Area
149,769 m²

Type
60-storey tower
with retail podium

Status
Concept complete

Date
2010

Kazan Riviera Tower
Kazan, Russia

Kazan is a true meeting point for many cultures. Here east meets west, Christian meets Muslim, Tatar and Bulgar come together with Russian and European. The new tower draws heavily on this duality in its basic form.

The tower also takes inspiration from Kazak artistic tradition, including folk dances and loose, woven clothing. The result is a shapely aesthetic, which subtly twists two strands into a single organic form as it rises into a powerful, confident statement. The patterns of local cloth are expressed in the treatment of the façade, which has clear references to the warp and weft of woven fabric. The result is a fascinating composition that is intriguing, beautiful and impressive, its fluid shape reflecting the river that flows around its exceptional site.

The tower accommodates a 220-key five-star hotel that incorporates ballroom facilities on two floors, along with restaurants and cafés. The hotel is complemented by 370 residential apartments, and some 7,800 m² of commercial office space. The podium comprises a 7,000 m² retail mall and a 3,200 m² health club, together with parking and service accommodation, while the top three floors of the tower – the highest point in Kazan – take the form of a spectacular viewing gallery, featuring a huge interpretive model of the city. The viewing gallery also features a restaurant, enabling visitors to take their time enjoying the stunning view by day or night.

Yiwu World Trade Center
Yiwu, China

MIXED-USE

Client
Confidential

Area
340,530 m²

Type
A new low-carbon, mixed-used development comprising a five-star hotel and apartment hotel, residential, offices, conference and banquet facilities and a retail mall

Status
Concept complete

Date
2009–2011

Yiwu sits some 100 km from the eastern coast of China, and is currently recognised as the world's largest commodity trade centre. Central to the Chinese economy as a shopping and tourism destination, it has a rich cultural history stretching back at least 2,000 years, and yet remains largely unknown outside China.

The brief calls for a development to project Yiwu onto the international stage. In more practical terms, as well as providing commercial accommodation, the building is required to create a covered link between the northern green belt and the southern river plaza.

The proposal places a mall at its core, surrounded by residential towers of 20 and 34 storeys respectively, a serviced apartment tower (36 storeys) and a combined office and hotel tower at a substantial 68 storeys. The towers are carefully spaced such that the rising and falling skyline circling the mall reflects the rippling form of the traditional Chinese dragon, rising in ever-taller arches from tail to head, a powerful image of strength and good fortune in Chinese mythology and culture.

Brisbane French Quarter
Brisbane, Australia

The competition-winning design for the Brisbane French Quarter project comprises a six-star hotel, residential apartments, restaurants and retail space, all linked by a Parisian-style podium. Designed to support the city's emergence as an international destination, the development is intended to bring a new level of high-end luxury and sophistication to the Brisbane skyline.

The design combines the street level 'French flavour' of the precinct with Queensland's own unique lifestyle. The concept features a pair of towers, one a luxury hotel, the other a residential grouping of luxury apartments and penthouses, that sit above a podium of retail accommodation. The architectural forms make use of glittering curtain walls in beautiful curved falls of glass, with creative rooflines providing a pleasingly articulated skyline in what will surely become Brisbane's landmark development.

MIXED-USE

Client
Confidential

Area
100,800 m²

Type
Mixed-use hotel,
restaurants,
commercial and retail

Status
Competition entry

Date
2008

Skygate City
Singapore

Skygate is a concept for a resort at Singapore's Bay Marina, constructed around the theme of entertainment. It incorporates many low-rise buildings, but the outstanding element is the Skygate Tower. The inspirations for the tower are sustainability and futurism, blended to create a piece of sculptural architecture that will become an internationally recognised symbol of Singapore.

The architectural forms are inspired by water, flight and technology. The tower is an elegant cone, its façade articulated using horizontal balconies and sky gardens to punctuate the elevations every 11 floors. This creates an ascending visual rhythm and reduces solar gain by 85%, as well as providing an attractive amenity for the 1,200-room, six-star hotel. At the tower's peak is a 145 m high open structure containing a dynamic but delicate, shimmering assembly of 60 vertical axis wind turbines. This takes the overall height of Skygate to 500 m, well into supertower territory and among the top 10 towers in the world in terms of height.

The project incorporates seven mid-rise buildings containing 1,800 rooms, a Guggenheim-like museum, a 600 m long mall, an indoor area for 10,000 people, an amphitheatre seating 7,000 with dancing fountains, and a sailing academy to animate the bay. The viewing deck at level 67, a VIP gaming area at level 68 and a helipad and revolving restaurant at levels 69 and 70 provide panoramic views of Singapore. An integrated mooring for Singapore's environmentally-friendly airship indicates the comprehensive approach to responsible energy generation and conservation, recycling programmes and contemporary communication systems that are central to Skygate's design.

MIXED-USE

Client
Peermont Global (Pty) Ltd

Area
1,000,000 m²

Type
500 m, 85 storey, mixed-use commercial development with 3,000-room six-star hotel

Status
Competition entry

Date
2005

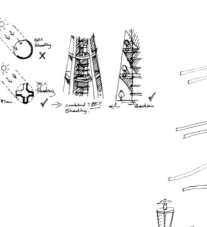

The conical centrepiece of the Skygate project was deliberately developed as an instantly recognisable landmark for Singapore.

FEBRUARY 2OC

LEVEL - 3

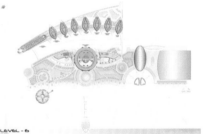

LEVEL - 6

LEVEL - 2

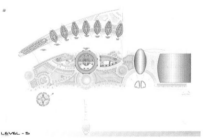

LEVEL - 5

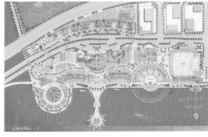

LEVEL - 1

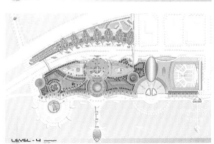

LEVEL - 4

Park View Towers
Dubai, UAE

This scheme addresses the problem of a city grid layout being bisected diagonally by a major, multi-lane highway. The result is a sequence of triangular sites, each with a major source of noise along their longest boundary.

Park View Towers provides a rational response to these difficulties with the less noise-sensitive retail accommodation being placed along the road boundary, elevated on the slender substratum of a dense concrete parking structure, and overlooking the road that they treat almost as a piece of kinetic art. Above this podium are towers of office accommodation at low level, with residential units above, rising through some 30 storeys to a height of 160 m.

The tower façades are beautifully modelled with subtly angled triangular facets of mirrored glass that provide a glittering sequence of intriguing reflections to the passing motorist. The raking edges of the triangles define the extent of the balconies, allowing them to increase in size as they rise above the noise and serve the higher-value penthouse units.

The massing is a dynamic composition of three-sided figures and acute angles, all clearly referenced in the modelling of the elevations to produce an elegant, integrated contribution to the cityscape.

MIXED-USE

Client
Confidential

Area
140,000 m²

Type
Mixed-use commercial towers

Status
Concept design

Date
2008

Padideh Shandiz
Shandiz, Iran

MIXED-USE

Client
Confidential

Area
950,000 m²

Type
Mixed-use
development

Status
Under construction

Date
2010–2013

Shandiz lies 35 km northwest of the city of Mashhad, near Iran's border with Afghanistan. The Padideh Shandiz Tourist Complex aims to provide the town with some much-needed services and tourist facilities, as well as catering to the 2.8 million residents of Mashhad and some 20 million pilgrims who visit the city annually.

The plan incorporates a shopping mall of 200,000 m² leasable area, a water park, a 600-room five-star hotel, 1,000 serviced and residential apartments, a flower garden and market, and a cultural centre. The total proposed gross floor area is approaching 1,000,000 m².

The concept is that of a Garden City, where exterior and interior spaces are given equal importance. Shandiz's climate is comfortably

cool for much of the year, enabling the development of a network of 'ecologically inspired' open spaces as an integral part of the concept.

The climate makes a particular contribution to the sustainability initiatives incorporated into the scheme. The complex aims to showcase a range of sustainable elements, setting a standard for the greater Mashhad region and for Iran. In comparison to contemporary benchmarks, the proposal will reduce energy consumption by 25%, water consumption and irrigation by almost half, and retain almost all stormwater on-site. Half of the infrastructure will be made with recycled material, and construction has been managed to ensure balanced cut-and-fill, minimising the quantity of material transported to or from

the site. A responsible solid waste management strategy will reduce waste taken to landfill by half, and a quarter of the water used on-site will be recycled from site drainage.

Environmental comfort, transport networks and natural resources have all been addressed, and the scheme considers social aspects such as public transport and access to community facilities. Particular care has been exercised in incorporating a range and gradation of civic spaces, and a network of public spaces and parks.

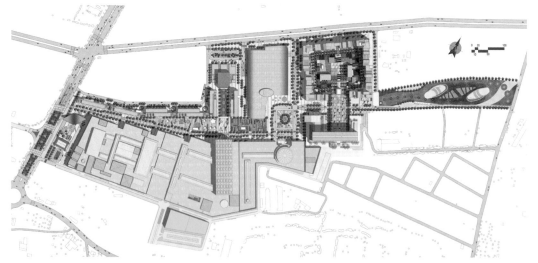

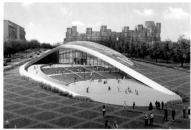

SPORT AND LEISURE

Wild Wadi Aqua Park
Dubai, UAE

SPORT AND LEISURE

Client
Confidential

Area
3 ha

Type
Themed water park

Status
Complete

Date
1996–1999

The Wild Wadi is a fully themed Arabic water park that, when completed in 1999, had some of the most technically advanced rides in the world. Its 24 exhilarating rides and water features, occupying a 3 ha landscaped garden within the Jumeirah Beach Resort, are designed to give guests an experience of a lifetime in a world away from reality.

The park was conceived as a wadi (a dry riverbed) that has been colonised and developed over time by shipwrecked sailors. It loosely interprets the legend of the famous seafarers Sinbad and Juha, who were caught in a terrible storm in the middle of the Arabian Sea and were washed up in a tropical paradise. This unashamedly free interpretation of a seafaring legend, with its particular local resonance, won the 1999 World Water Park Association's Industry Innovation Award for Outstanding Design and Theme.

The design employs the best of contemporary water park technology, such as the Master Blaster™ that creates an uphill flow of water linking 16 of the exhilarating rides. In total there are 2.4 km of interconnected waterways, together with restaurants, a souk and shaded picnic areas, set in a park with more than 40,000 plants.

In 2005 Atkins was asked to update the attractions, developing both existing and new facilities that continue the original theme. That process is currently being repeated in 2010, with three new rides ensuring that Wild Wadi retains its position as the number one water park in the Middle East.

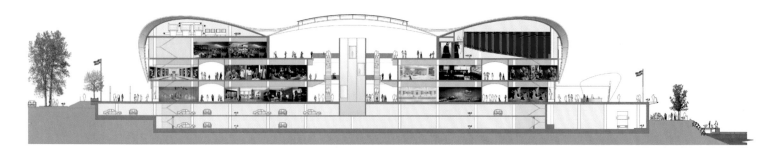

Kazan Zoo and Botanical Gardens
Kazan, Russia

SPORT AND LEISURE

Client
Invest-City,
Government of Kazan

Area
40 ha

Type
Three adjacent
central city sites

Status
Design

Date
2007

Prompted by the declaration of the Kazan Kremlin as a World Heritage Site and the imminence of Kazan's 200th anniversary, the Kazan government has initiated some significant improvements to the city centre. This particular project addresses the conceptual masterplanning of three adjacent city centre sites, totalling 40 ha, to incorporate the existing Kazan Zoo and Botanical Gardens.

The existing zoo is relocated to a greenfield site across a lake from the city, linking back to the retail development by means of a signature bridge that represents the body of the 'Strikaza' (dragonfly) upon which

the extended masterplan is themed. The tubular bridge encompasses a winter garden at the retail end, housing an historically significant collection of subtropical plants, while at the zoo end the bridge terminates in a spectacular tropical house.

The zoo component was developed in conjunction with the Zoological Society of London. Due to the harsh winter conditions in Kazan, the zoo layout clusters 'warm' species around the central tropical house to give visitors a mini zoo experience in winter without the need to venture outside. Colder creatures are housed in enclosures

on radiating circular paths that guide visitors back to the main tropical house.

Its 'Flora and Fauna' theme makes the retail component unique in Kazan. Its 80,000 m² of retail and leisure space are contained within a building of reptilian appearance, a reference to the Zilant – a mythical winged dragon and the symbol of Kazan.

The zoo layout invites exploration. The recreation facilities overlook the lake towards the lions, tigers and bears, while the reptile house and aquarium are placed within the mall to entice visitors across the bridge.

The lake is the focus of the new layout, defining the major zones of the site.

The new zoo buildings provide a spectacular backdrop to the lakes.

Driffield Pool
Driffield, UK

SPORT AND LEISURE

Client
East Riding of
Yorkshire Council

Area
2,750 m²

Type
New leisure facility
adjacent to Driffield
High School

Status
Complete

Date
2006–2008

In line with the UK government's
desire for schools to offer extended
services, a new leisure facility adjacent
to Driffield High School has made the
school a hub for the local community.
The Driffield Community Leisure Centre
houses a 25 m six-lane pool, with a
learners' pool, a four-court badminton
sports hall with room for spectators, a
gym and several community rooms.

The facility makes a fresh and positive
statement to the public and students.
The simply articulated building sits

on a cleanly landscaped site. Colour
and pattern guide people to a light
and airy lobby with direct access to
all the facilities. Bright colours are
used to link and identify the various
components. The introduction of
trees and structured planting into the
landscape complements the existing
flora and softens the appearance of
the car park. It also provides solar
shading for the building and buffers
the prevailing winds on the exposed
boundaries while still maintaining
clear sightlines for security.

Leisure facilities are traditionally large
consumers of energy and emitters
of CO_2. The energy consumption at
Driffield Pool is reduced by the use
of natural ventilation and daylighting
wherever possible, underpinned
by high levels of passive insulation.
The swimming pool spaces, for
example, incorporate innovative
insulated translucent wall panels
that maintain privacy, but reduce
daytime reliance on artificial light
and minimise the heat loss normally
associated with glazed areas.

Dubai Creek Restaurant
Dubai, UAE

Client
Confidential

Area
2,400 m²

Type
Restaurant and
event space

Status
Design complete

Date
2008

This small, refined building is a response to a pleasantly simple brief and a superb site at the edge of the Dubai Golf Course, overlooking the creek. The brief required panoramic views of the creek to be a feature of the building.

The proposal achieves this aim by means of a cantilevered structure, enhanced by the introduction of an elevated, landscaped hill, linking the building to the golf course at the lower level and concealing the kitchens within. The double-tiered

restaurant with terraced floors nestles below an elegant, deeply cantilevered roof that is in effect a floating shade plane, providing diners with a comfortable, clear view of the creek. Externally, the floors are treated in similar fashion and form a series of floating and curved planes.

Below the restaurant is an amphitheatre, focussed on a simple stage floating above the waters of the creek. It provides a supremely elegant venue for fashion shows, theatre displays and events.

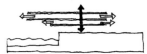

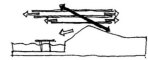

Enchantment of the Seas
Miami, USA

Cruise liners and buildings have much in common, not least in terms of planning and scale. Recent developments have seen liner design extended to incorporate many elements of contemporary urban design disciplines.

This commission involved elongating the cruise liner *Enchantment of the Seas* by cutting it in half and inserting a new 22 m long mid-section. The new 15-storey high mid-body element contains an additional pool, adjacent bars and an interactive children's fountain that becomes an illuminated feature at night, along with staterooms and storage accommodation.

Weighing 2,666 tonnes, the new section was constructed in Finland and floated 800 km across the Baltic and the North Sea to Rotterdam, where the mother ship was being prepared. The modifications were completed in 28 days: six days to cut through 600 m of steel, and another 22 days to insert, weld and fit-out the new section.

Enchantment of the Seas, with 151 new staterooms and new bridges linking the decks, subsequently won the 2005 Shippax Award for Outstanding Sundeck, a gratifying reward for all involved in the highly complex design, planning and coordination of this innovative scheme.

SPORT AND LEISURE

Client
Royal Caribbean International

Area
Increased length by 22 m

Type
Lengthening and revitalisation of luxury cruise liner

Status
Complete

Date
2004–2005

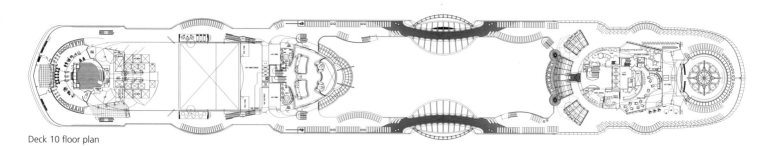

Deck 10 floor plan

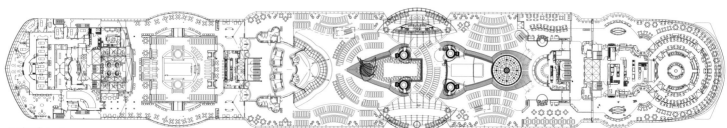

Deck 9 floor plan

The new prefabricated section is readied to be slipped into place and welded in position.

The design process involved the creation of new 'flying bridges' that, as well as providing elevated walkways along the length of the deck, define and enclose the play areas, introducing some intimacy into an otherwise exposed space.

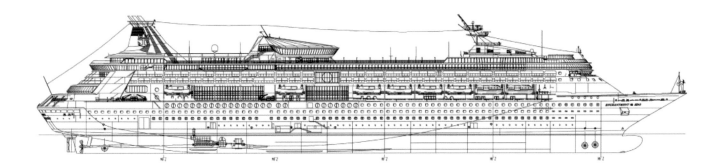

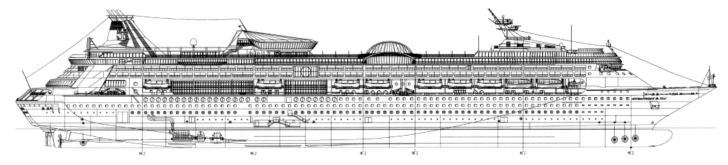

Oman Botanical Gardens
Muscat, Oman

**SPORT AND
LEISURE**

Client
Diwan of Royal Court

Area
420 ha

Type
Habitat-based botanic
garden

Status
Concept complete

Date
2006–2007

Set in a beautiful location close to a large wadi, these gardens have been designed to reproduce the different habitats of northern, central and southern Oman. The north and south extremes are so different to the local microclimate that they will require enclosure in biomes: large, transparent, highly-serviced structures, amorphous in form and unashamedly contemporary in appearance and specification. These contrast vividly with the other buildings in the reserve, which celebrate the traditional crafts of stone, mud brick and areesh (woven palm) construction.

The first biome is 1,200 m², and recreates the climate of southern Oman, notable for the monsoon that occupies the summer months in the Quarra mountains that surround the town of Salalah. The monsoon exerts a powerful influence: three months of almost constant gentle

rain and humidity turn the mountains green and temperate, and enable the vegetation bordering the seashore around the town to achieve a jungle-like lushness. The size and form of the biome will be determined by the particular topography of its site, but it will incorporate a cliff face with waterfalls, the green landscapes of both hill and plain and examples of the *Boswellia sacra* tree, Salalah's celebrated source of frankincense.

The second biome reproduces the habitat of northern Oman, the Jebel Akhdar mountain range, which rises to a high plateau 3,000 m above sea level. Cut by deep limestone valleys filled with juniper and palm trees, the range is subject to sporadic winter floods. Even in summer the air is cool at this elevation, which makes the fundamental function of both biomes that of keeping the heat out.

This may seem somewhat counter-intuitive for structures that so closely resemble traditional hot-houses, but the durable ETFE glazing and carefully developed passive convection system achieve it with great efficiency.

At the heart of the project is a hotel and reception centre, inspired by Omani architectural forms and suggesting an oasis settlement within a date palm grove. There is also a sanctuary that features indigenous Omani plants in a contemporary setting, supporting one of the themes of the garden – that of restoring the balance between the indigenous flora and the alien species currently used for domestic and municipal gardens. Taken as a whole the project reflects Oman's recent development, combining as it does contemporary advances with carefully preserved cultural traditions.

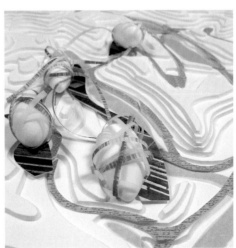

The golden cladding is 'peeled' away at the corner, allowing an interchange of light and views.

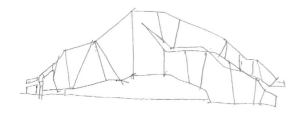

SPORT AND
LEISURE

Client
University of
Northumbria

Area
7,265 m²

Type
Three joined sports
halls, a training hall,
a 25 m pool, 40 m
sprint straights, high
performance training
facilities and a gym

Status
Under construction

Date
2007–2010

University of Northumbria Sports Centre
Newcastle, UK

This new sports facility for Northumbria University will provide spaces for indoor sports, high-performance training and leisure amenities for the university and local community. Its urban location posed a number of significant architectural challenges.

The centre features three joined sports halls, a 25 m swimming pool, 40 m sprint straights, high-performance training facilities and a gymnasium. Telescopic bleacher seating, contained within six cassettes just 0.8 m wide, enables the multi-purpose main sports hall to be transformed into

an event arena for 2,600 spectators. Architecturally, the building takes its compact form from two simple elements – the sports hall on one side, and ancillary accommodation edged by a garden on the other, which are connected by a bank of fixed seating. The clear layout is immediately understood by the visitor, allowing easy navigation and a quick grasp of the facilities on offer.

The spaces within the centre do not easily lend themselves to external expression. Coloured and perforated aluminium cladding, faceted and

folded to give depth and dynamism to the façade, is used to convey at street level some sense of the energy, space and movement contained within. This outer skin is cut away in places to allow approaching visitors glimpses of activity inside, and to harmonise the scale of the building with its smaller neighbours. The external lighting has been designed to enhance this effect while meeting the practical requirements of security and safe wayfinding.

The cladding system
has been treated as a
loose 'wrapping', pulled
away and distorted
in places to provide
intrigue and interest,
always with a functional
rationale behind
each intervention.

Barnard's Meadow
Lowestoft, UK

Barnard's Meadow is a 4.5 ha playing field adjacent to a sixth form college in Suffolk. This project involved the creation of changing facilities and the introduction of an all-weather pitch to complement the grass playing fields.

The pavilion building uses modular construction to reduce construction waste and optimise environmental efficiency. The flexible teaching space faces north to provide diffuse daylighting and control solar gain. A high-performance thermal envelope minimises air permeability and hence reduces heating demands, and carefully controlled ventilation maintains high comfort levels. All materials are sustainably sourced, and where possible 'A-rated' as defined in the *Green Guide*. The building is configured to allow for future expansion to the south and east.

The façade is composed of vertical composite panels, finished in a palette of eight colours drawn from the building's surroundings, which, seen from a distance, merge into a single neutral tone. Vertical black-framed window and door openings continue the rhythm, and a simple canopy helps define the main entrance.

SPORT AND LEISURE

Client
Suffolk County Council

Area
425 m²

Type
Sports pavilion

Status
Design complete

Date
2009–2011

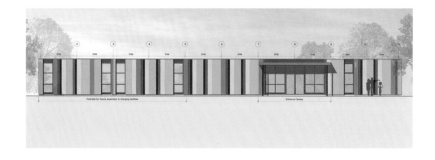

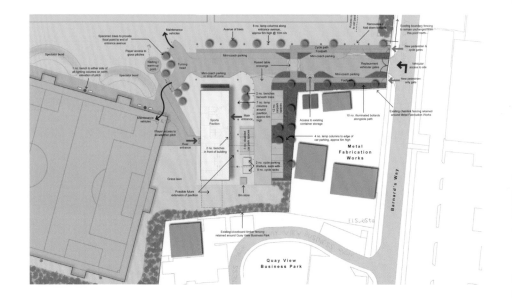

Oasis of the Seas
Miami, USA

SPORT AND LEISURE

Client
Royal Caribbean International

Area
220,000 gross tonnes

Type
Cruise ship

Status
Complete

Date
2005–2009

For Royal Caribbean, their guest experience is paramount, and this commission was a means of introducing innovation and excitement into a highly competitive environment. Not only were the design team able to use their creative skills to the full, but they could call on Atkins' broad range of engineering expertise to make their innovations work.

Oasis of the Seas is the largest cruise ship in the world, stretching from a remarkable 47 m wide at the waterline to over 65 m in width on the upper decks. It has 2,700 staterooms, providing the capacity to accept 5,400 guests at full occupancy. At 360 m long and 65 m high, this ship would constitute a significant building project if static, let alone floating. It set sail for the first time in November 2009.

The design team worked closely with Royal Caribbean on the early masterplanning of the vessel, and introduced an innovative interlocking stateroom concept allowing for more guest rooms between the bulkheads. The team was also awarded design responsibility for three of the seven 'neighbourhoods' on board, and developed the Rising Tide concept – a 'floating' bar elevating passengers between decks – to address the passenger circulation challenges that arise in such a large edifice.

Plaza Dubai
Dubai, UAE

In the urban growth of Dubai the tower has come to represent the nature of the city. The search to define a city centre has led to taller and taller towers, with Dubai's Downtown today defined by the tallest tower in the world, the Burj Khalifa. However, as the towers have reached greater and greater heights, the spaces inside become more and more exclusive, and the spaces outside more constricted and less significant.

The Plaza Dubai was conceived as a response to the privatisation of public space in Dubai. It offers a completely open and democratic venue for Dubai's inhabitants and visitors, and as such forms a new centre-point for the city.

The 20,000 m² of public space created within Plaza Dubai is on par with the great public spaces of the world – Tiananmen Square, Trafalgar Square, St Peter's Square, La Défense, Red Square – and at 160 m in diameter forms an amphitheatre that can seat 5,000 spectators. A permanent stage provides an arena for shows, displays and presentations of all types.

Comfort is provided by a shade structure in the shape of the crescent moon, a subtle reference to the local Islamic culture. The shading revolves in concert with the sun and is driven by solar power. At times of low occupancy, especially during summer days, the Plaza can be flooded using Dubai's plentiful ground water to produce a giant mirror pool for the city, reflecting the surrounding buildings and sky. The combination of pool and shade will provide a calm, contemplative space for relaxation and discussion, reflecting a strong element of Arabian tradition and culture.

SPORT AND
LEISURE

Client
Confidential

Area
20,000 m²

Type
Public plaza with an amphitheatre for 5,000 spectators

Status
Competition entry

Date
2008

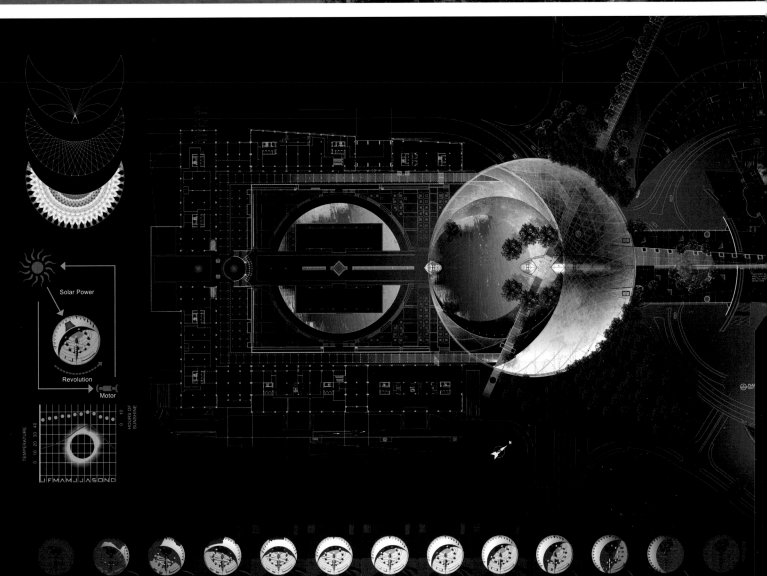

Solar Power

Revolution

Motor

TEMPERATURE
0 10 20 30 40

HOURS OF SUNSHINE
0 10

J F M A M J J A S O N D

N

06:00 07:00 08:00 09:00 10:00 11:00 12:00 13:00 14:00 15:00 16:00 17:00 18:00

Zabeel Park
Dubai, UAE

SPORT AND LEISURE

Client
Dubai Municipality

Area
48 ha

Type
Technology theme park

Status
Complete

Date
2003–2005

Zabeel Park is a 48 ha technology theme park that has vitalised a previously vacant area, linking the original urban settlements of Al Karama and Al Jafiliya to the DIFC, the new financial district. The park occupies two sites on either side of a major highway, linked by a soaring, curved footbridge.

The park has a lively side, boasting an amphitheatre, exhibition galleries, a bowling alley, an Imax theatre, a Techno Zone and an Alternative Energy Zone. Surrounding these are large landscaped gardens that provide the perfect location for calm relaxation and quiet, secluded family events.

The buildings for administration and various support facilities are used to form gatehouses, solid elements that punctuate the boundary fence and serve to indicate access points and ticket offices. Further pavilions and kiosks are located at strategic nodes in the park, connected by wide sweeping paths lined with palm trees. Picnic and barbecue facilities are sprinkled liberally throughout the green areas, and offer varying levels of privacy.

The materials employed for the built forms are principally stainless steel panels and fabric, tent-like roofs, the latter just one example of the wide use made of Arabic motifs. Footpaths scattered amongst the recurring landscaped themes are finished in an attractive blue exposed aggregate.

Atkins undertook the commission in conjunction with landscape architects Al Khatib Cracknell. This successful collaboration for a committed client resulted in the development of a valuable and well-patronised resource for the people of Dubai, and is a clear demonstration that the city has a real interest in developing a rich urban culture, rather than in the exclusive pursuit of commerce.

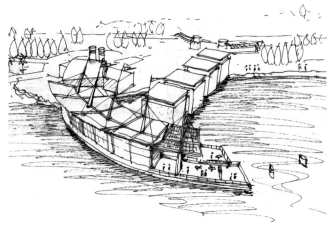

Daegu Stadium
Daegu, South Korea

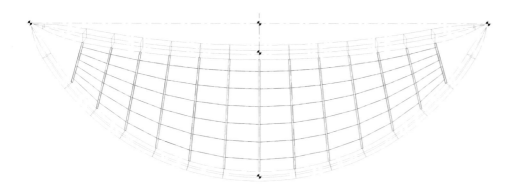

Like two cupped hands, the roof structure of the stadium embraces the pitch and the spectators.

To prevent light pollution the floodlighting is located on the inner rim of the roof structure.

Daegu Stadium co-hosted the 2002 FIFA World Cup. Located on the outskirts of Daegu City it is the 'jewel in the crown' of the Daegu Grand Park.

The design is a collaborative endeavour between Atkins and the Idea Image Institute, and notionally represents two giant cupped hands. Atkins was initially responsible for the structural concept and later undertook the detailed design on behalf of the Samsung Corporation.

The roof consists of a 23,000 m² PTFE-coated glass fibre membrane stretched across tubular arches, supported by prismatic steel trusses and spanning a dramatic 270 m over the 70,000-seat stadium. A great deal of attention was paid to the configuration of the supporting structure to minimise clutter and thus ensure the result is as elegant as it is spectacular.

SPORT AND
LEISURE

Client
Daegu City Council

Area
Roof covers 23,000 m²

Type
70,000 seating
capacity stadium

Status
Complete

Date
1996–2002

World Cup Bid Stadiums
Tripoli, Libya

SPORT AND LEISURE

Client
Libyan Football
Federation

Area
Various

Type
Development of eight
stadiums

Status
Concept design

Date
2003

Libya's national game is soccer. In September 2003, Libya submitted a competitive bid to FIFA in Zurich to host the 2010 World Cup. Atkins' multidisciplinary team was engaged to support the bid, designing eight new stadiums to be built in major cities on the Mediterranean coastline, accompanied by training centres for the competing national teams.

The stadiums were to be built in locations already passionately represented in the thriving Libyan national league, with the intention of providing them with high-quality legacy venues. In parallel with this, important infrastructure works were to be designed, together with new hotels across the country and a new media centre in Tripoli.

Atkins prepared concept designs for eight stadiums and a training centre, and went so far as to offer a ninth stadium option showing a 'legacy mode' appropriate to sustainable use in Libya after the World Cup event. The event was eventually awarded to the Republic of South Africa, but the exercise was a superb chance to really develop contemporary stadium design and reflect growing recognition of Libya as a positive contributor to the world community.

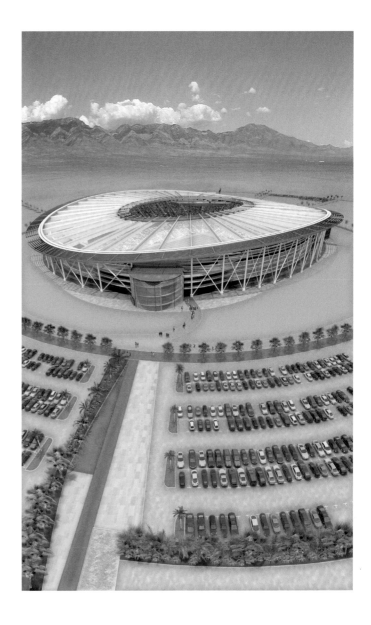

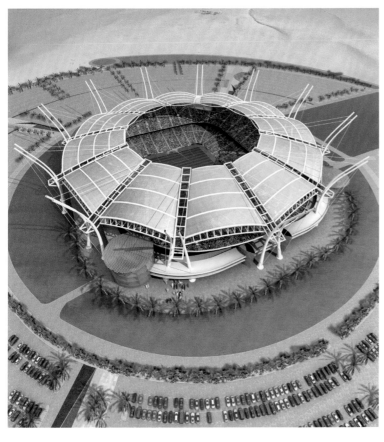

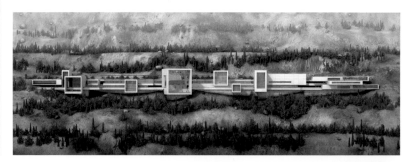

Qassioun Steps
Damascus, Syria

SPORT AND LEISURE

Client
Confidential

Area
41,500 m²

Type
Leisure development including an amphitheatre, hotel, conference centre, restaurants and retail

Status
Design

Date
2009

Damascus is the oldest continuously inhabited city in the world, and home to a truly fascinating combination of mysterious history and bustling modern urban life. Qassioun Steps is designed to convey and interpret the richness of that relationship.

Study the old city of Damascus and you will find a largely orthogonal arrangement of narrow, shaded alleyways linking self-effacing, traditional Arabic houses and community structures. Step through the low doorways, however, and you discover magnificent courtyards, jewel-like gardens, pools and terraces artfully concealed from the public gaze. Plotting these exquisite tiny oases on a plan of the old city reveals an intricate urban pattern of rectangular courtyard spaces, varying in size and following the rhythm of an urban grain that has grown up over millennia. That rhythm provides the inspiration for the massing of Qassioun Steps, both in plan and in elevation.

The same rhythm dictates the irregular but controlled interior layout of restaurants, souks, shops, a boutique hotel, a conference suite and a large open amphitheatre with spectacular views over the city below.

The rhythm and layout of the courtyards of ancient Damascus inspired both plans and elevations for the Qassioun Steps project.

The plan follows the orthogonal layout of the old city, and is carefully organised to follow the axis of the main thoroughfares in the city below, while stepping backward and forward on plan to follow the contours of the hillside. The exception is the amphitheatre, which is set slightly off-axis, oriented instead towards the Grand Mosque. This introduces a slight disturbance in the grid, characteristic of the historic city layout.

The elevations are given a scale that distinguishes them from the informal housing extending up the hill from the edge of the city below, and the clearly defined rectangles of the individual components relate strongly to both the historic courtyards and the crisp elevations of Damascus' modern buildings. Like the Acropolis in Athens, the complex is a civic construct that provides a range of buildings of varying size and mass, which work together to create a sense of presence and gravitas.

Qassioun Steps is clearly visible from almost anywhere in Damascus, and while its purpose is not immediately apparent, its careful design ensures that it is immediately recognised as part of both the old and new cities. The spectator will be compelled to investigate, and in so doing will be presented with a series of rewarding experiences. It is an object lesson in the sophistication and subtlety that are so often embodied in apparently simple eastern architecture.

Yas Island Water Park
Abu Dhabi, UAE

SPORT AND LEISURE

Client
ALDAR Properties PJSC

Area
22 ha

Type
Water park

Status
Detailed design

Date
2010–ongoing

Yas Island is home to the new Yas Marina F1 circuit, and the water park is one of a suite of theme parks that are developing around it. Covering an area of 22 ha, the park is positioned to make best use of an interchange between two major highways, providing excellent access and a prime local point of exposure.

The proposal is intended to produce the "greatest water park in the world". It will employ the ultimate collection of world-class rides and experiences in richly textured and themed surroundings, based on the compelling legend of The Lost Pearl. This is a theme intimately related to Emirati Arab culture and history, and recalls a time, easily within living memory, when pearl diving was a staple industry in the coastal Emirates and a defining image in its recent past.

The colours and materials for the attractions take into account ambient conditions; generally bright sunlight and in the summer months, intense heat. They must be durable, resistant to fading and UV degradation, and most importantly, remain cool to the touch and be chemically benign. Natural tones, inspired by earth, vegetation, water and sand are sought for their calming and comforting presence. They support the park's naturalistic themes and add 'reality' to the experience, providing a restful background for relaxation between thrills.

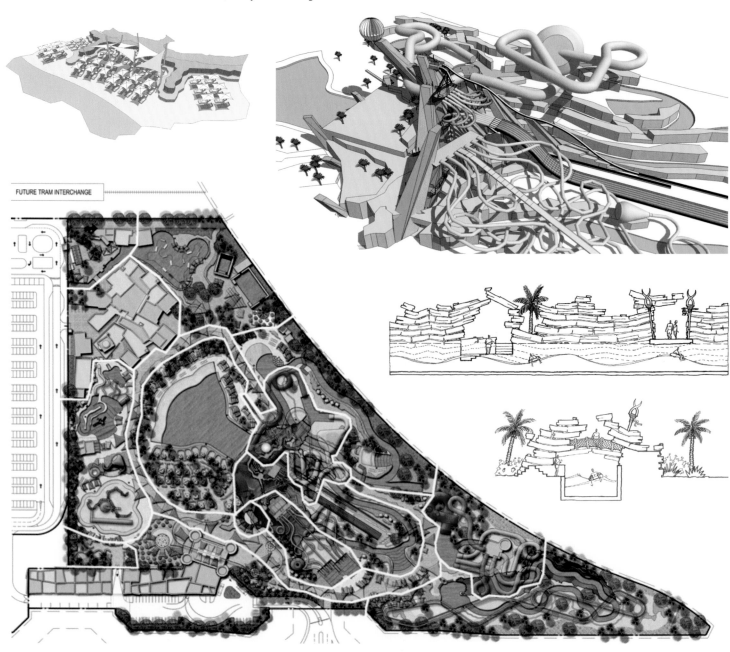

FUTURE TRAM INTERCHANGE

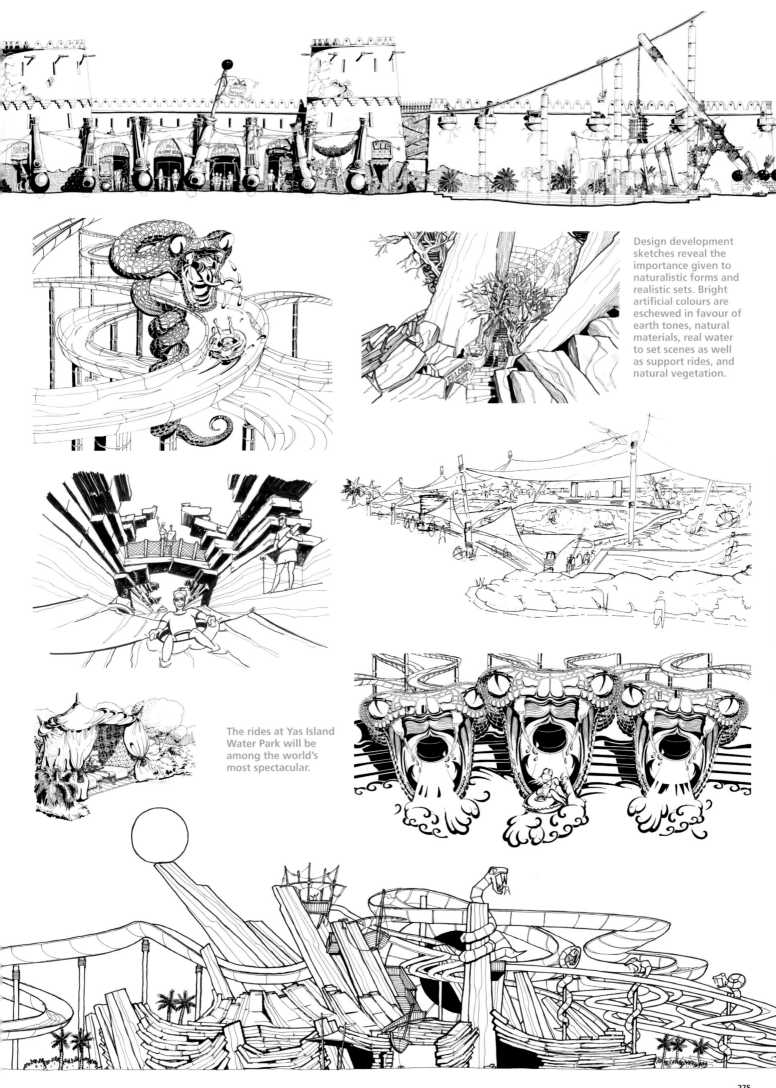

Design development sketches reveal the importance given to naturalistic forms and realistic sets. Bright artificial colours are eschewed in favour of earth tones, natural materials, real water to set scenes as well as support rides, and natural vegetation.

The rides at Yas Island Water Park will be among the world's most spectacular.

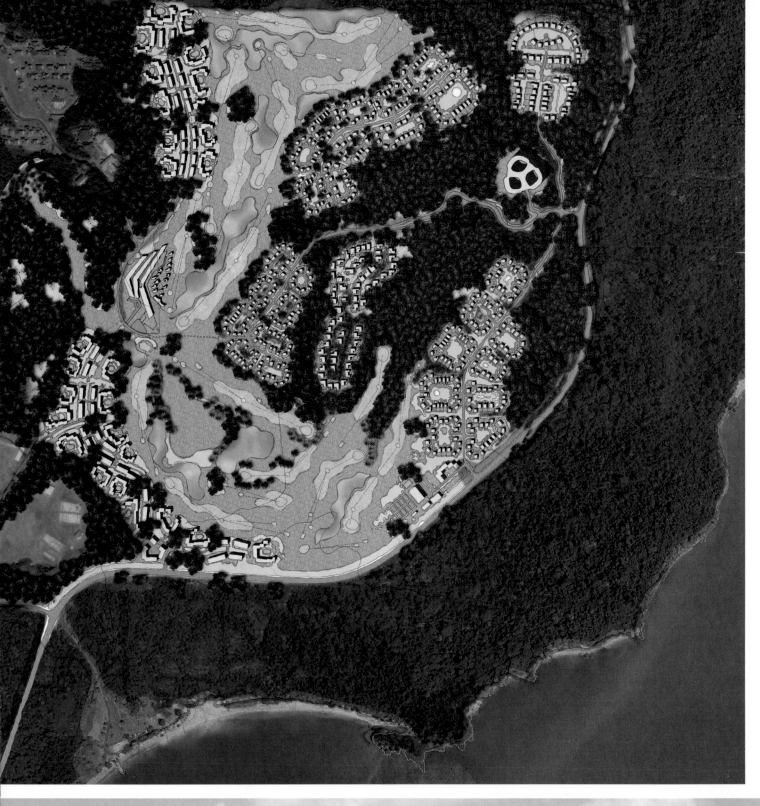

Kobbe Hills, Panama Pacifico
Panama

SPORT AND LEISURE

Client
Confidential

Area
600 ha

Type
Residential development and golf course

Status
Concept design

Date
2008

One of the new residential neighbourhoods within Panama Pacifico will be the exclusive community of Kobbe Hills. Featuring luxurious new housing disposed around a championship golf course with an adjacent resort and business hotels, the new community forms the first phase of the approved master development plan.

This exclusive development will consist primarily of luxury villas and townhouses, with residents enjoying membership of the adjoining golf course and country club. These occupy the lower ground, while the highest point of the Kobbe Hills provides the site for a 350-bed conference hotel, with easy access from the Kobbe Coastal Parkway.

The country club hotel and golf club house are sited on a spur of land overlooking the start and finish of the two golf nines. The par-72 golf course occupies the valley floor within a 'Wetland nine' to the north and a 'Savannah nine' to the south, both bordered by discretely landscaped residential accommodation with views across the open courses.

A key environmental objective of the masterplan has been to minimise the removal of forest on the steeper slopes. Where development is proposed in existing forest areas, the approach has been to create glades into which clusters of housing are introduced. Sufficient areas of forest will be retained between housing clusters to provide a strong green framework to contain the development and maintain corridors for wildlife.

The golf course at Kobbe Hills provides the framework for the development, with luxury houses set around the course perimeter in grassland and wetland zones.

HEALTHCARE, SCIENCE AND TECHNOLOGY

Client
Durham University

Area
2,400 m^2

Type
Research Institute

Status
Complete

Date
2008

Institute for Hazard and Risk Research
Durham, UK

The Institute for Hazard and Risk Research is an extension of the existing Durham University geography department. Its prominent position adjacent to the campus entrance is intended to give the department a new status within the university.

The institute has been designed to fully utilise current low-energy technologies and ecological best practice. The new building is set into a natural bank, and its laboratories have been given green roofs that control drainage run-off, provide a useful habitat and 'heal' the landscape disturbed by building. Externally, natural materials are used for both appearance and durability; internally, natural light and ventilation penetrate the building, providing a benign environment for users that is enhanced by high levels of insulation.

Glazed study bays flank the connecting link to the existing geography building. Offices enclose a dual-level winter garden, providing a place for staff and students to meet in the best campus tradition.

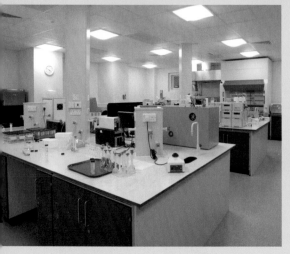

Heartlands Hospital Research Unit
Birmingham, UK

Client
Heart of England NHS
Foundation Trust

Area
3,600 m²

Type
Medical innovation
development, research
unit and diabetes
centre

Status
Complete

Date
2009

This specialist outpatient and medical research facility occupies the site of a demolished Victorian ward block. It is the first of a number of research and development buildings that the local NHS Trust is seeking to develop under its 'Outline Planning Approval' granted in 2006 for a medical park campus extension to their current hospital site.

The new unit will provide day care for diabetes patients, and separate but associated research facilities for medical staff. The building takes the form of a pair of long, two-storey blocks arranged on either side of a full-length, double-height atrium, with a footprint of around 1,800 m².

Attention has been paid to daylighting and comfort levels, and the provision of a bright, pleasant yet ordered ambience. The design includes a number of features aimed at improving the sustainability of the building, including rainwater harvesting, solar water heating and ground sourced space heating.

The atrium not only provides a linking concourse and waiting area, but it allows both natural light to flood the core of the building and the adoption of natural ventilation. Both approaches enable a significant reduction in the unit's power consumption and have a marked positive effect on the recovery times of its occupants.

The double-height street space with its bright glass roof and soaring volume is intended to lift the spirits of patients.

Particular attention was paid to getting light into the deeper volumes of the building without unnecessarily increasing solar gain in summer.

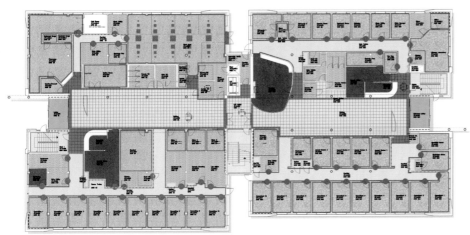

Ground floor plan

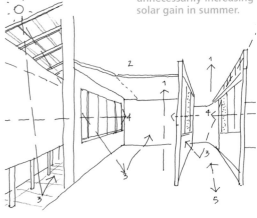

Anchor at West Hall
West Byfleet, UK

HEALTHCARE, SCIENCE AND TECHNOLOGY

Client
Anchor 2020

Area
10,250 m²

Type
Care home

Status
Design

Date
2008–2010

Within a long-term care community, the most vital element for the residents is a sense of belonging, to substitute for the familiarity of the home environment. Anchor at West Hall addresses this by providing a series of 'home-sized' house units set into individual garden landscapes.

The units contain large, comfortable en-suite rooms arranged in clusters around a kitchen and living space. The leaf-shaped plan allows for a friendly irregularity of spaces and for rooms to be fed directly from a central area without recourse to long corridors.

The leaf forms of the plan sit particularly comfortably in their rural surroundings.

282

The ground plan is repeated on the upper two levels, where the floor plates are shortened in length to accommodate a sweeping green roof that curves downwards, giving an individul atmosphere to each of the shared external terraces. These soft roofs with large chimneys are the main architectural features of the four residential buildings, and provide the whole development with a strong ambience of home, comfort and shelter.

The buildings are arranged in a freeform landscape of curved banks, planting and paths that lead to the existing Manor House. This will be restored and extended to provide an aqua-therapy pool, physiotherapy area, hair and beauty centre, library, cinema and restaurant. A renovated boat house provides facilities for venturing onto the River Wey, which borders the site.

Special attention has been paid to the selection of materials, levels of lighting, and visibility and contrast of colours to balance the needs of the elderly without detracting from the homeliness of the scheme.

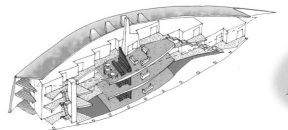

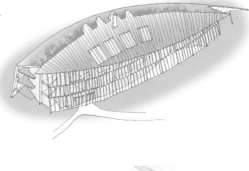

The buildings combine natural materials with sustainable technologies and careful design to produce comfortable but stimulating architecture.

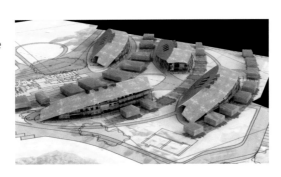

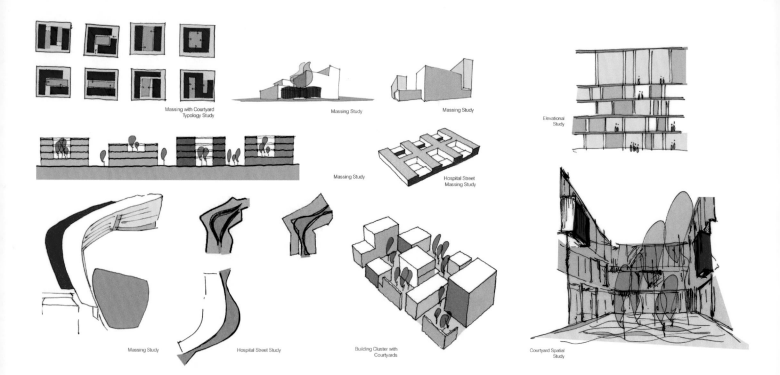

Massing with Courtyard Typology Study

Massing Study

Massing Study

Elevational Study

Massing Study

Hospital Street Massing Study

Massing Study

Hospital Street Study

Building Cluster with Courtyards

Courtyard Spatial Study

Kazan hospital renders orthogonal concepts as fluid, organic designs in reference to the human body.

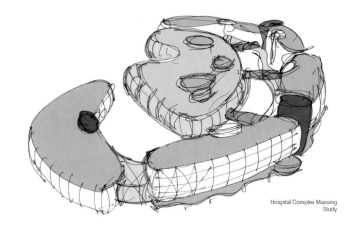

Hospital Complex Massing Study

Emergency Hospital
Kazan, Russia

HEALTHCARE, SCIENCE AND TECHNOLOGY

Client
Tatarstan Government

Area
72,000 m²

Type
Accident and emergency facility for the citizens of Kazan

Status
Masterplanning and design complete

Date
2007

Hospitals are powerful symbols of the social value placed on healthcare. As community venues, they directly affect patients, visitors and medical staff and provide strong landmarks in the urban fabric, acting as catalysts for further development.

Kazan's Emergency Hospital incorporates the latest in hospital design thinking and is conceived as part of the urban development for the entire area. It will be highly visible from the city's administrative heart across the Kazanka River to the southwest, from which it is easily accessible via the new Millennium Bridge. Its soft curves symbolise caring and protection, and its modern materials and finishes project a reassuring confidence.

Running north–south through the central building is a covered street that connects ancillary buildings and is strung with well-proportioned open spaces for visiting relatives and a treatment waiting area for patients. The individual buildings derive their character and identity from the shape of these courtyard spaces.

It is well known that patient experience and recovery can be improved by architecture that incorporates art and landscaping. A long external courtyard parallels the indoor street, providing a series of relaxed, landscaped spaces to aid relaxation and recovery, outdoor physical therapy areas and offering social settings for both staff and visitors. The vista from the recuperation wards is one of pleasant parklands and water.

The hospital design represents the best in contemporary standards, and incorporates sufficient flexibility to ensure it continues to function effectively through the many changes of health policy, technological advances, demographic trends and public expectations that will invariably occur.

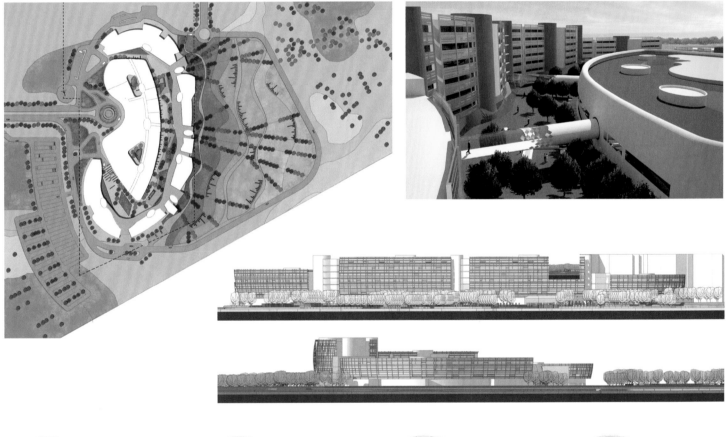

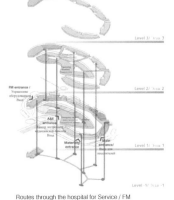

Routes through the hospital for Service / FM

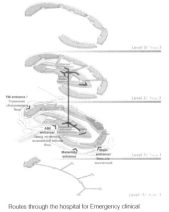

Routes through the hospital for Emergency clinical

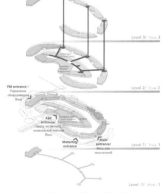
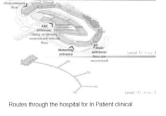

Routes through the hospital for In Patient clinical

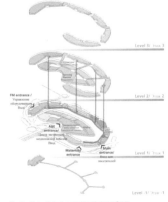

Routes through the hospital for Visitors / Staff

Wiltshire and Swindon History Centre
Chippenham, UK

HEALTHCARE,
SCIENCE AND
TECHNOLOGY

Client
Wiltshire County Council/
Swindon Borough Council

Area
3,900 m²

Type
Archival storage with
public access

Status
Complete

Date
2007

The new £11.8 million Wiltshire and Swindon History Centre preserves documentary, object and archaeological evidence of the county's past and supports important custodial, educational and promotional roles. As such, it was an ideal project for the substantial Heritage Lottery Funding, which was granted in 2003 following the preparation of an expansive set of bid documents by Wiltshire County Council and Atkins.

Since it opened in 2007, the building has provided services to over 25,000 people per year, either through direct personal research in the new building or through its postal and internet enquiry service.

The new building has been licensed to house the significant collection of ancient documents held by the County Council in purpose-designed, environmentally controlled strong-rooms on behalf of The National Archives. A large new public reading room allows members of the public direct access to thousands of library books, Record Office documents and digital microfilm and microfiche copies of historic information.

In addition, the County Archaeologist's Office administers the County Sites and Monuments Record Office from the new reading room, and the County's Objects and Archives Conservation Unit occupies new north-facing, state-of-the-art laboratories and workshops.

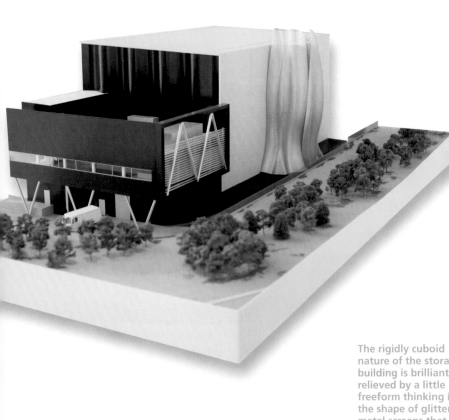

The rigidly cuboid
nature of the storage
building is brilliantly
relieved by a little
freeform thinking in
the shape of glittering
metal screens that
turn mundane
service components
into artworks.

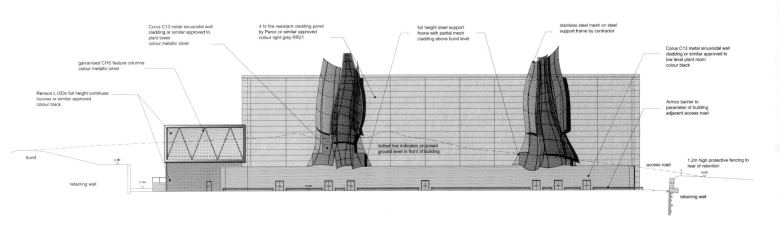

British Library Archive Unit
Boston Spa, UK

HEALTHCARE,
SCIENCE AND
TECHNOLOGY

Client
British Library

Area
5,800 m²

Type
Archive repository

Status
Complete

Date
2004–2008

The British Library's collection contains over 150 million items including printed books and serials, manuscripts, maps and stamps, newspapers and sound recordings. This new archive storage facility is for high-density, low-usage materials, suitable for handling by a range of access equipment.

The document retrieval system is capable of supplying 250 documents per hour, and provides a fully automated response to the four million requests that the Library responds to each year. The 1.5 million items currently stored can be managed by a maximum of five staff.

The facility is a very large building located in a rural setting and the first phase of its planned growth is complete. It satisfies contradicting demands of 'low visual impact' and 'architectural statement', by combining simple massing with fascinating detail. The long, sky-grey walls of the main building are interrupted by fluid forms in punched stainless-steel mesh, shrouding access towers and air handling ducts. Raking columns support the administration centre, and are replicated in the supports for the louvre panels that flank the unit.

The building allows for storage growth, with 12.5 kilometres of shelving being added every year to accommodate a variety of media in a low light, oxygen-controlled environment. It is expected to solve the British Library's archive storage requirements for the next 15–20 years.

Paul O'Gorman Leukaemia Research Centre, Gartnavel Hospital
Glasgow, UK

HEALTHCARE,
SCIENCE AND
TECHNOLOGY

Client
NHS Greater Glasgow
and Clyde/University
of Glasgow

Area
2,500 m²

Type
New-build laboratories
and leukaemia
research centre

Status
Complete

Date
2004–2008

This new building, together with an existing refurbished laboratory to which it is linked at the second floor level, provides an integrated service related to blood disorders in Glasgow. The UK's National Health Service operates three of the laboratories – Oncology, Immunology and Haematology – while Glasgow University, part owner of the building, operates the specialist Leukemia Research Unit.

Each floor is arranged around a large central laboratory space, with specialist rooms and offices located alongside. Externally, the layout is expressed by patinated copper cladding on the vertical circulation and administrative accommodation, with laboratory space enveloped in an appropriately sterile white finish. The upper floor is set back from the main two levels, minimising the apparent height of the building and enhancing the horizontal lines.

The plant room at roof level is contained in a giant blue tube, an exaggerated air extract cowl. At ground level the whole composition 'floats' above a recessed undercroft, enabling old and new floor levels to be comfortably matched.

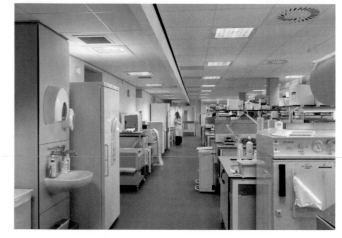

The County Hospital
Hereford, UK

HEALTHCARE,
SCIENCE AND
TECHNOLOGY

Client
Hereford Hospitals
National Health
Service Trust

Area
35,000 m²

Type
General hospital

Status
Complete

Date
2002–2003

This £65 million project is a mixture of new-build, refurbishment and extension of an existing hospital for Hereford Hospitals NHS Trust. It will enable all of the acute services, at present spread over three sites, to be rationalised and provided from a single location in Hereford.

The main accommodation of the new-build facility is provided in wards and rooms housing 250 inpatient beds for acute, coronary, intensive and high-dependency care. Medical services include day surgery and general operating theatres, emergency, orthopaedic and a full range of outpatient facilities, along with diagnostic imaging services. Maternity accommodation includes paediatric, obstetrics and neonatal services, and at the other end of the spectrum is a full range of care and rehabilitation facilities for the elderly. Support facilities include sterile services and catering.

The building has been purposely provided with a narrow plan to enable natural light and ventilation throughout its depth, enhanced by the enclosure of three themed courtyards with hard and soft landscaped gardens. High-quality materials ensure durability and reduced maintenance costs, with particular attention paid in the design to reducing both material wastage and fabrication timescales. The external use of red brick provides a link to the surrounding vernacular architecture, with aluminium cladding and white rendered panels reinforcing the image of its clean, sterile interior. A full interior design was developed and incorporated with the cooperation of the Trust.

The interior continues the clean, bright theme, with colours chosen for their therapeutic as well as aesthetic value.

Milton Keynes Hospital
Milton Keynes, UK

HEALTHCARE,
SCIENCE AND
TECHNOLOGY

Client
Milton Keynes
Hospital NHS
Foundation Trust

Area
3,500 m²

Type
Women's and
children's healthcare
services

Status
Design

Date
2009

This new maternity and children's hospital is a response to a challenging brief. In addition to the usual conundrums of planning an open, accessible, yet intensely private, highly serviced and technically demanding facility, significant problems were added by virtue of its site.

It sits at the edge of an existing hospital, to which it will be linked and which it must respect in terms of massing and materials. It also needs to provide opportunities for future expansion, and its construction must not disrupt the business of the existing hospital. Emphasis is placed on integration with the existing corridor and travel routes, ensuring practical locations for new units adjacent to existing services, and, in consideration

of its funding through charitable donations, making the best use of the existing buildings on site as well as offering outstanding value for money.

The result is a fascinating new addition that enfolds and re-uses the frame of an existing building. It features light-filled and airy interiors with beautiful views, and yet complete privacy is achieved thanks to the clever use of levels, angled windows and the provision of delightful contained gardens that both landscape the site and provide a living screen.

The gardens provide therapeutic benefits and are an integral part of a comprehensive range of carbon critical design features.

The heavily glazed internal courtyard allows light to flow into the circulation spaces, bringing well-understood therapeutic benefits to the occupants.

Slagelse Psychiatric Hospital
Sjaelland, Denmark

**HEALTHCARE,
SCIENCE AND
TECHNOLOGY**

Client
Region Sjaelland

Area
44,000 m²

Type
Healthcare facility

Status
Competition
entry, Purchase –
Honourable Mention

Date
2009–2010

Psychiatric illness is a difficult branch of medicine. Sufferers frequently have not only their illness to contend with, but the difficulties that it poses in relation to their surroundings. Slagelse Psychiatric Hospital has been designed to address this by providing a simple, easily comprehended environment that promotes a feeling of wellbeing and safety. This directly assists the patient's recovery, and also provides a 'dynamic' response to the return to health, in that as patients recover, they can increasingly be left to manage their own lives and treatment, further increasing their confidence and wellbeing.

Patients are housed not in wards, but in houses, accessible from the hospital via glazed links that run through internal courtyard gardens. Each has an individual character, providing a sense of place and easy wayfinding. Access to the houses

is by 'streets' rather than corridors, designed as a string of spaces, again given individual characters and linked through windows and glazed walls to internal courtyards or the external landscape. This connection with the outdoors is not only pleasant, but also has proven clinical benefits in terms of speed and quality of recovery.

The same streets also provide access to the treatment areas, functional spaces based on the same comforting architecture that are grouped into wings, accessible directly from the main foyer in accordance with a readily grasped layout. The foyer is a large, comfortable space, highly glazed to maintain links with the outside, and open enough to be immediately apprehended by the visitor.

There is a café, screened by walls of planting and subdivided into intimate niches of various sizes, in which

inpatients and visiting relatives can meet in semi-private surroundings. There's a large auditorium opening off the foyer, too, so that conference delegates do not have to penetrate and disrupt the calmer internal spaces. The foyer doubles as ante-room and support space for auditorium events.

The same careful thinking has been applied to the selection of materials, colours and textures, the integration of the myriad services a modern hospital demands and the changes that will be demanded by future developments in medical science, demographics, population numbers and so forth. The building's efficiency and sustainability are of the highest current standards, with a comprehensive scheme to make the best use of renewable energy and on-site recycling integrated into the project from the start.

Slagelse attempts
a delicate balance
between unresricted
wandering and
safe containment
for vulnerable but
active patients.

Cork Medical Clinic
Cork, Republic of Ireland

The Cork Medical Clinic is a major private healthcare facility located on the outskirts of the city of Cork in the Republic of Ireland. The site is a prominent, steeply sloping greenfield with dramatic views of the north of the city and along the valley to the southwest.

The hospital incorporates the latest technological advances in healthcare treatment facilities and advanced IT support systems. Although primarily an outpatient centre, the clinic has 78 inpatient beds including nine intensive care beds, a full suite of operating theatres, radiotherapy and same-day surgery facilities, a private medicine wing and support accommodation including kitchen and dining facilities and a conference suite and administration centre featuring an electronic medical records system. These facilities are all supported by 450 car parking spaces, service roads, landscaping and a utility authority infrastructure.

The concept design developed three functional zones – patient accommodation, clinical services and consultancy – all linked by a central circulation spine. This approach provides clarity for the visitor and patient and also allows a clear servicing strategy to be developed to meet the differing needs of each functional group. The building form was developed in response to the demands of the site, with consultancy suites located in the curved element to the western boundary and conference and administration functions on the upper level to take advantage of the impressive countryside views.

The building services systems contribute to an environmentally sustainable design and are as innovative as the healthcare model. They incorporate renewable energy technologies including ground source heat pumps, photovoltaic panels and solar panel arrays to make maximum use of renewable energy sources, backed by highly effective energy reduction measures.

HEALTHCARE,
SCIENCE AND
TECHNOLOGY

Client
Sheehan Medical

Area
20,000 m²

Type
New-build clinic

Status
Complete

Date
2005–2007

Royal Hospital for Sick Children
Yorkhill, UK

HEALTHCARE,
SCIENCE AND
TECHNOLOGY

Client
NHS Greater Glasgow
Health Board

Area
3,000 m²

Type
Pediatric intensive
care unit and high
dependency unit

Status
Complete

Date
2004–2006

This state-of-the-art paediatric intensive care unit and high dependency unit has been inserted into existing buildings at the Royal Hospital for Sick Children, Yorkhill. It overcame not only severe planning constraints, but construction and phasing difficulties too. Added to that was a requirement to provide scope for future expansion.

To create the new facility of 28 beds and associated support accommodation, the team designed a link bridge structure at the second floor level to provide a floor plate that enables the siting of the two new units next to each other. The single floor makes support and ancillary facilities considerably more efficient and enables staff to share the running of both wards.

This project was constructed while the main hospital building was operational, meeting a number of logistical, safety and health challenges. The result is a layout that not only accommodates the requirements of patients and staff now, but which can also be adapted to future clinical needs.

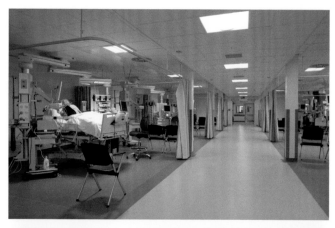

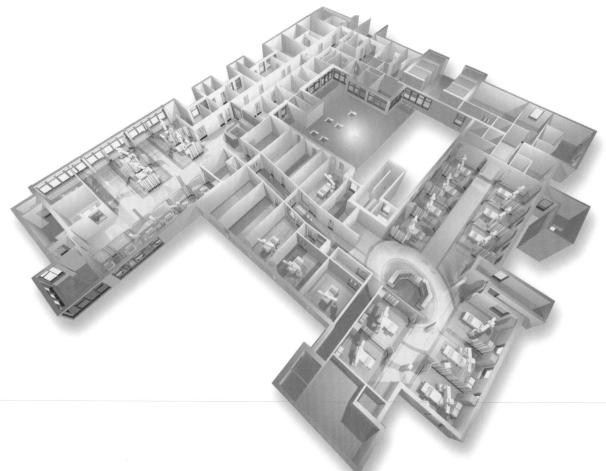

No dramatic gestures here – just solid attention to detail and the creative use of space.

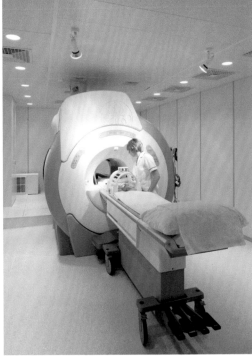

A vibrant splash of yellow and a stylish canopy highlight the main entrance.

The plan is rigorous and efficient, ensuring that the majority of the spending goes into services rather than structures.

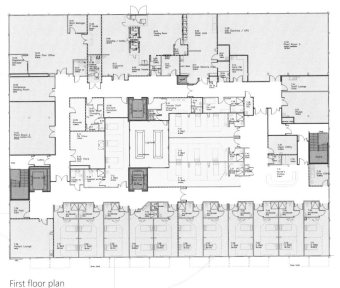

First floor plan

Independent Sector Treatment Centre
Shepton Mallet, UK

HEALTHCARE, SCIENCE AND TECHNOLOGY

Client
UK Specialist Hospitals Limited

Area
4,250 m²

Type
New-build

Status
Complete

Date
2004–2005

This project was undertaken in consortium with OR International, an American developer of speciality hospitals, and New York-Presbyterian Healthcare, one of the leading healthcare systems in the United States. The new facility cost nearly £12 million, and is expected to complete some 11,000 surgical operations each year.

Designed to provide additional capacity for NHS patients and thus contribute to reducing waiting times, this technically advanced centre is one of the first

of its type in the UK. It will focus on hip, knee, cataract and general surgery, and serve residents within a 40 mile radius of Shepton Mallet.

The architecture is simple, with a rigorously efficient plan reflecting the project's main focus. Colour and texture have been used to enliven the exterior and combined with a stylish sweeping canopy, give the building a cheerful atmosphere of competence and confidence – good health should be enjoyed and celebrated.

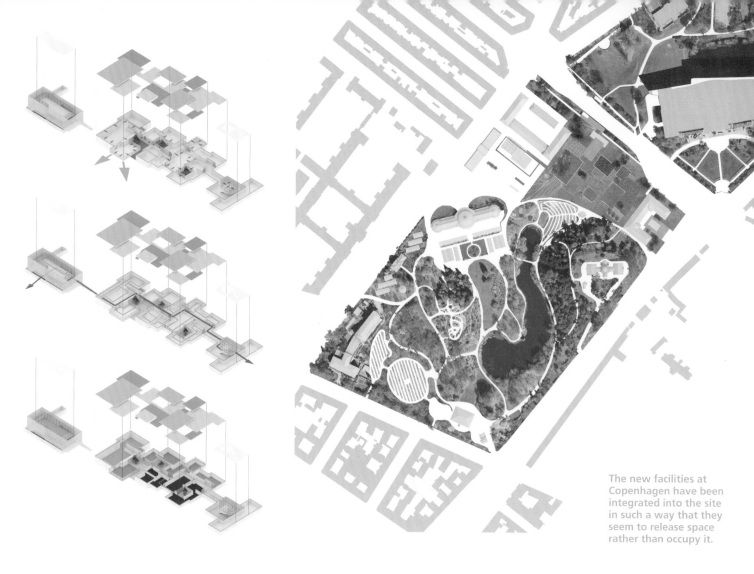

Natural History Museum
Copenhagen, Denmark

Client
Copenhagen
University

Area
30,000 m²

Type
Museum and
educational facilities
(new-build and
refurbishment)

Status
Competition entry

Date
2009

The parkland around Copenhagen is much loved by the city's occupants, none more so than the section that houses the three scientific establishments that concern themselves with the natural world: the Zoological Museum, the Geological Museum and the Botanical Museum and Garden. This project sought to link these individual buildings to form a single entity, the Copenhagen Natural History Museum, and at the same time to restore the plaza in front of the Botanical Garden glasshouse and improve the appearance of the site generally.

The existing Zoological and Botanical buildings to the north and the Geological building to the east are solid brick structures, and caused a certain amount of disquiet when they were first constructed. Their site is a remnant of the historical defensive space that surrounded the old city and their intervention changed the nature of this much-valued space quite markedly.

A fundamental requirement of the new scheme was that the remaining open space between the two blocks be preserved, ensuring open views from both within and outside the site.

The new link addresses these concerns by being located below ground. It connects the two existing brick complexes with a new subterranean string of exhibition halls, designed in such a way that any of the new spaces can be closed off without disrupting access to another or interrupting the primary link. This is important: changing displays are a fundamental means of keeping the museum lively and giving patrons a good reason to revisit.

The roof of the underground section is organised as a series of shallow terraces, which provide a perfect pattern for experimental new garden beds. As well as being scientifically valuable, their frequent replanting again refreshes and revitalises the

museum. The terraces have been judiciously spaced to allow daylight to filter into the exhibition spaces below. Although a simple device, this has to be controlled very carefully – daylight may reduce artificial lighting costs and provide excellent colour rendition, but it can be extremely harmful to exhibits.

The connection to the fourth element of the site, the greater garden and glass palm house, is made by a new entrance pavilion, placed in a corner of the northern complex of existing buildings where it will not disrupt the all-important views. This new pavilion controls access to the site, and the design team has made the most of its brief chance to introduce some drama to the new museum complex by creating the ultimate green building. Its façade consists of walls of live vegetation, reflecting its function, its green credentials and its botanical connections. It is a traditional greenhouse turned inside out: literally, a green house.

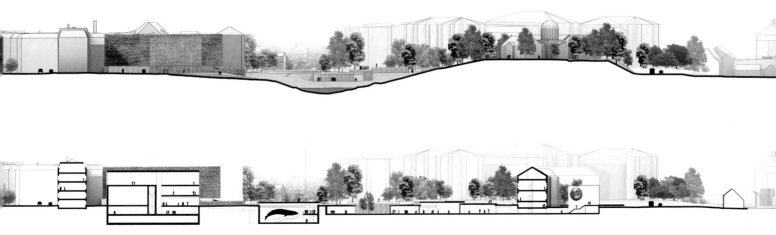

Tayside Mental Health
Perth and Angus, UK

HEALTHCARE, SCIENCE AND TECHNOLOGY

Client
NHS Tayside

Area
29,200 m²

Type
New-build mental health developments

Status
Under construction

Date
2009–2012

Tayside, in the heart of Scotland, is developing an enviable mental health unit with the assistance of Atkins' comprehensive multidisciplinary team. The new facility is spread over two sites and involves three separate units – two at Murray Royal Hospital in the city of Perth, and one in the small town of Stracathro in nearby Angus.

The integrated campus will cost nearly £100 million in total and will provide 235 beds to support adult and elderly psychiatric care, split between both sites, along with the North of Scotland's new medium security unit for mentally disordered offenders at Perth. The new facilities will be combined with the best of the retained buildings (some of which are protected as being of historical importance) to create an enhanced patient environment that supports human dignity, wellbeing and growth.

Of course, the final designs have been developed not only to meet the challenging functional requirements of modern mental healthcare, but to incorporate the best of sustainable design. In terms of daylighting, they take the concept further to ensure that the proven health benefits of natural light, fresh air and views of the beautiful rural surroundings are brought deep into the hospitals and made available to every patient.

At Murray Royal Hospital, the new facilities replace existing, outdated Victorian and post-war buildings, and provide a new expanded mental health service comprising a 66-bed General Adult Psychiatry (GAP) ward and a 50-bed Psychiatry of Old Age (POA) ward. These are linked through a central patient and public support unit incorporating an ENT/dental suite, outpatient facilities, a day hospital,

a therapies department and social facilities including a café and a shop. Due to the security implications, the 67-bed Secure Care Centre (SCC) has been developed as a separate building, albeit linked as part of a cohesive architectural solution run by an integrated mental health service.

At Stracathro Hospital, outdated facilities spread throughout the county of Angus are replaced by a new, integrated mental health hospital. A 25-bed GAP ward and a 27-bed POA ward share a single building, together with social and patient support accommodation including a day hospital, tribunal services and a gymnasium. The position and orientation of the new unit was carefully considered in order to make the most of the dramatic external landscape and an adjacent, historically significant walled garden.

Left and *right*: Stracathro Hospital in Angus, where clean new buildings are replacing a hodge-podge of tired old structures.

Above: An aerial view of the Murray Royal Hospital in Perth, where new buildings are integrated with historic structures to create a new mental health hospital.

Seafield Residential Care Home
Ayr, UK

One result of an increasingly elderly population is that diseases of old age are becoming more prevalent. This project, commissioned in late 2007, addresses the problem with a 54-bed residential care home for the elderly, with particular attention paid to the care of those with dementia.

While medical treatment is part of the regime, the basic foundation of care is the provision of a tranquil, peaceful environment in which the occupants can rest. The building supports this approach by being arranged to enclose or define calm, safe courtyard spaces, internally and externally.

On the ground floor are continuing care houses for those suffering from dementia, with general access rooms (alternative therapy, physiotherapy, administration) wrapped around the central courtyards, linked by 'wandering routes'. These are strung with 'pausing' spaces, providing rest and courtyard views. The residents' bed spaces are arranged around the perimeter of the building, giving each resident access to the wider landscape. The upper floor houses respite and rehabilitation accommodation.

The building and landscaping are also used to define 'external' courtyards. One is located at the entrance, a shared surface for cars and people, another is the private back garden that provides space to wander and a greenhouse.

Privacy is important – it allows patients to remain safe, and enables them to enjoy the therapeutic benefits of outside life and the freedom to wander. The attention paid to the building form and landscaping strives to enhance this quality of free access to nature.

HEALTHCARE,
SCIENCE AND
TECHNOLOGY

Client
South Ayrshire Council

Area
4,400 m²

Type
Mental healthcare facilities

Status
Concept design complete

Date
2007–2009

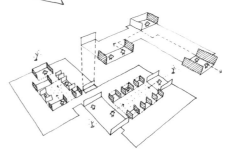

The central public realm consists of common townscape events. The use of shop, park, office and spa scenes distances them from institutional functions and attempts to evoke universal memories.

A bench along a public route becomes an event commited to memory, assisting in visually mapping the interior.

A graduation of shelter and enclosure creates an outside space veiled with internal public spaces, retaining a close bond between inside and out.

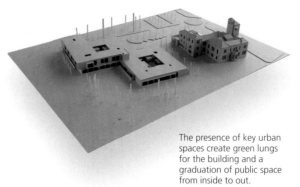

Each bed space extends into a small, private garden where further opportunity exists to colonise independently or with family.

The building's form is at once similar and dissimilar to the listed building through the creation of considered contrast and the subtle repetition of a clustered building type.

The presence of key urban spaces create green lungs for the building and a graduation of public space from inside to out.

HEALTHCARE, SCIENCE AND TECHNOLOGY

Client
NHS Lothian

Area
45,000 m²

Type
New-build/hospital refurbishment

Status
Complete

Date
2000–2007

Royal Edinburgh Hospital Redevelopment
Edinburgh, UK

Updating old hospitals is challenging, and invariably leads to designs diluted by compromise. Their replacement, on the other hand, is an opportunity to produce a new state-of-the-art facility without compromise, and this can be a joyful experience.

The replacement of the old Victorian Royal Edinburgh Hospital in Morningside on an adjoining greenfield site will provide a landmark world-class mental healthcare facility. The accommodation includes a main reception hub with social facilities, outpatient departments, a day care unit, a life-skills centre, a clinical centre, a university education suite and 354 inpatient beds to cater for dementia, general and acute psychiatry, intensive care psychiatry, rehabilitation, substance misuse, alcohol dependency and care of the elderly.

The multidisciplinary design team worked particularly closely with the future users of the hospital, including having key design staff seconded to the hospital for a period. This provided valuable insights, and empathy with the difficulties that both patients and staff experience in their day-to-day endeavours. The architectural proposal takes advantage of this insider knowledge, combining a confident and efficient layout with the wonderful views and natural south-facing slope offered by the new site to maximise the theraputic benefits of both the internal and external environments for patients, visitors and staff.

Sustainability initiatives are intrinsic to the design proposals and include thermodynamic modelling to determine optimum orientation and solar treatment, zoning for daytime and 24-hour occupancy, natural ventilation strategies, rainwater harvesting and CHAPS (combined heat and power systems). A significant component of the sustainability strategy is the decision to design for off-site prefabrication, which reduces construction time, raises construction quality and reduces construction waste.

Towards the end of the technical commission Atkins also developed initial designs for a new £5 million stand-alone unit housing Scotland's national brain injury centre, the Robert Ferguson Unit, on the nearby Astley Ainsley Hospital site.

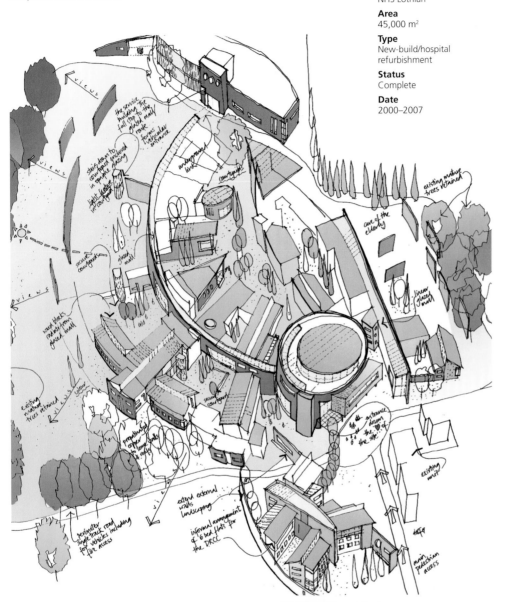

305

Wellness Resort
Dubai, UAE

HEALTHCARE, SCIENCE AND TECHNOLOGY

Client
Dubai Healthcare City (DHCC)

Area
19 ha

Type
Healthcare resort

Status
Design ongoing

Date
2008–2012

The UAE is intent on becoming an internationally recognised location of choice for quality private healthcare, and to this end is developing as a centre of excellence for a full range of medical and associated treatments. As part of this plan, the Wellness Resort will become the premier integrated centre of excellence for clinical and wellness services, medical education and research in the Gulf.

Incorporating hospital inpatient facilities, outpatient clinics, healthcare education facilities, hotels, spa resorts, long-term care facilities and residential areas, the Wellness Resort will occupy an exciting waterfront building on a 19 ha campus that has been designed to make the most of a superb site and to convey the idea of a healthy zest for life.

Gynaecology Unit, Glasgow Royal Infirmary
Glasgow, UK

HEALTHCARE, SCIENCE AND TECHNOLOGY

Client
NHS Greater Glasgow and Clyde

Area
3,000 m²

Type
New-build and refurbishment

Status
Complete

Date
2005–2009

This £8 million development of women's medical services in Glasgow involved the improvement of the gynaecology inpatient facilities at Glasgow Royal Infirmary. It provides 33 beds and a suite of two operating theatres, directly below the well-known Princess Royal Maternity Hospital.

The facilities have been developed by altering and extending existing hospital installations around the hospital's main outpatient entrance. This involved a great deal of careful design and management to mitigate the health, safety and infection control risks associated with working in a live hospital. Atkins was able to undertake this as part of the full multidisciplinary consultancy provided for the project.

A challenging brief involved replanning the interior of this unit without disrupting the work of the busy hospital around it.

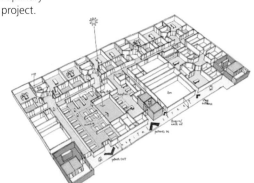

Tepnel Life Sciences
Livingston, UK

HEALTHCARE,
SCIENCE AND
TECHNOLOGY

Client
Thermal Transfer

Area
480 m²

Type
New-build laboratory
and offices

Status
Complete

Date
2007–2008

Tepnel Life Sciences is a provider of outsourcing services for the UK pharmaceutical, biotechnology and healthcare industries. The design of their new facility on Livingston's Eliburn Campus in south-central Scotland was undertaken with specialist design and build contractor, Thermal Transfer.

The facility contains a range of highly serviced accommodation, incorporating some demanding technical requirements. Laboratories, incubator rooms and instrument rooms are connected internally by a 'racetrack' of glazed circulation around the ground floor, which enables visitors to receive a guided tour without disturbing the activities within. The building also accommodates an administration suite and a boardroom, and makes careful provision for future expansion.

Externally the massing is simple, with clean white cladding reflecting the precise, controlled nature of the business within. The form is largely influenced by the cross section, which was developed efficiently to distribute ventilation throughout the building. Large glazed areas overlooking the adjacent pond give the intensely introverted interiors a link with nature and daylight.

Clean lines and white cladding clearly express the sterile internal functions of this laboratory building.

EDUCATION

Northumbria University City Campus East

Newcastle-Upon-Tyne, UK

This award-winning sustainable design creates a new landmark law, business and design school for the Northumbria University city campus. It incorporates a distinctive detached, double-curvature outer layer, shading and enclosing the buildings and making a confident new contribution to the urban fabric of Newcastle-Upon-Tyne.

Located to the east of Newcastle city centre within a contained site, the new school is the latest in a sequence of distinctive projects. Newcastle is undergoing an architectural renaissance, of which the new campus is a significant component.

EDUCATION

Client
University of Northumbria

Area
24,000 m²

Type
Schools of law, business and design faculties

Status
Complete

Date
2005–2007

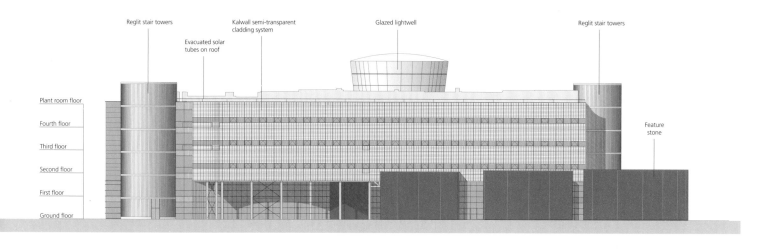

Reglit stair towers

Evacuated solar tubes on roof

Kalwall semi-transparent cladding system

Glazed lightwell

Reglit stair towers

Feature stone

Plant room floor
Fourth floor
Third floor
Second floor
First floor
Ground floor

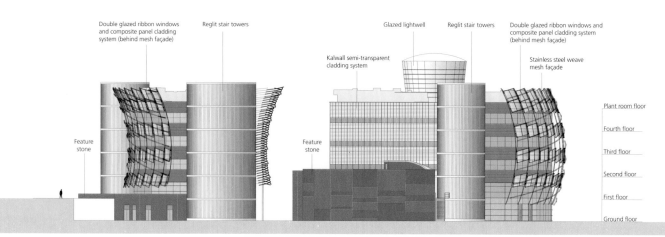

Double glazed ribbon windows and composite panel cladding system (behind mesh façade)

Reglit stair towers

Glazed lightwell

Reglit stair towers

Double glazed ribbon windows and composite panel cladding system (behind mesh façade)

Kalwall semi-transparent cladding system

Stainless steel weave mesh façade

Feature stone

Feature stone

Plant room floor
Fourth floor
Third floor
Second floor
First floor
Ground floor

To the east and west a 'solar veil' is created by a stainless steel mesh frame. This shades the buildings against 50% of the sun's radiation and reduces air conditioning loads without adversely affecting interior lighting. The structure is facetted, but reads as a gentle compound curve thanks to its scale. It also provides some drama to what would otherwise be simple, efficient but somewhat bland elevations.

The design school is a single structure, while the law and business schools are combined on the other side of a shared space that is thus enclosed to form an external courtyard. Internally, the buildings incorporate flexible office and teaching spaces, raked and flat floor lecture theatres and hospitality suites, with the distinctive curved plans resulting in some dramatic but efficient interior spaces.

The design incorporates the use of recycled materials and boasts a host of other sustainable initiatives. It has received numerous accolades, including the CIBSE Low Carbon Performance Award for Low Carbon New Build Project of the Year, the RICS Sustainability, Design and Innovation Award and the overall Building of the Year Award 2008 for Northern Region.

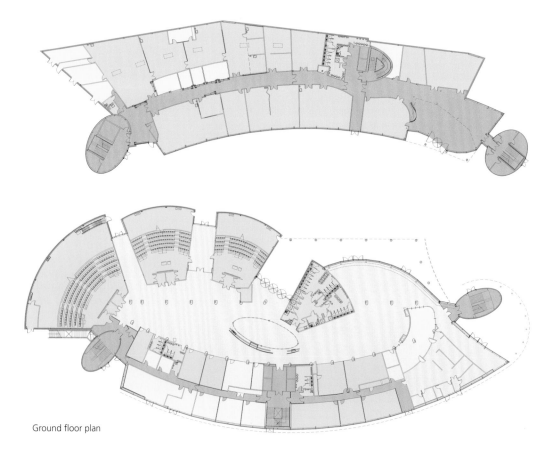

Ground floor plan

Social interaction, impromtu meetings and discussion in passing are an important part of academic life. Creating interesting circulation spaces promotes these activities.

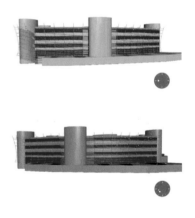

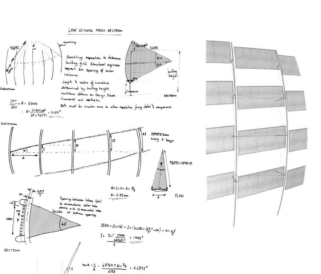

The solar grids are a disarmingly simple means of making best use of the sun's gifts, capturing and transferring heat while enabling daylight penetration, and simultaneously providing solar shading. That they also provide some architectural drama is a valuable bonus.

Penistone Grammar ALC
Barnsley, UK

EDUCATION

Client
Laing O'Rourke

Area
13,600 m²

Type
School

Status
Under construction

Date
2008–2010

This modern addition to the small Yorkshire market town of Penistone was developed through an intense engagement with the school. It captures the school's vision and ethos in a way that will reinforce its culture, heritage and aspirations for the future.

The school's key Business and Enterprise facilities are used to define the main entrance. This is presented in a contemporary setting, separate from the new Sixth Form centre, access to which is via a linked building with a dedicated entrance.

The school is divided into learning zones organised around a central 'heart' space that makes the most of daylight, fresh air and countryside vistas. Each class can break out into this space, and movable partitions enable adjacent classes to be combined.

The new school nestles comfortably into the hillside in the same fashion as the town, forming another piece in the patchwork of buildings and fields. The natural beauty of the landscape has clearly influenced the design – views over the fields and the

town are maximised by the careful placement of building elements, and framed views of St. John's Church, the local railway viaduct and the Pennine hills reinforce the school's position within a rural setting.

Penistone Grammar ALC is an adaptable building in which structure, services, environmental, infrastructure and building fabric present little or no impediment to change. Teachers and students can use it in many ways to explore new ways of teaching and learning.

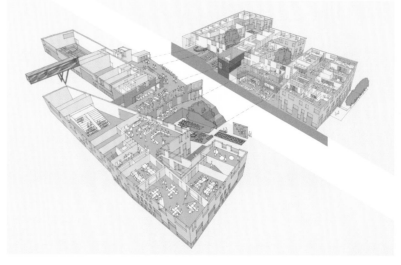

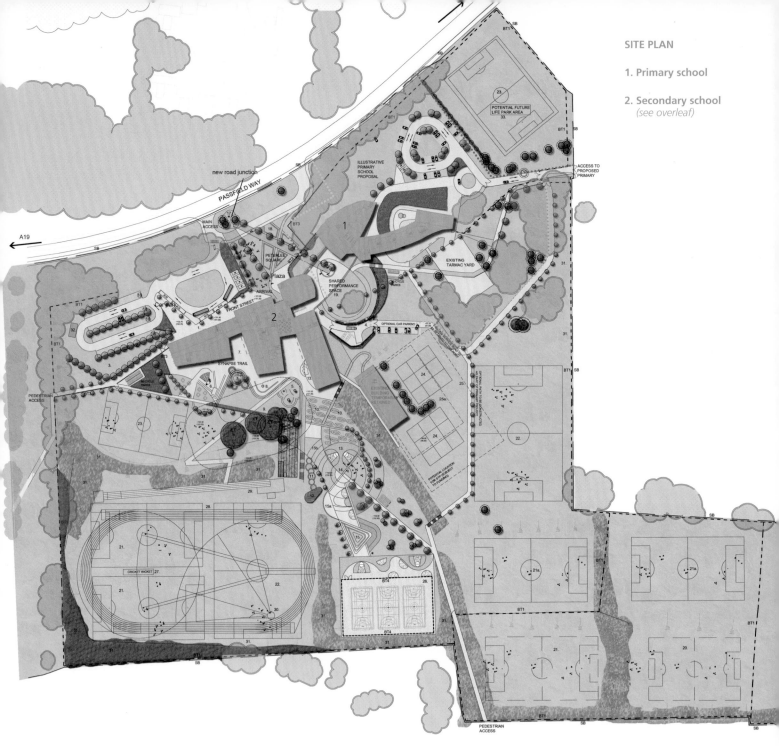

SITE PLAN

1. Primary school

2. Secondary school
(see overleaf)

Shotton Hall Primary School
Peterlee, UK

EDUCATION

Client
Inspired Spaces

Area
2,145 m²

Type
Primary school

Status
Under construction

Date
2009–2010

The redevelopment of Shotton Hall Primary School is taking place simultaneously with that of The Academy at Shotton Hall as part of Durham's education programme. The existing infant and junior schools will merge into a new all-through primary school to serve the Shotton Hall community.

The ethos of the school promotes the development of children as rounded individuals, knowledgeable and aware of society and able to contribute fully to their community. Adopting this as the basis of the design approach generated a progressive, responsive learning environment, with vibrant social spaces for staff, pupils and visitors in a friendly, safe and secure building.

The class bases surround a central zone that acts as a social anchor to the three elements of the school – the community zone, an administration area and the main teaching wing. This social 'heart' is the key to the flexibility of the design, allowing it to be tailored to the needs of the school or community groups.

The existing landscaped grounds feature groups of mature trees, grassland and wetland. New gardens have been introduced to provide outdoor learning spaces, and a nature trail leads to the entrance, further drawing the outdoors into the learning environment as a significant part of the school curriculum.

As well as learning, these two new schools support social activities for the broader community. They are set to transform education and provide a community focal point.

main hall   main entrance   class base entrance   heart space   class base entrance   class base entrance   external play

Long, low elevations feature recessed outdoor classrooms and are carefully integrated into the landscape.

The plan is centred on a social gathering space, providing a venue for the interaction that is seen as increasingly fundamental to effective learning.

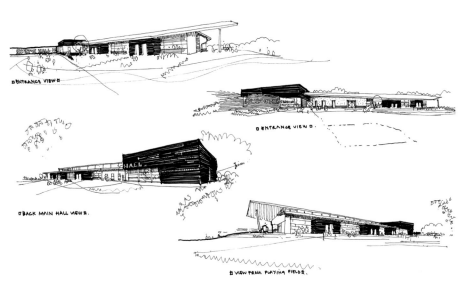

ENTRANCE VIEW

ENTRANCE VIEW

BACK MAIN HALL VIEW.

VIEW FROM PLAYING FIELD.

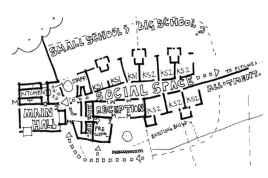

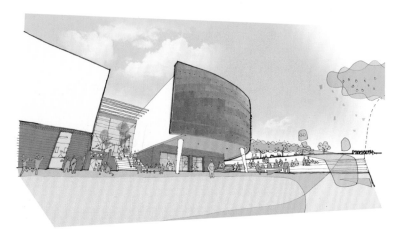

The entrance is defined by the bronze-clad volume of the school's performance space, clearly indicating the importance that the faculty places on this activity.

Performance pervades the school's ethos and architecture. Many of the internal spaces evoke images of theatre – foyer, box office and access deck as well as auditorium.

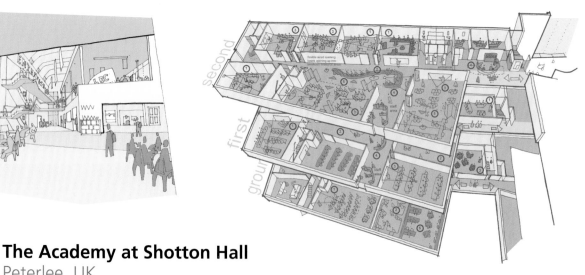

The Academy at Shotton Hall
Peterlee, UK

EDUCATION

Client
Inspired Spaces

Area
8,470 m²

Type
Secondary school

Status
Under construction

Date
2009–2010

The Academy at Shotton Hall is a new 910-place secondary school that uses the performing arts to improve pupil motivation and achievement. The school's aim is to inspire pupils to succeed in all areas of school life, and the building is a physical representation of this ethos.

The school's performance space, curved and clad in metallic shingles, proudly announces itself as the main feature, with its elevated position flanking the main entrance. The buildings and materials allude to the local geological strata and the area's mining heritage, with textured bands of white render floating above a plinth of dark brick in an allegorical reference to the seams of black coal to be found in the local chalk cliffs.

The school is respectful of its climate, culture and context. The buildings are arranged along a north–south axis to control solar gain and create sheltered south-facing outdoor spaces that are protected from the harsh coastal wind. The school departments are placed within this framework in a pattern reflecting their degrees of interdependency.

A primary school is included in the site masterplan (*see previous page*) and, when completed, the two schools will share the benefits of an outdoor performance area and a combined heat and power plant.

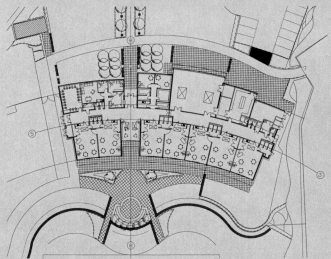

Chancellor Park Primary School
Chelmsford, UK

EDUCATION

Client
Essex County Council

Area
1,200 m²

Type
Primary school

Status
Complete

Date
2003–2004

Chancellor Park is a purpose-built primary school that opened in 2004. During the initial stages of the school design it was agreed that it should provide a powerful statement about sustainable architecture.

The result is a striking building with a strong organic form. The teaching spaces are arranged in a gentle arc oriented to the south to maximise solar energy inputs, and the internal environment is tempered by a carefully considered energy management strategy. Roof lights are employed to improve natural illumination and support a passive ventilation system. Shallow plan depths, deep eave projections, high thermal mass and extensive glazing, incorporating trickle ventilation, are further components of this sustainability strategy.

The emphasis on 'green architecture' is reflected in the construction of the building envelope, which incorporates laminated timber structural beams, heavily insulated cedar cladding on the north elevation and recyclable finishes elsewhere. The use of timber in structure and external finishes is commonly questioned in temperate climates, but its durability is excellent if properly detailed.

The school was awarded a commendation in the 2005 Civic Trust Awards, in recognition of a high-quality design that makes a positive contribution to the local environment and helps the community to become more sustainable.

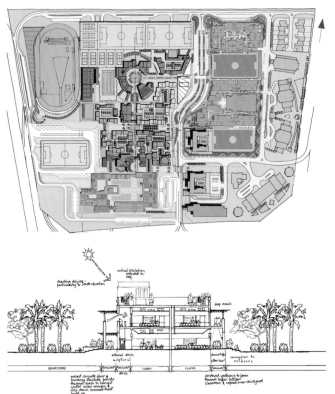

Flagship Campus
Dubai, UAE

EDUCATION

Client
Taaleem Education

Area
137,878 m²

Type
Educational facility comprising academic facilities and accommodation

Status
Design complete

Date
2005–2010

This world-class centre of educational excellence is planned for Dubailand, some 30 km south of Dubai. The development will offer educational facilities from crèche through to junior college, and includes staff and student accommodation as well as sports facilities that can also be used by the wider community.

In creating indoor and outdoor spaces between the schools, the plan responds to the location, climate, local culture and architecture. Connections are crucial, but individual buildings are allowed their own identity within the scheme as a whole.

Zones to the north of the site are developed as a community centre, while to the south facilities for polo, riding and horse racing add an extra dimension to the normal educational amenities and reflect a proud aspect of the local culture. In keeping with the ethos of an open campus environment, much of the car parking will be housed beneath the sports pitches.

Exterior materials are hard-wearing and sourced locally, while interior materials are cost efficient, functional, durable and elegant. Appropriate porcelain, granite and marble finishes are complemented by timber wall panelling and decorative metal ceilings to provide texture and visual interest to both school accommodation and public areas.

Jumeirah English Speaking School
Dubai, UAE

EDUCATION

Client
Jumeirah English
Speaking School

Area
18,000 m²

Type
12 buildings ranging
from single storey
to G+2

Status
Complete

Date
2004–2005

The generator for the design of the Jumeirah English Speaking School at Arabian Ranches was the notion of a 'journey' through school life. This was transformed on plan into a figure-of-eight, with an amphitheatre at the intersection point defining the heart of the school.

In form the design is inspired by vernacular villages and towns, which also inform the choices of material and the colour palette. Narrow streets and shady squares, focal landmark buildings and activity nodes under palm trees, towers and gateways are orchestrated to create a framework for the social and academic life of the students.

The auditorium and amphitheatre are the equivalent of a public building and a village square. Following a similar theme, the architectural language is a hybrid of Arabian and Mediterranean townscapes – pantile roofs, extended eaves, rendered walls, pergolas, pavilions, arches and arcades contrast with modern components in the form of tensile structures over the play areas.

In both planning and services terms, sustainability is intrinsic to the design. The result is a rich, supportive learning environment, safely contained within an attractive, secure campus.

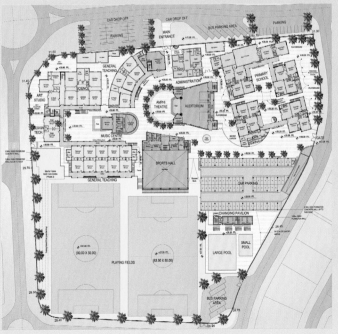

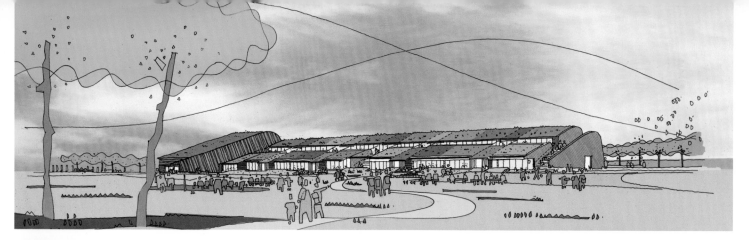

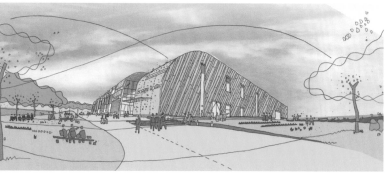

Green roofs provide recognised benefits in terms of sustainability, and in this case a valuable teaching resource as well.

Below, a series of sketches illustrate the conceptual development of the form – almost pulling the landscape up into a shelter.

Living walls to the north, and timber walls to the east and west provide a rugged, natural atmosphere.

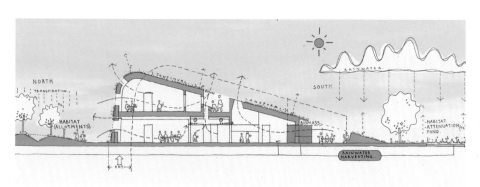

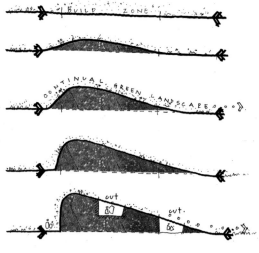

Northwood Primary School
Darlington, UK

EDUCATION

Client
Darlington Borough Council

Area
2,875 m²

Type
Primary school

Status
Complete

Date
2008–2010

Northwood Primary is one of the pathfinders for the UK Primary Capital Programme. It is an exemplary education building that embraces sustainable design and provides an open learning environment to serve the needs of the whole community.

Both the ground and first floor levels are deliberately given a southerly aspect, allowing controlled solar gain while exploiting the views and providing access onto outside teaching spaces. The garden terraces are pleasant and secure areas, with shelter from both the climate and busier areas of the school.

The school has an extensive sedum patchwork roof that was inspired by nearby allotments, with the building appearing to 'grow' out of the surrounding landscape. The effect is heightened by selected areas of the roof being carried down towards the ground as green walls.

The sedum roof and walls offset CO_2 emissions and reduce rainwater run-off, mitigating the risk of flooding while providing a natural habitat for flora, insect and bird life, and creating an inspirational learning resource in the process. Students are able to investigate the life forms

that live on their school, and grow strawberries and the like in the walls, interacting positively with their unusually ecologically sound building.

This marriage of outdoor teaching space and sustainable thinking leads the way in innovative, low-carbon primary school design. It is intended to bring nature into an urban context, enabling children to learn from the landscape and support the school's sustainable curriculum, contributing to the development of a new carbon-conscious generation.

The school was given a simple, regular plan and a rational zoned layout.

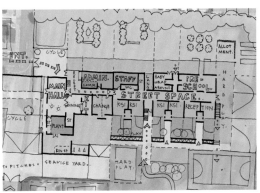

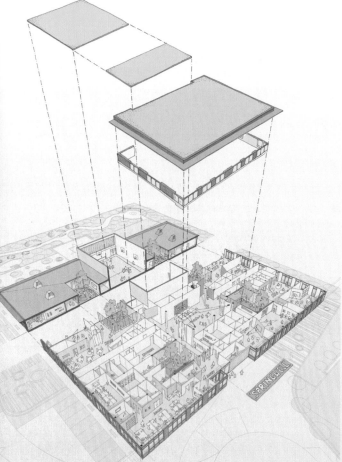

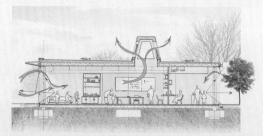

Natural ventilation and enclosed courtyards provide a safe, healthy atmosphere and controlled access to the outside environment.

Springwell School
Barnsley, UK

EDUCATION

Client
Laing O'Rourke and
Barnsley Metropolitan
Borough Council

Area
3,526 m²

Type
Community
special school

Status
Under construction

Date
2008–2011

Springwell is a specialist BESD (Behavioural, Emotional and Social Difficulty) school. Its design springs directly from considerations of the challenges posed by children with such problems. Dispersed around a central space, each quarter of the plan layout is devoted to particular age groups, with the key feature being that any one quarter can be closed to contain 'behavioural outbreaks' while preventing disruption to the rest of the school. This arrangement provides a central 'heart' around

which the whole school can come together at key times of the day.

All stages of learning within a BESD school are based on the creation of a safe and familial setting with socialisation and community at the heart of the learning process. The teaching system also defines the sequential stages of the curriculum, and its relationship to the outside world and the 'life skills' the child develops. Within this school there is an emphasis on kinaesthetic learning – that is,

learning through physical activity rather than simply listening and watching. Accordingly, at the centre of the school is a multi-use space for drama and sports, surrounded by specialist drama therapy and music rooms.

The quarters each contain combinations of learning spaces, providing the wide range of features and environments that are so important in schools of this type. Each is provided with an enclosed courtyard and links to the surrounding landscaping.

Selby College
North Yorkshire, UK

EDUCATION

Client
Selby College

Area
7,853 m²

Type
Further education
college

Status
Complete

Date
2008–2010

The redevelopment of Selby College redefines the College's image and rationalises its facilities, strengthening its current position among England's top-performing colleges. The proposals integrate masterplanning, building and landscape design.

The new campus buildings are arranged around a central landscaped 'heart' space. This provides a new focal point for the college while facilitating clear wayfinding and offering a range of spaces from quiet sitting areas to busy circulation routes.

The three-storey, glass-fronted Jubilee Building houses the College's

mathematics centre, science laboratories, a sports hall and fitness suite, health spa, hair and beauty therapy salons and treatment rooms, training kitchens and restaurant, student services, refectory and general offices. Entered through the light-filled atrium, the interior has a clean, sharp aesthetic with minimalist detailing and is highlighted with panels of bright colour.

The result is contemporary and vibrant, creating an inspirational learning environment.

Lowestoft Sixth Form College
Lowestoft, UK

EDUCATION

Client
Suffolk County
Council

Area
8,027 m²

Type
Sixth form college

Status
Under construction

Date
2009–2011

Suffolk County Council has commissioned this college to serve 950 16–18-year-olds, with the ability to engage 14–16-year-olds and adult learners as part of a broader curriculum and as a contributor to regeneration and training. The curriculum focus will be predominantly academic to complement the vocational training available through the adjacent Lowestoft College.

The site for the sixth form college is being leased from Lowestoft College and lies at the northern end of its campus. The intention is that the two establishments will provide academic and vocational education in a mutually supportive way, giving students a choice of approaches.

The building has been developed to provide a vibrant and exciting learning environment with a strong

sense of identity. The accommodation is arranged around an enclosed rectangular atrium that provides a real sense of arrival upon entry. This space is enhanced by open platforms suspended within the atrium at each level, linked by bridges to the decks that surround them.

The open core is more than a means of enhancing social interaction and a sense of connection among the students – it also provides an efficient means of introducing passive natural ventilation and allows daylight to penetrate the deepest recesses of the building. The sustainability initiatives continue externally, with horizontal sun shades controlling summer heat gain, and high levels of insulation, reflective surfaces and a technologically advanced glazing system controlling energy transmission through the external walls.

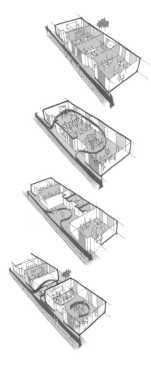

Flexible partitioning makes the building highly adaptable to changing spatial requirements.

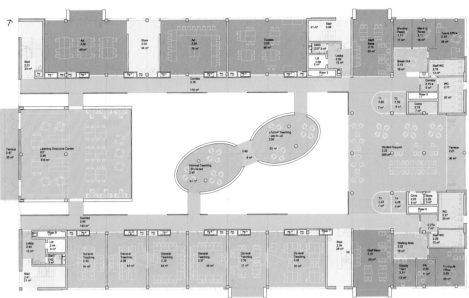

2nd floor plan

A simple, easily comprehended plan is enlivened by the two social spaces filling the atrium.

Particular attention has been given to context and orientation, and the integration of the college into its neighbourhood.

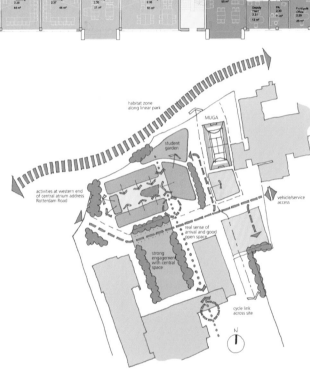

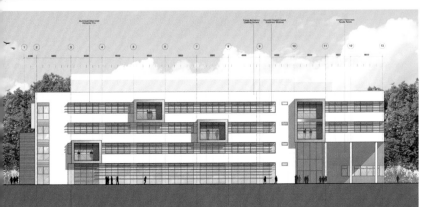

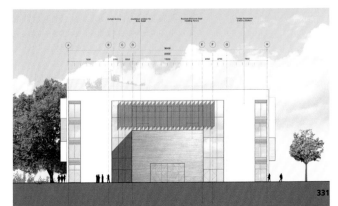

Wharton Community Library
Winsford, UK

EDUCATION

Client
Cheshire West
& Chester

Area
575 m²

Type
Community library

Status
Complete

Date
2008–2009

The original Wharton Library and Community Hall were built in the 1960s. In March 2008 Atkins was commissioned to carry out a feasibility study to consider either refurbishment or replacement of the existing buildings with a fully integrated library and community facility fit for the new century.

With lottery funding underpinning the project, a comprehensive community consultation process was undertaken, which was used in the establishment of a project brief and the preparation of comprehensive design proposals. These were presented at a public consultation meeting, at which the scheme received overwhelming support from residents and community groups.

The final design incorporates library and community accommodation on a single level, along with associated toilets, shared offices and catering facilities. A public space, 'Willow Square', was created between the library and adjacent shops, which

opened a link between residential areas, the library and a recently completed children's centre. Previously, the library and community hall formed a physical barrier to integration.

The security measures incorporated are subtle, with all glazing below 2 m being protected by integrated security shutters, but most light and ventilation being delivered through high-level bay windows. External render received a vandal-resistant coating, and self-cleaning glass removes the requirement for window-cleaner access and enables the use of discreet anti-vandal planting to form a barrier around the building perimeter.

To achieve the sustainability requirements a timber frame was specified, with only isolated structural steel members where absolutely necessary. The materials used were generally recycled or recyclable, and high insulation values and sunlight penetration were optimised to minimise energy consumption.

Ground floor plan

University of East Anglia
Norwich, UK

EDUCATION

Client
University of East
Anglia

Area
1,500 m²

Type
Central university
catering facilities

Status
Complete

Date
2006–2007

This refurbishment and extension of the central catering facilities at the University of East Anglia provides a new social centre for the campus. An inviting, modern interior has enhanced the popularity of the venue, and the changes have helped integrate the building into the masterplan for the university.

The facilities comprise three separate floors for refreshments, and a main food preparation and distribution centre in the basement. The ground-floor student refectory opens off the main campus square, and has been designed as a cool, modern restaurant. The coffee shop on the first floor offers snacks on a self-serve basis, and provides space and flexible furnishing layouts for informal student meetings. On the third floor is the staff restaurant and bar. This is an adaptable space, capable of hosting private lunch events, seminars and conferences.

The brief also provided the opportunity to introduce a minimalist glass pod that serves as the main entrance and provides access to new stairs and a passenger lift. At night this new transparent pavilion becomes a beacon for students on campus.

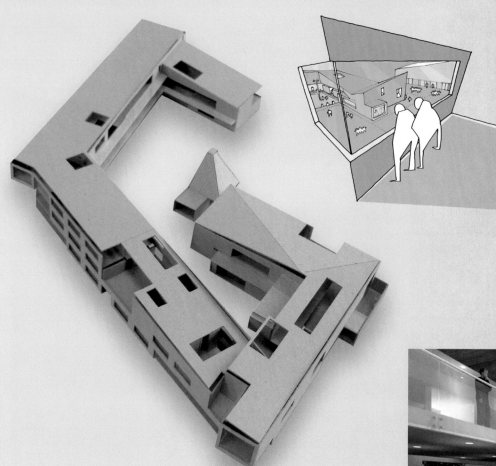

St. John Rigby College
Wigan, UK

EDUCATION

Client
St. John Rigby College

Area
10,500 m²

Type
Sixth form college

Status
Concept design

Date
2008

St. John Rigby College's new campus at Orrell in Wigan is unusual in that it sits in a greenbelt environment. Greenbelts are areas of protected countryside around urban conurbations and as such are usually not available for buildings. In response to its exceptional rural site, the new college has adopted the form and materials of agricultural buildings, albeit used in extraordinary ways.

The college has been kept low – never more than three storeys in height and with the ground floor sinking below ground level in places – to minimise the apparent mass of the structure and provide a more intimate engagement with its surroundings. It also adopts a narrow, ribbon plan form, ensuring that the occupants are never far from a window or glazed wall, invariably framing an exceptional view. The ribbon is folded to enclose a modest public courtyard, designed to provide a sheltered venue for *al fresco* study, socialising or even a theatre performance in the round.

At once self-effacing – long, low and partially buried – and bursting with civic pride, St. John Rigby College is a fascinating building in an exceptional setting.

Newcomen Primary School
Redcar, UK

Inspired by a fisherman's haven, the new £3.5 million Newcomen Primary School in Redcar, Cleveland is a new-build project that replaces an old school on the same site, constructed in the 1950s but never modernised. The new school makes innovative use of outdoor space, enabling pupils to both delight in and learn about their environment.

The school's management was determined to create large spaces to support innovative and creative ways of delivering the curriculum. This aim was satisfied when local fishermen's huts inspired the design team to create four 'breakout' areas between classrooms, bringing the outside in and enabling staff and children to take their classes outdoors.

These breakout areas, accessible from a central corridor, give a relaxed and open feel to the school, providing flexible spaces for creative play, art classes and IT bases for use by the staff, pupils and visitors. Three of the areas are unheated, covered outdoor spaces that are bounded by classrooms and cloakrooms. They contain plots of soil, enabling pupils to conduct environmental projects and planting experiments.

This innovative use of space has increased the usable footprint of the building without significantly increasing costs or contravening the DCSF guidelines concerning floor area and funding. The additional usable space is equivalent to six extra classrooms, and has provided the school with a useful adaptable learning resource should it wish to expand the building in the future.

'External classrooms' and an architectural form derived from local building types give this school a strong local character.

EDUCATION

Client
Redcar & Cleveland
Borough Council

Area
2,900 m²

Type
Primary school

Status
Complete

Date
2008–2009

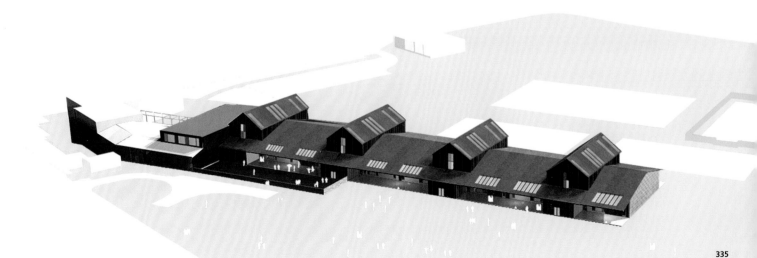

Community College Whitstable
Whitstable, UK

The redevelopment of Whitstable Community College is part of the UK's large-scale capital investment programme, Building Schools for the Future. Demolition of existing education buildings will make way for a new 1,232-place secondary school for pupils aged 11–18 with associated services, car parking and landscape improvements.

Significant new components are based on the concept of small learning communities within a large educational facility. Among them are the Creative School and the Global School, new buildings that will sit alongside the existing Logic School with its technical workshops, laboratories and open-plan learning areas.

The Global School provides event-based teaching of humanities, and focuses on film and media, publishing, citizenship and the integration of a business-like ethos. Its flexible design allows for the future introduction of additional business units or conference facilities.

The Creative School provides an environment that emphasises more artistic forms of learning, including music, art and drama. It incorporates a dance studio and activity hall, and is connected to the sports hall, promoting physical as well as academic development.

A vibrant addition to the existing library block that fronts the main road, the new community entrance serves both the sports hall and the College, giving it a new heart and identity. It is designed to extend a positive welcome to visitors, promoting the fact that the facilities have been designed to support the local community.

EDUCATION

Client
Skanska

Area
8,000 m²

Type
Community college

Status
Concept

Date
2007

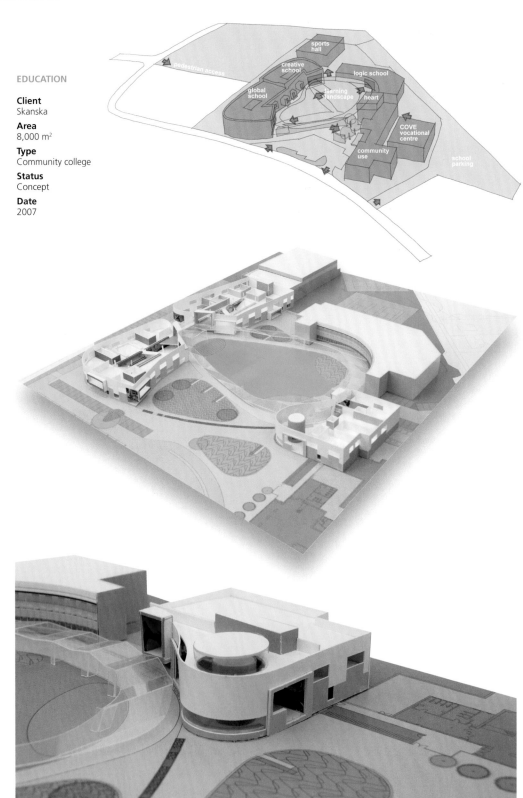

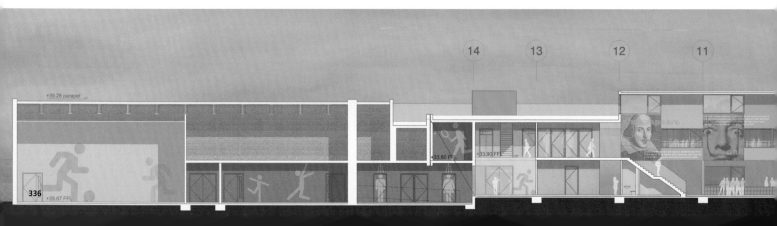

A powerfully individual design reflects the school's particular approach to learning, which concentrates on drama and performance as teaching tools.

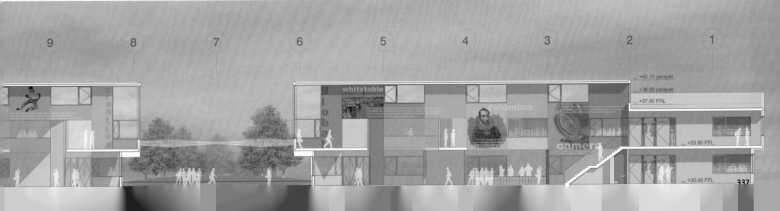

Grimsby Institute of Further Education
Grimsby, UK

EDUCATION

Client
Grimsby Institute

Area
25,000 m²

Type
Further education
college

Status
Concept design

Date
2007–2011

As with all publicly financed education projects, an ability to show 'best value' in design and operation is a prerequisite for funding. This project meets that requirement by delivering an exciting building using an economical set of components that, in combination, create spaces that are functional and flexible.

Buildings that are 16 m wide are placed 16 m apart, and the space between them is covered to form atriums. These are all linked to a common end volume that extends the length of the school. This 'spine' is the main organisational space, and is defined on one side by the secondary curriculum blocks and perpendicular atria, and on the other side by more recreational areas such as catering, hair and beauty care centres, health and fitness facilities, and social spaces.

The only exception is an irregular block that houses the higher education area and also defines the entrance. This is denoted by a sculptural roof element that is repeated on the internal atria.

This simple, modular set of spaces can be occupied in a highly flexible way, which will facilitate change and internal expansion in the future. Most importantly, all of the proposed space is enclosed in a single large envelope, giving significant savings in overall costs and easing the management of the institute.

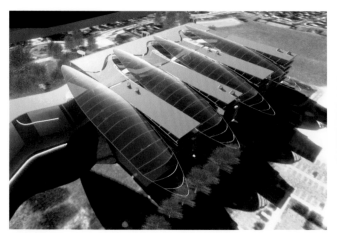

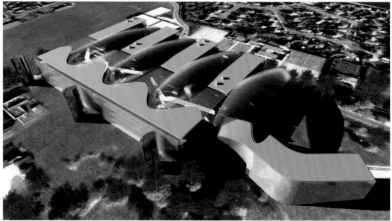

City College Plymouth
Plymouth, UK

EDUCATION

Client
City College Plymouth

Area
37,000 m²

Type
Redevelopment of
college campus

Status
Design

Date
2008–2016

City College occupies seven different sites in Plymouth. The brief was to concentrate all operations onto a single site in a distinctive, world-class building.

The response proposes three crystalline towers, rising to a height of nine, eight and seven storeys respectively, carefully placed on parallel axes with the intervening spaces filled by opaque and translucent blocks with the same trapezoidal crystalline structure. The transparency inherent in the proposal is important, with technology designed to be on show throughout the building.

The massing of the buildings arises from phased demolition and construction, and the release of as much land as possible to landscaping. The project is a carbon-critical exemplar, integrating solar, thermal and wind energy, photovoltaic panels, natural ventilation, natural daylighting, *brise soleil* and thermal chimney techniques, among others.

Nescot
Epsom, UK

EDUCATION

Client
Nescot

Area
25,000 m²

Type
Further education
college

Status
Design

Date
2008–2010

Nescot provides highly respected educational courses in a range of theoretical, practical and vocational subjects, including construction work training, sports therapy, visual and performing arts and business studies. It occupies an attractive sloping site in the greenbelt of the North Downs in Surrey.

The project addressed the replacement of an existing college with a new purpose-built structure, split conceptually into two parts: a learning centre for traditional student teaching, and a skills park concentrating on vocational courses for public customers and trades-

people. The massing was deliberately fragmented and limited to a maximum of three storeys to reduce the impact on the landscape and improve the environmental performance.

A series of large, connected atria form the communal hub of the college, opening out onto a shared external court on the northern, 'urban' edge of the site. Wings of prime teaching space are arrayed in an east–west orientation, facing south over the North Downs with horticultural, animal husbandry and sports spaces extending further into the greenbelt.

Incorporating a series of carbon-critical design features, the form of the college incorporates shallow, single-aspect teaching spaces that 'breathe' into the atria, optimised orientation, high levels of daylighting and *brise soleil* to control solar gain.

Green roofs and living walls were incorporated to improve thermal performance and to embed the scheme into its rural context. Timber cladding and planar glass engage with the natural landscapes of Surrey and provide an openness and accessibility that reflect the college's educational ambitions.

Richmond School
Richmond, UK

EDUCATION

Client
North Yorkshire
County Council

Area
8,000 m² of new-build
accommodation

Type
Masterplanning and
remodelling existing
school campus

Status
Complete

Date
2006–2011

Richmond is a small market town, but it has a large catchment area. Its redeveloped school will serve 1,700 students and 120 staff. The new facilities will give it the means to operate a more flexible curriculum, offer more facilities to the wider community, provide high-quality working environments for its staff and state-of-the-art learning spaces for its pupils.

In addition to an upgrade of the eclectic mix of historically significant buildings on the 70-year-old campus, the design provides a substantial amount of new accommodation, sympathetically linked to the existing campus in ways that provide a revived sense of cohesion. The new buildings respect the old in terms of form and massing, but in detail – particularly energy efficiency – they are very different.

The approach to sustainability was particularly thorough and wide-ranging, considering elements such as transport, food miles, healthy lifestyles and energy use. Measures to reduce energy consumption include the use of natural light and ventilation, integrated solar shading and insulation systems, and additional thermal mass in the form of heavy, exposed concrete. Renewable energy sources include solar water heating and a 250 kW biomass main boiler, together with six wind turbines.

This comprehensive contemporary design so impressed the British government that it released an additional £2 million in funding to support the development. Richmond School is now one of three UK government-funded exemplars of sustainability.

York University
York, UK

York University's campus at Heslington West is undergoing a programme of significant modernisation, and a parallel programme of major expansion will create a new Heslington East campus. This ambitious project is the largest development to occur on the university's estate since the existing campus was built in the 1960s. It will be one of the largest capital developments in the UK's higher education programme during the decade leading up to 2020.

The new development will incorporate sustainable architecture and building systems designed to be appropriate to the university, the community and the surrounding landscape. The designs draw inspiration from an altruistic desire to protect the biodiversity and habitats of the campus wildlife, and include woodland, lakes and associated wetlands.

EDUCATION

Client
York University

Area
180,000 m²

Type
Masterplan of university faculty building and campus

Status
Concept design

Date
2007

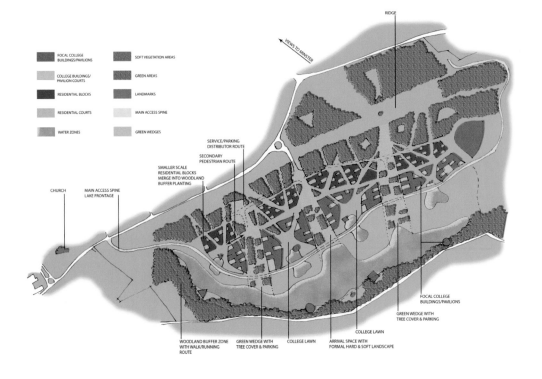

Legend:
- FOCAL COLLEGE BUILDINGS/PAVILIONS
- COLLEGE BUILDINGS/ PAVILION COURTS
- RESIDENTIAL BLOCKS
- RESIDENTIAL COURTS
- WATER ZONES
- SOFT VEGETATION AREAS
- GREEN AREAS
- LANDMARKS
- MAIN ACCESS SPINE
- GREEN WEDGES

Labels on plan:
RIDGE
VIEWS TO MINSTER
SERVICE/PARKING DISTRIBUTOR ROUTE
SECONDARY PEDESTRIAN ROUTE
SMALLER SCALE RESIDENTIAL BLOCKS MERGE INTO WOODLAND BUFFER PLANTING
CHURCH
MAIN ACCESS SPINE LAKE FRONTAGE
WOODLAND BUFFER ZONE WITH WALK/RUNNING ROUTE
GREEN WEDGE WITH TREE COVER & PARKING
COLLEGE LAWN
ARRIVAL SPACE WITH FORMAL HARD & SOFT LANDSCAPE
COLLEGE LAWN
GREEN WEDGE WITH TREE COVER & PARKING
FOCAL COLLEGE BUILDINGS/PAVILIONS

St. Jean's Molenbeek
Brussels, Belgium

EDUCATION

Client
Commune of
Molenbeek

Area
2,500 m²

Type
Nursery and
primary school

Status
Complete

Date
2007

Molenbeek is a new town with a high concentration of poorly paid immigrant workers. This scheme for a new 2,500 m² primary and nursery school was personally supported by both the Minister for Education and the Mayor of Brussels, who were determined that this would be a flagship school for community education.

St. Jean's was the first new school to be built in central Brussels for over 25

years. It opened in September 2007, and has been designed to offer a secure haven as well as a supportive learning environment for its pupils.

Children may be dropped off early and collected late, allowing parents to work the hours required to support their families, safe in the knowledge that their children are occupied and supervised. The school also provides facilities aimed specifically

at supporting the local community, such as its very large refectory that ensures pupils always enjoy at least one substantial meal a day.

The project was a particularly rewarding one for the design team, which was able to build on its experience of working with educational departments of UK local authorities, and develop its expertise in working with local communities.

A restrained use of colour, a limited palette of natural materials and a considered, precise composition of masses give St. Jean's a pleasingly calm atmosphere, ideally suited to a place of learning.

Greenfield Community School
Dubai, UAE

EDUCATION

Client
Taaleem Education

Area
25,000 m²

Type
Kindergarten, primary
and secondary school

Status
Under construction

Date
2006–2011

Greenfield Community School can provide a student's entire basic education, progressing from kindergarten at the north of the site, through the primary school in the centre, to the secondary school at the south. Given the care exercised in the design of the campus, that should be an uplifting and pleasant journey.

Facilities within the primary and secondary schools include an ICT space, a library with associated spaces, toilets, cloakrooms, changing rooms, stores, a gymnasium, and large and small swimming pools. The layout follows a rational plan and accords with the best of contemporary practice.

The senior school circulation areas have been developed into a series of open, airy indoor and outdoor spaces. These are filled with daylight internally but shaded from Dubai's searing sun externally, providing a range of plazas, squares, courtyards, open rooms, enclosures, verandahs and galleries, frequently overlooking each other and ranging in feel from intimate to wide-open.

These spaces are used to articulate the façades, giving the school the form of a series of grouped pavilions rather than three solid blocks. The spaces created by this approach support a wide range of social activities and promote a real

sense of community in the school – you know you're part of a greater community if you can see it, meet it and interact with it between lessons.

The school buildings adopt a cool and ordered interpretation of traditional Gulf architectural forms, with functional elements – pergolas, screens, windows – developed as decorative devices. Combined with the light and shade introduced by the planning approach, the result is a range of buildings that accord closely with the history and culture of their location, at once contemporary and Arabian.

Hipperholme and Lightcliffe School
Halifax, UK

EDUCATION

Client
Calderdale
Metropolitan Borough
Council

Area
2,000 m²

Type
Secondary school

Status
Complete

Date
2005–2007

Hipperholme and Lightcliffe High School and Sixth Form Centre currently has a capacity for some 1,100 pupils. This commission involved the provision of extra teaching space and improvements in circulation, while in the process giving the school a complete facelift and a new architectural cohesion.

The design features a bold curved façade, which encompasses both new and existing buildings. This is not simply a screen – it is a three-dimensional structure that generates interest through an intriguing combination of opacity and translucency, solidity and space, with accents in colour and texture. Within the school a judicious reworking of the existing facilities has been combined with the careful integration of a series of new spaces, including a new high-tech resource centre, a two-storey design and technology block, additional changing rooms, improved sixth form facilities and classrooms, and a new administration block and staff area.

The revamped accommodation achieves all the requirements of the brief. As a bonus, the change in the physical character of the school has provided it with an opportunity to improve morale and create a brand new image.

The new curved façade provides a united front at Hipperholme and Lightcliffe School.

North Liverpool Academy
Liverpool, UK

EDUCATION

Client
North Liverpool City
Academy

Area
14,000 m²

Type
School

Status
Complete

Date
2003–2006

An innovative approach was adopted for the design of the 1,750-pupil North Liverpool Academy. Two parallel rectilinear blocks house the main teaching spaces, which are grouped around internal top-lit activity courts. A strongly contrasting organic form, expressed externally as a 'tube' that wraps over the building, activates the 'street' space between these linear elements. This core space houses and defines the academy's social and shared spaces, and is a visual key to the building's organisation, as well as an instantly recognisable feature from outside the site.

The design is highly integrated in terms of structure, finishes and environmental behaviour with the use of extensive fenestration to optimise natural lighting, high thermal insulation and passive ventilation systems for cooling in hot weather. The exposed concrete structure provides both a durable finish and reduced loading on heating systems through thermal lag, supported by the use of natural ventilation wherever possible to minimise installation and running costs and to reduce noise.

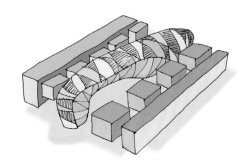

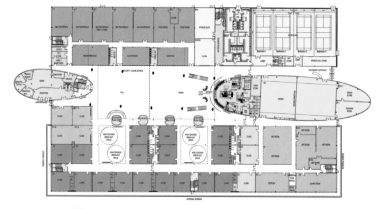

Ground floor plan

The combination of a strictly orthogonal plan with a large 'fluid' intervention creates a striking composition.

The internal street space is undeniably dramatic and provides the social heart of the school.

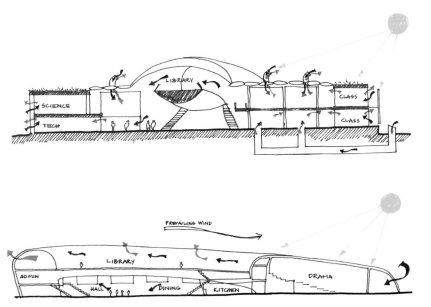

TRANSPORTATION

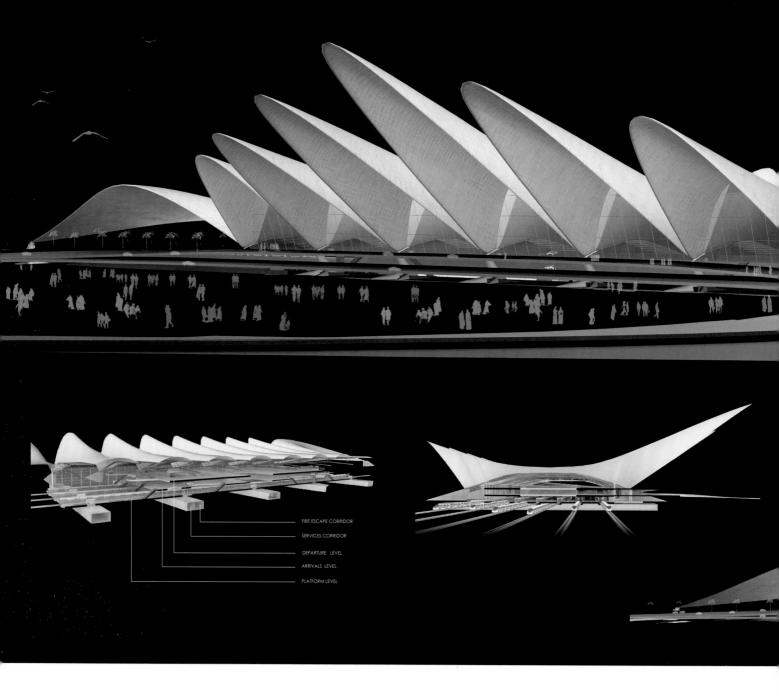

FIRE ESCAPE CORRIDOR

SERVICES CORRIDOR

DEPARTURE LEVEL

ARRIVALS LEVEL

PLATFORM LEVEL

Haramain High-speed Rail Link Stations
Makkah, Saudi Arabia

TRANSPORTATION

Client
Confidential

Area
64,000 m²

Type
Four iconic stations,
each 450 m long

Status
Competition entry

Date
2008

The Haj, the fifth pillar of Islam, is the pilgrimage to Makkah that should ideally be made at least once by every able-bodied Muslim. Some two million Haj pilgrims arrive annually in Makkah and Medina, from at least 150 different countries, for the four-day period of Dhu al-Hijjah. The number of pilgrims rises annually.

The new Haramain high-speed (360 km/h) rail link is designed to ease travel between Medina and Makkah for the pilgrims. This project concerned the design of four new stations at Jeddah, Makkah, Medinah and King Abdullah Economic City. A key challenge was to enable construction of each station to take place around a separate contract for the creation

of the railway tracks themselves, without compromising the safety or programme for either contract.

The proposal resolved this by adopting a modular system, using a series of prefabricated, lightweight components for each of the architectural elements. The external structure of each station is created from a series of arches arranged in sequence along either side of the track and connected with tensile members supporting translucent, insulated canopies. The canopies provide a bright, dramatic enclosure and reduce cooling loads, covering a large floor area without introducing the need for daytime artificial lighting.

The modular approach is continued at platform level, with the creation of units that can be combined to form kiosks containing shops, waiting rooms and services enclosures. Again, the size of each kiosk can be tailored to its location simply by varying the number of modules it employs.

The considerable volume of the stations would have created a challenge for a traditional air conditioning system. Instead, computational fluid dynamics are used to develop a system of highly efficient air conditioning binnacles to cool the air at low level.

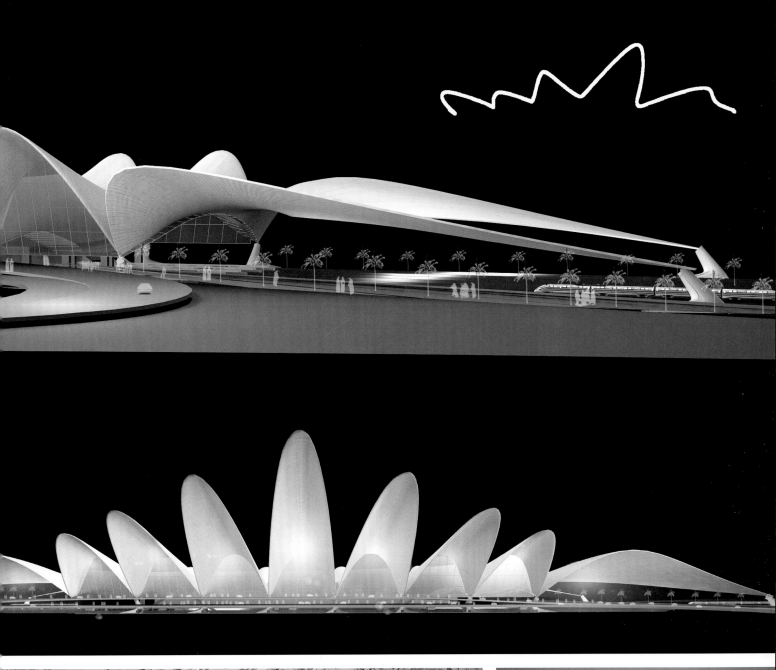

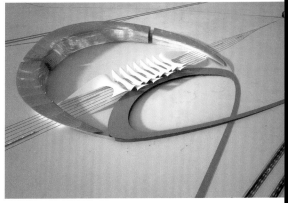

East Station
Hangzhou

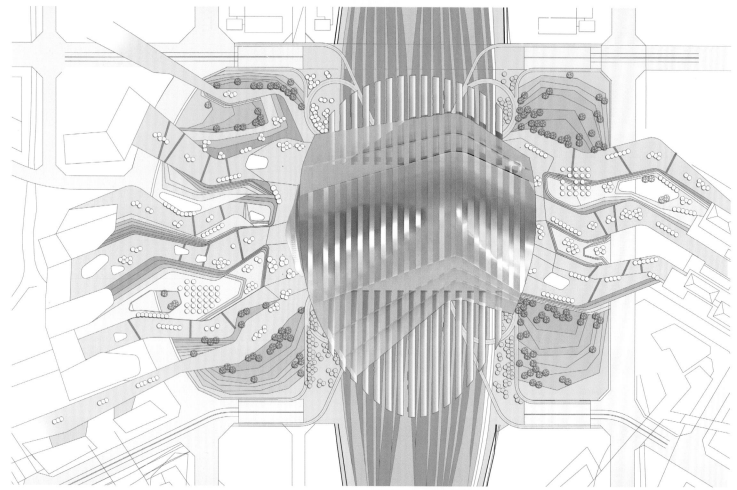

Hangzhou Railway Station
Hangzhou, China

TRANSPORTATION

Client
Hangzhou Municipal
Government/
Hangzhou Urban
Planning Bureau

Area
357,700 m²

Type
Transport interchange
and railway station

Status
Competition entry

Date
2008

This concept is a competition entry for the railway station and transport interchange that will form the centrepiece of the new 64 ha central business district in the city of Hangzhou. The building is a major interchange linking two underground metro lines with six national high-speed rail lines, and providing a connection to the extremely high-speed 'maglev' line connecting Shanghai city and Pudong airport.

The station will handle up to 180,000 people daily, and will occupy a total of eight levels within the building, five above ground and three below.

The three-dimensional form of the station takes its inspiration from West Lake, the focus of Hangzhou. The sweeping glass and metal roof suggests a series of ripples spreading across a body of water. The central 'wave' that extends across the tracks enfolds grand entrance façades looking out over new public plazas at each end of the station, and also incorporates passenger drop-off points fed by the Hangzhou road network.

The structure has been designed to be light and transparent, with materials chosen to allow the main internal volumes of the public space to be seen, as well as clearly expressed. The bright, airy interior is intended to be welcoming, with natural light and ventilation creating a comfortable, efficient environment.

The atmosphere will be enhanced by interior planting – indeed, the scale of the building is such that it is not unreasonable to characterise this as 'indoor landscaping'.

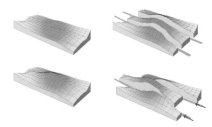
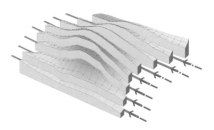

The ripples in the roof were developed by displacing slices of a double-curvature form.

Taiyuan Wusu International Airport
Taiyuan, China

TRANSPORTATION

Client
Shanxi Province
Civilian Airport Group

Area
55,000 m²

Type
Airport

Status
Complete

Date
2008

Taiyuan Wusu airport is located to the southeast of Taiyuan, the capital city of Shanxi Province and its political, economic and cultural centre. It has a long history – in ancient times, Taiyuan was an important military town, but now it is one of China's most important centres of heavy industry, using more than half the nation's coal output to power its factories.

A particular challenge in the planning of this new terminal was maintaining the efficient relationship between the terminal and the flight area. Also, the terminal zone had to satisfy the demands of both short-term and long-term operation.

A building form incorporating 45° angled junctions is used to develop the character of the site, providing a functional and clearly visible link between the existing terminal and the new main building and its gate piers. The existing building and the new extension merge around three courtyards that evoke traditional Shanxi courtyards, a feature of this region of China.

The courtyards are open internal spaces, functional in that they separate the domestic and international passenger areas, but also in that they bring daylight and fresh air into the depths of the plan, enhancing the environment and appearance of the terminal.

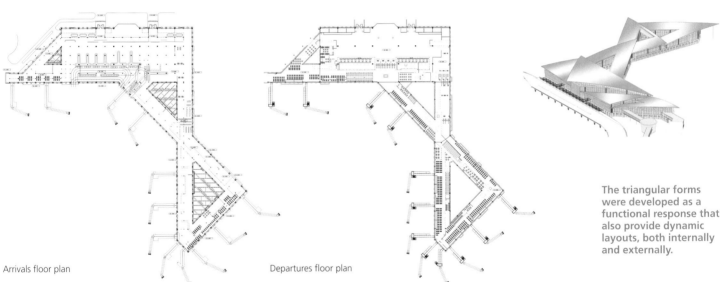

Arrivals floor plan

Departures floor plan

The triangular forms were developed as a functional response that also provide dynamic layouts, both internally and externally.

Urumchi Diwopu International Airport
Urumchi, China

TRANSPORTATION

Client
Urumchi Airport
(Group) Co Ltd

Area
200,000 m²

Type
Airport terminal
extension

Status
Competition entry

Date
2005

Urumchi Diwopu International Airport is the gateway to western China, and is typical of many Chinese terminals in that it needs to be expanded. It is expected to accommodate an annual passenger volume of 16 million people by 2015, rising to 26 million by 2022. Annual cargo handling capacity will rise in parallel to reach 275,000 tonnes and 430,000 tonnes respectively.

Its shape and structure are based on a south-facing 45° isosceles triangle, which satisfies the demands of function, land use and integration with the existing terminal. The inner courtyard neatly separates domestic and international traffic and also provides a welcome terminal garden. The departure and arrival areas are separated by placing them on different levels.

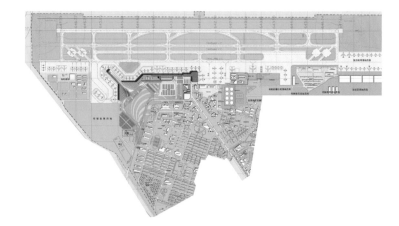

The terminal design takes inspiration from the unique topographic and geomorphic features in Xinjiang, with the roof's stretched curves derived from the region's migrating sand dunes. Evidence of climatic response is present in the use of daylighting, solar energy, photovoltaic technology, energy-saving glass curtain walling, recycled evaporative cooling, rainwater harvesting and water recycling. The atrium plays an important role in adjusting the microclimate in the waiting areas.

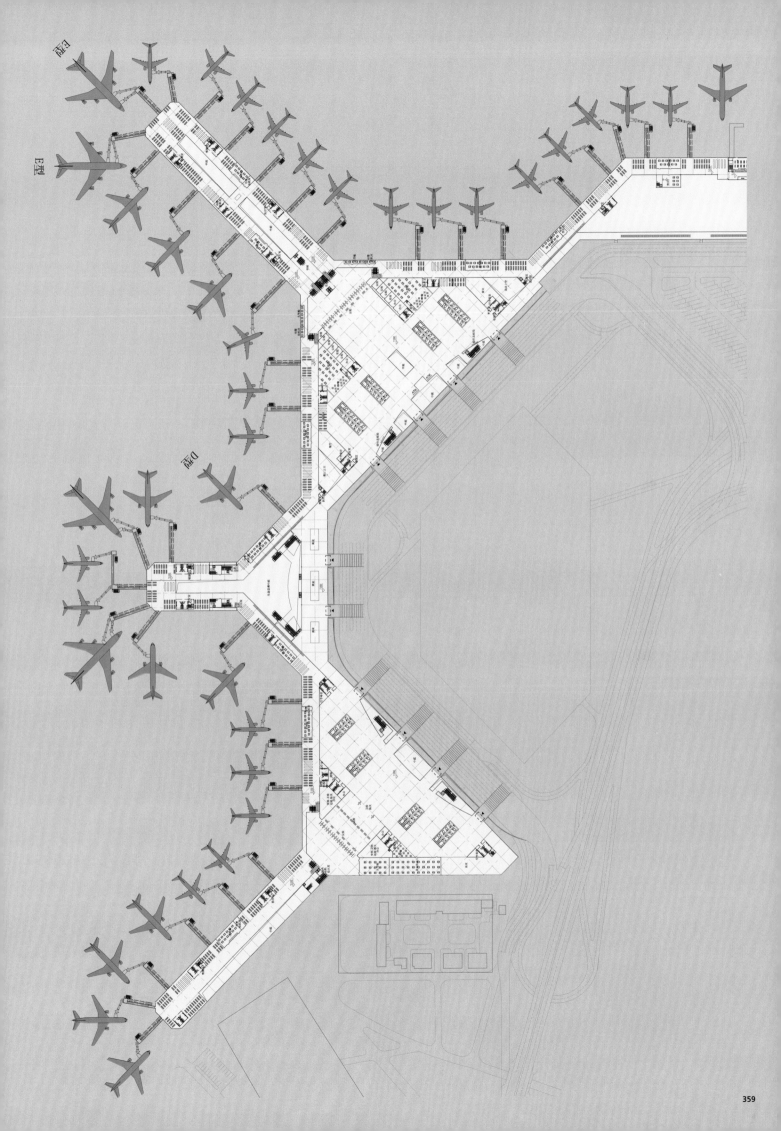

E型

D型

Xian Xianyang International Airport
Xian, China

TRANSPORTATION

Client
Western Airport
Management Group
Co. Ltd

Area
270,000 m²

Type
Airport
masterplanning and
Terminal 3 design

Status
Design

Date
2007

Xian Xianyang International Airport is set to become one of the most important airports in central and western China. Located in the north of Xianyang district, it is some 26 km from the centre of Xian, one of China's largest cities and home to the historic 'terracotta army' archaeological site.

The new Terminal 3 is to be sited to the southwest of the current terminal, and will provide 270,000 m² of additional floor space. When the airport expansion is complete, it is anticipated that its passenger volume will rise to 31 million people per year, with a peak handling capacity of 11,150 people per hour.

The terminal plan employs a symmetrical finger pier layout, which as well as being efficient and legible has the grandeur and formality that characterise the higher forms of traditional Chinese architecture. Passengers are separated onto three levels – domestic departures and arrivals are placed at ground level, with international arrivals and departures on two elevated levels.

The sculptural arcing roof rises in symmetrical layers towards the central axis. This is a form inspired by the historic architecture of the Han and Tang dynasties, but is also an architectural device providing natural light and fresh air, as well as making a significant contribution to the terminal's external appearance. Formal planting helps root the terminal in the historic landscape.

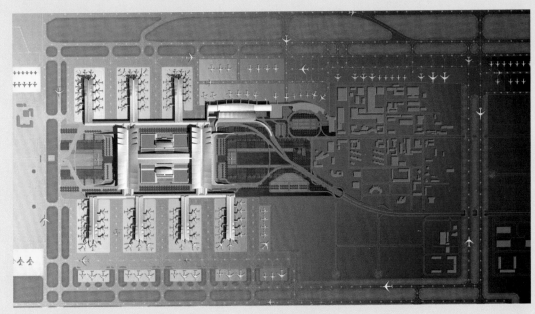

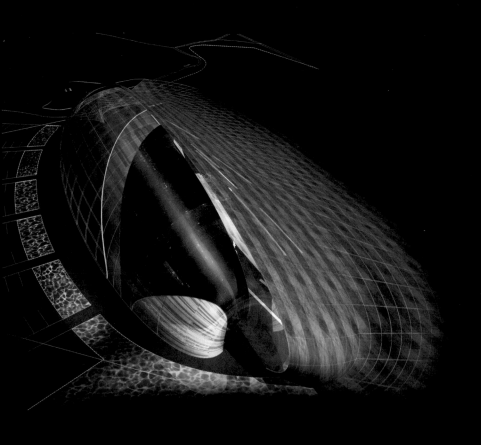

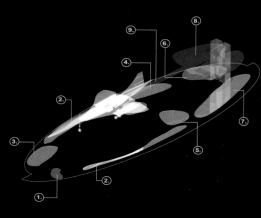

Axonometric Plan

1. Foyer entrance
2. Interactive historical displays
3. Retail / café
4. Simulator / pilot training
5. Exhibition areas and suspended components
6. Wind tunnel visible from exterior
7. Construction techniques and testing
8. Education and conference area
9. Walkway to Concorde

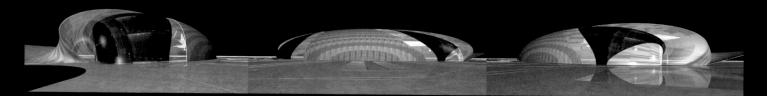

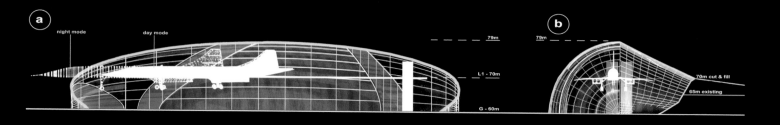

a

night mode   day mode

79m

L1 - 70m

G - 60m

b

79m

79m

70m cut & fill

65m existing

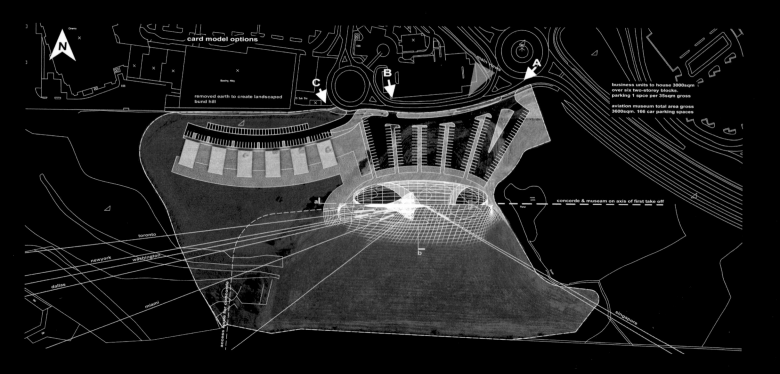

N

card model options

removed earth to create landscaped bund hill

B

C

A

main road

business units to house 3000sqm over six two-storey blocks. parking 1 spce per 35sqm gross

aviation museum total area gross 3600sqm. 166 car parking spaces

concorde & museam on axis of first take off

toronto

newyork   washington

dallas

miami

singapore

Filton Concorde Museum
Bristol, UK

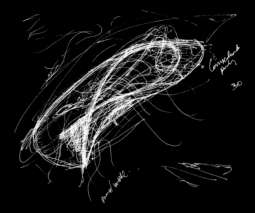

TRANSPORTATION

Client
Confidential

Area
3,600 m²

Type
Museum
commemorating
lifetime and
achievements of
Concorde aircraft

Status
Concept

Date
2008

Concorde, whose lifetime and achievements are commemorated in the museum, was by common accord one of the most beautiful and dramatic aircraft ever to take to the skies. The Filton Concorde Museum is intended to convey and enhance that drama, despite being firmly fixed to the ground.

The spectacular curves of the building form are derived from the aeroplane's sweeping wings. Top-lit vents are used to depict original Concorde destinations, and expressive metal walls, which reflect the prevailing weather conditions, are inset with glazed panels to provide glimpses of the aeroplane inside. At night, hydraulic apparatus moves Concorde forward so that its distinctive needle nose pentrates the building envelope.

Visitors to the museum can explore both Concorde in particular and aspects of flight more generally. Interactive displays, simulator training, teaching areas and wind tunnel demonstrations are enhanced by the conference facilities and café.

The Concorde Museum is a long-term resting place, requiring precise environmental control to limit degradation of its precious charge. The system has been designed to be as sustainable as possible: internal temperature fluctuations are minimised by passive means such as orientation, solar shading and the thermal mass of the natural earth bank and green roof, while rainwater harvesting, greywater recycling and reed bed filtration service the visitor amenities.

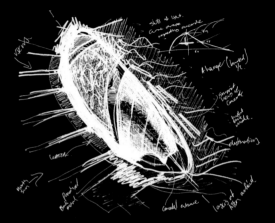

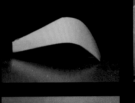
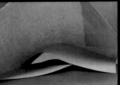
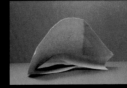

Yinchuan Airport
Yinchuan, China

TRANSPORTATION

Client
Yinchuan He Dong
Airport Expansion
Project Headquarters

Area
33,000 m²

Type
Airport
masterplanning and
Terminal 2 design

Status
Complete

Date
2008

In tandem with China's economic expansion there has been exponential growth in air travel. Cities that were caught up in the first wave of growth are rapidly being overtaken. So-called 'second tier cities' are now building airports – it is predicted that more than 1,000 new airports will be built in China in the near future.

The winning entry in a limited competition, this design for the new domestic terminal building

for Yinchuan in China's western province of Ningxai reflects the Islamic influence of the minority groups in this, the most important Muslim port of China. The 53 m clear-span roof encloses a light and airy space, with its sweeping aerofoil shape intended to express the concept of 'flight'.

The structural frames of the terminal buildings are representative of the pointed arches of traditional Muslim architecture.

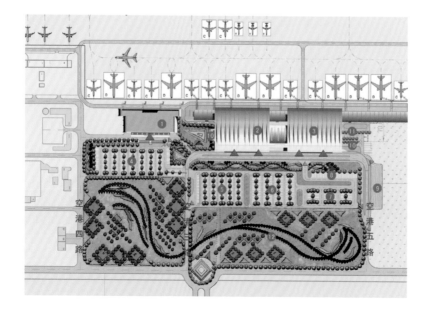

Dubai Metro
Dubai, UAE

TRANSPORTATION

Client
Japan-Turkey Metro
Joint Venture

Area
N/A

Type
Metro system

Status
Complete

Date
2006–2011

The advantage of a multidisciplinary workforce is that help and advice on almost any matter affecting the practice of architecture is available from within the organisation, and nowhere has this been more thoroughly demonstrated than on the Dubai Metro. Atkins was the lead designer for the joint venture, with a team of as many as 60 architects forming part of a total of some 600 professionals in Atkins offices all over the Middle East, Europe and Asia at the peak of the design period.

Atkins provided design, project management and construction support for all the civil works and coordinated this with Mitsubishi Heavy Industries, who were responsible for the rolling stock and train control systems.

Red Line: 52.5 km of track; 47 km of viaduct; four underground and 25 overground stations; 5.5 km of tunnels; two maintenance depots.

Green Line: 22 km of track; 14.5 km of viaduct; six underground and 12 overground stations; 7.5 km of tunnels; one maintenance depot.

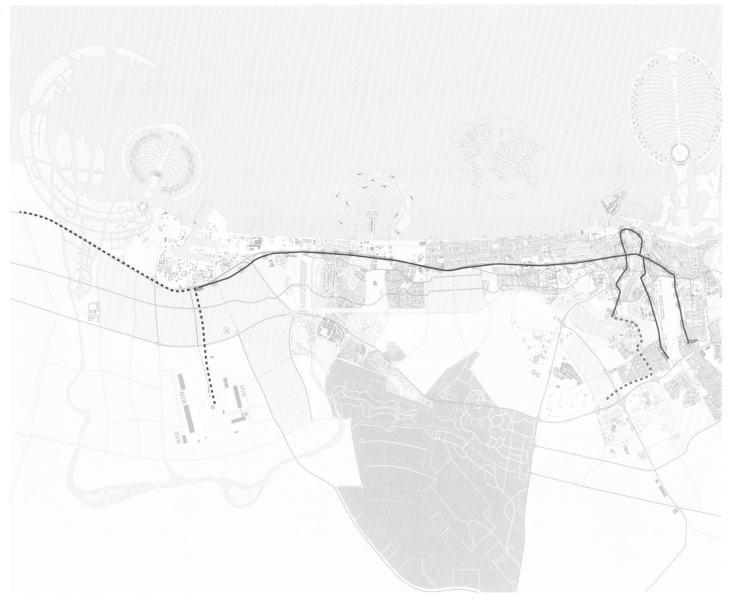

369

ABU BAKER AL SIDDIQUE STATION

Abu Baker Al Siddique Station is one of the Dubai Metro's 37 overground stations. Its position, directly below the main flight path of Dubai International Airport, necessitated a unique design some 5 m lower overall than the other elevated stations.

The result is a sleek variation on the standard station theme. The simple, rational layout has the station concourse slung below the main line and terminated at either end by service rooms clad in aluminium louvres. Public access to the platforms is by means of escalators, stairs and lifts.

The exterior of the station is a straightforward enclosure of aluminium roofing panels and expansive glazed façades, the latter providing spectacular views of the city and easing passengers through the transition between the noisy, bustling streets below and the cool, quiet calm of the Metro. The glazed walls are relieved by horizontal blades that combined with the inclination of the façade, serve to combat solar gain.

The horizontal lines of the station façades and the textures that enhance the walls of the services rooms are back-lit at night, producing a dramatic image suggestive of movement and speed.

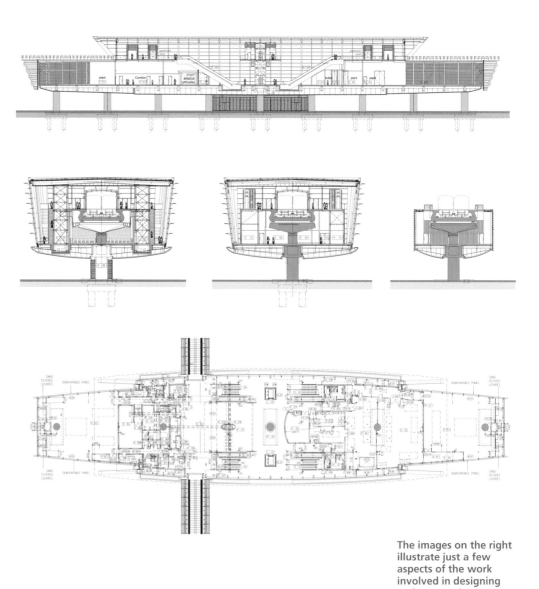

The images on the right illustrate just a few aspects of the work involved in designing and constucting the Dubai Metro.

Sustainable Monorail Station
Dubai, UAE

TRANSPORTATION

Client
Confidential

Area
6,000 m²

Type
Metro station

Status
Concept design

Date
2008

For this monorail system in Dubai, Atkins adopted the high-sustainability approach it applies to all new projects, developing a range of passive systems applicable to all future transport projects.

The most obvious feature of the station is its arresting cladding, a highly insulated panel-based system that can be tailored to suit orientation, fine-tuned during the design phase and easily modified once commissioned. The cladding controls infra-red light penetration into the internal volume, which is already carefully organised to minimise the air conditioning load while providing a bright, airy interior.

The provision of controlled natural lighting for platforms and concourse areas naturally minimises power consumption, and also enhances the aesthetics and atmosphere of the station interior, providing the connection with the outside that people find so desirable. The north façade of the station is heavily glazed, giving views over a palm garden and the nearby university.

The roof of the station has a dedicated passive smoke exhaust system in case of a train fire, minimising the need for mechanical extract fans and ducts within the platform level, saving expense and increasing internal space and light.

This new station will connect the Palm Monorail to the Dubai Metro *(see preceding pages)*. The scheme also incorporates 1,000 m² of stabling for trains, which follows the same sustainable design principles as were developed for the station.

Sustainable Tram Depot
Dubai, UAE

TRANSPORTATION

Client
Confidential
Area
8,500 m²
Type
Tram depot
Status
Concept design
Date
2008

Depots provide a hub where trams or trains are stabled, cleaned and maintained, and from which they are often controlled. While often utilitarian in nature, and of little or no architectural merit, depots can actually be attractive and efficient parts of an environmentally responsible transport system if given a little care and attention at the design stage.

In this case Atkins developed an aesthetic approach that responded to the broad range of building sizes and types that are gathered together to make a depot. The intention was to provide a coherent means of creating a stylish and attractive group of buildings despite their widely disparate functions and forms.

The copper roof is carried through the entire scheme, including stations, to provide a unifying identity, and the way in which it will patinate to an attractive shade of green is a subtle pointer to the attention that has been paid to minimising energy use.

An expansive green roof is planted with specific species to act as a biofilter for tram wash water, provide an attractive view for surrounding high-rise buildings and a thermal mass for the depot, enhancing comfort by slowing heat gain during the

day and heat loss during the night. Photovoltaic cells drive pumps for the roof irrigation and filtration system, and venturi skylights provide natural ventilation, cooling and lighting. Each of these inititives reduces the requirement for powered alternatives.

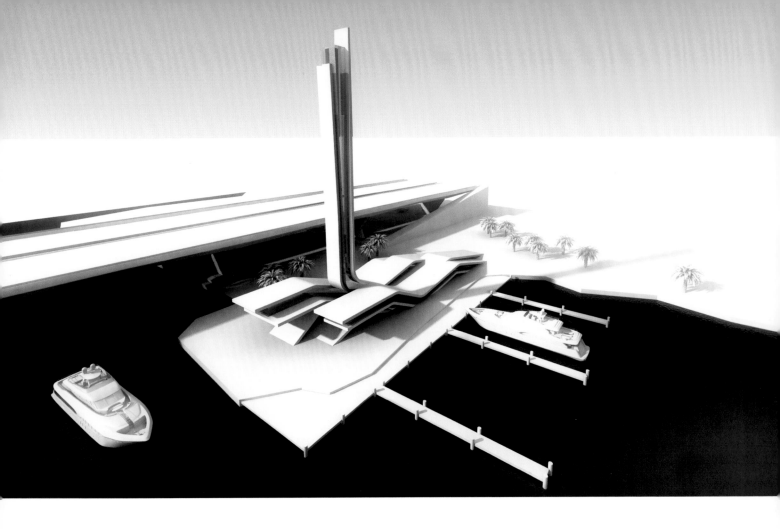

Ferry Terminal
Dubai, UAE

TRANSPORTATION

Client
Confidential

Area
2,400 m²

Type
Ferry terminal

Status
Concept design

Date
2008

The dual demands of this project were for a ferry terminal for passenger handling and an observation tower. The obvious response would have been to adopt the form of pier and lighthouse. Instead, the design team chose to blend the two units together to form a single flowing element that starts from the ground as a pedestrian-accessible roof, rises to form the ferry terminal and then divides into separate 'flows', two of which rise to form the observation tower and two of which form the cantilevered restaurants and viewing platforms.

The dynamic, fluid lines can be read as waves, or seen as evocative of the concept of water more generally, with the tower providing a pleasing splash.

The roof and tower are expressed as waves, ripples and splashes in the water that the terminal addresses.

Signature Bridge
Dubai, UAE

TRANSPORTATION

Client
Confidential

Area
5,600 m²

Type
Bridge spans 200 m
providing a three-lane
dual carriageway

Status
Design complete

Date
2008

Bridges are intriguing structures. At their simplest they can be little more than a log over a stream. Expand the brief a little to introduce further functional requirements and the result can be spectacular.

The structural problem of bridging a new canal is straightforward, but in this case the challenge was enhanced by the client's requirement that it be sympathetic to its residential context. Most difficult of all was achieving the specified minimum vertical clearance beneath the bridge without extending the approach roads and, by so doing, isolating the adjacent retail malls from passing traffic. Too high a bridge would make the retailers unhappy; too low, and the inability of boats to pass beneath it would reduce the value of the upstream waterside residential plots.

The means of realising this aim was to minimise the deck thickness, which effectively mandated a tension structure. The result of a creative refinement process is an elegant, functional structure that delivers excellent aesthetic and functional value for money.

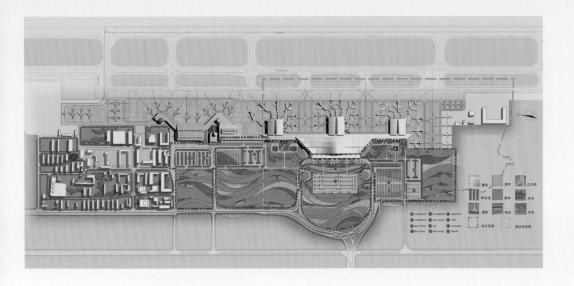

The simplicity of the layout belies the sophistication in the design. The beautiful landscaping makes reference to the ripple of the terminal roof in its layout of terraces and ponds.

Changsha Huanghua International Airport
Changsha, China

TRANSPORTATION

Client
Changsha Airport
(Group) Co.Ltd

Area
154,220 m²

Type
Airport terminal
extension

Status
Design

Date
2008

Changsha Huanghua is an important principal airport serving the south and east of mainland China. It is located 24 km east of Changsha city and, when complete, will be able to accommodate up to 15.2 million passengers per year, with a peak hourly throughput of 5,340 people.

The new terminal adopts a peninsula layout parallel to that of the existing Terminal 1. It has the standard separation of spaces, with arrivals at ground level and departures

at the second floor level, 8 m above. Over the latter, a high roof encloses a mezzanine floor with clear heights of more than 10 m.

The building's hybrid structure employs concrete for the lower terminal levels and steel for the upper levels and roof. It uses a series of gentle curves to express the logic of the plan and section. Deep overhanging eaves exaggerate the form and create shading for the glass walls. The principal finishes are aluminium

cladding and high-performance double glazing for the walls, with aluminium sheets for the roof articulating the simple forms with a subtle mix of reflection and translucency.

Distinctive landscaping builds on traditional Chinese elements such as terraces and waterways, in this case with a partiular local relevance. The curves relate to those incorporated in the built forms, and ease the transition between buildings and surroundings.

Crossrail
London, UK

TRANSPORTATION

Client
Crossrail Ltd

Area
N/A

Type
Rail infrastructure

Status
Detailed design

Date
Completion 2017

Crossrail is a new high-frequency railway that from 2017 will link the counties of southeast England to and through the centre of London, and on to Heathrow and the west. Atkins, in partnership with Arup, Grimshaw, GIA Equation and Hawkins Brown, is playing a key role in the project through multidisciplinary joint venture contracts to design tunnels and stations, either in total, or in the design of the common finishing components that will provide Crossrail with so much of its clear, strong identity.

The sprayed concrete lining the tunnels has been exploited by the designers to create smooth, curved junctions that allow spaces to flow from one axis to another. This helps passenger orientation and minimises the need for complex signage. An architectural cladding system using three-dimensional curved GRC panels is proposed to develop this aesthetic, by expressing the fluid, seamless tunnel construction.

An assessment process has been used for material and product selection that takes account of whole-life carbon footprint and embodied energy. For example, Crossrail will be the first metro network to embrace the use of new LED long-life lighting technology. LED technology is now advanced enough to support some sophisticated design subtleties. It

can provide warm, indirect light to calm passengers within spaces where they may feel stressed – complex junctions, say – but bright cool lighting in places where they have made decisions and want to move quickly.

It is intended that Crossrail will be the first fully digital network, providing entertainment, art and

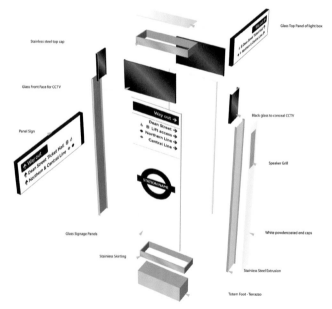

Broad flowing thoroughfares, bright finishes and superb lighting will characterise the completed Crossrail scheme in 2017.

travel information by means of large-scale multimedia displays, centrally controlled and coordinated across all Crossrail stations. The services connections supporting these and all the other facilities are to be contained within ducts at low-level, making access for maintenance or repair quick, easy and safe.

The design intent has been summarised in a single statement. "To design a modern, minimal, elegant and functional transport system that enhances the passenger experience".

British Airways World Cargo Centre
London, UK

TRANSPORTATION

Client
British Airways

Area
84,500 m²

Type
Automated cargo
centre and offices

Status
Complete

Date
2000

The British Airways World Cargo Centre and Corporate Headquarters incorporate numerous innovative technical and operational features in this commended design. Of particular interest is the radar-absorbent cladding, derived from stealth aircraft technology and used to reduce the disruptive radar image of the the 300 m long, 95 m wide and 36 m high building. A saw-tooth profile is built into the north elevation for the same reason, in this case by deflecting radar waves down onto the concrete.

The 84,500 m² building uses a state-of-the-art mechanical cargo-handling system capable of managing and distributing a million tonnes of freight per year. Heavy transfer structures, used in conjunction with

raking piles, bridge the Heathrow Express and Piccadilly Line tunnels. Designed around a three-storey atrium, the open-plan offices of the staff business centre are an integral part of the overall development.

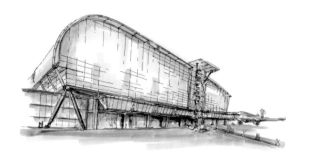

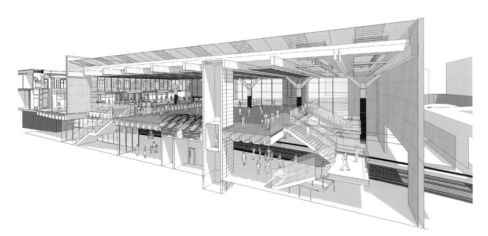

Farringdon Station
London, UK

TRANSPORTATION

Client
Transport for London

Area
7,500 m²

Type
Station

Status
Under construction

Date
2007–2017

Clean, bright, and immediately comprehensible to the passenger, the revised Farringdon Station is a fine example of the best in contemporary transport design.

Atkins' multidisciplinary design team is responsible for both the original railway infrastructure refurbishment plans and the design and integration of a new ticket hall building at Farringdon Station in London. The ultimate aim of this project is to enable Thameslink to operate longer trains at increased frequencies, and to improve disabled access and integration with new railway lines in the process.

Farringdon Station is a complex structure. It serves a number of surface and underground lines and has legal protection for its historic buildings, which adjoin the Charterhouse Square Conservation Area. The station is unique in that it provides connections to three of London's major airports. In addition, the new ticket hall will serve the new Crossrail link when it becomes operational in 2017, and appropriate provision had to be incorporated for this future development.

The ticket hall is a modern intervention within a group of historically significant buildings, some of which had to be demolished to make way for it. The new proposal is a clean piece of modern architecture, respectful of its high-quality historic surroundings. It attempts to match them as an equally high-quality contemporary design, avoiding any hint of pastiche. That it succeeds was confirmed when planning consent was granted for the proposals in 2009 after protracted and careful consideration.

This involvement of historic structures in contemporary schemes is important. It ensures a useful life for the older buildings, something that experience has shown offers them by far the best chance for survival. It also enables some of their character to inform the newer structures, enhancing the whole design by providing a historical context, enriching it and providing a relationship with place that helps to root a new structure in its surroundings.

The contemporary interventions were carefully integrated with the refurbishment proposals made by the same multidisciplinary team. Aesthetically, the result is a cohesive overall concept, despite the disparity in age of the various buildings involved. Practically, it will provide universal access for all, with an entirely step-free 'mainstream' route from pavement to platform.

Tianjin Train Station
Tianjin, China

TRANSPORTATION

Client
Tianjin Municipality

Area
80,000 m²

Type
Central railway and
transit hub

Status
Competition entry

Date
2006

This was an international design competition entry for a major new city-centre railway and transit hub. The scheme included the masterplanning of the surrounding 95 ha inner city traffic system.

The scheme encompassed the architectural and traffic planning for the junction of a high-speed rail system, the national rail system, a metro system, an inter-city long distance bus terminus, a municipal bus station, taxi stands, underground vehicle parking and pedestrian traffic from the new commercial city centre and a public landscaped plaza.

This project was the focus of Tianjin city's rejuvenation efforts, and a landmark for the 2008 Olympic Games.

The concept, called 'shifting horizons', represents forms in motion, capturing the traditional excitement and romance of rail travel. This is expressed as a sequence of sublime, light-filled spaces that subtly transform themselves as one moves through them, and as the natural lighting conditions transmute from day to night.

The development of modern railway stations is an exercise in planning as much as in design.

Identity, comprehension and functionality are the three main axes of the discipline. An understanding of vertical zoning for pedestrians and horizontal interconnection for transport systems was critical to understanding the problems and developing a circulation system for this centre.

The architectural forms are derived directly from the east–west formal organisation and the north–south functional connections. The forms are used to fulfill their functional roles only and are never forced to extend beyond their functional boundaries. A harmonious and efficient relationship

between form and function is thus ensured, and a comfortable, elegant composition is created.

The importance of the linear roof is stressed to reflect the linear nature of the huge space that is at the heart of the scheme. The roof planes are angled to allow natural southern daylight to penetrate, while also maximising the spectacle and size of the main space. The forms attempt to integrate and develop the original station building as much as possible, creating lively, interesting views from many urban vantage points.

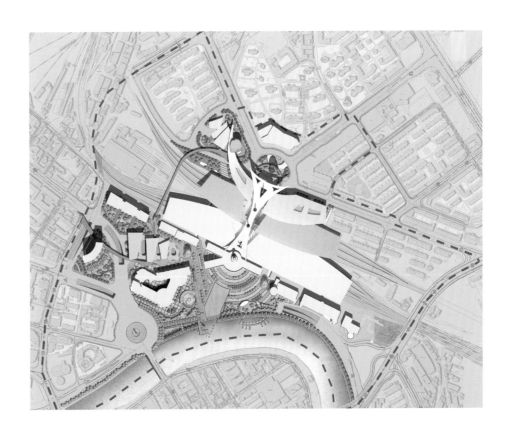

MASTERPLANNING AND URBAN DESIGN

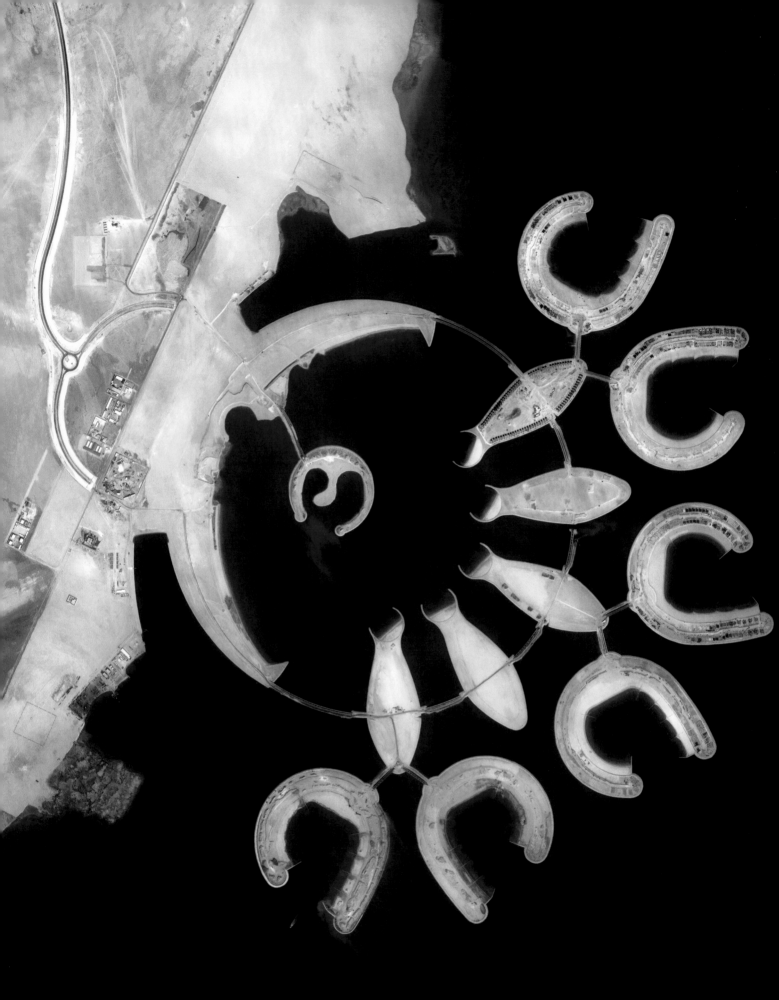

**MASTERPLANNING
AND URBAN DESIGN**

Client
Durrat Khaleej Al
Bahrain

Area
20 km²

Type
Residential,
commercial and
leisure resort

Status
Under construction

Date
2004–2012

The sustainable residential, commercial and leisure resort community of Durrat Al Bahrain is conceptually a 'necklace of pearls' suspended from the southeast shoreline of Bahrain. Intended to provide an exotic resort lifestyle, the 20 km² masterplan proposes a broad arc of six created, serif-shaped atolls, each with an exclusive community of 172 villas that boast either individual yacht moorings or private beaches.

The atolls are linked, like pendants on a necklace, by slender bridges to an inner ring of five 'petal-shaped' islands. These each have 1.5 km of water frontage with moorings and act as neighbourhood nodes, with community facilities and a shared white sand beach serving up to 90 villas. At the heart of the 'necklace' and linked to the individual petals is a crescent-shaped promontory with shops, cafés, leisure facilities and 2,000 apartments.

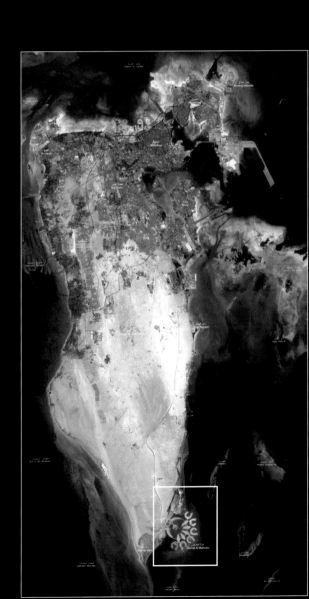

The architectural language employed for the residential units is unashamedly modern and plays off the crystal-clear aquamarine and emerald water. A 'grand canal' separates the crescent from the mainland, where there are additional facilities including a golf course and marina.

Built around the concept of a 'toy box' and a place for fun, a hotel with a rippling roof profile occupies a prominent position at the geographical centre of the development.

While the infrastructure of Durrat Al Bahrain is an artificial construct, not untypical for the region, the geometric arrangement of islands, canals and waterways is hydrologically sympathetic to the environment. The reclaimed land development will eventually be home to 60,000 people.

Tidal flow pattern analyses were undertaken for various land configurations and tide patterns to ensure the continued health of the marine environment.

Durrat Al Bahrain Marina
Bahrain

**MASTERPLANNING
AND URBAN DESIGN**

Client
Durrat Khaleej Al
Bahrain

Area
68 ha

Type
Residential,
commercial and
leisure marina

Status
Masterplan complete,
under construction

Date
2007–2010

Durrat Al Bahrain Marina extends over a 150 ha site, of which 68 ha is reclaimed. Together with its neighbouring golf course, it forms an extension of the highly successful main development and complements it in both role and character.

While smaller than its parent development, it shares physical similarities. A crescent-shaped island continues the main theme, and is separated from the mainland by a canal. Its seaward-side partially encloses the 400-berth marina, while a central spine road links the crescent to two further crescent islands with private beaches, which provide the remainder of the marina perimeter and come together to frame its seaward entrance.

The compact and efficient scaling of this development allows nearly all of the single- and multi-level apartments, lofts and townhouses to have water frontages and sea views.

In addition, all residences will have convenient access to public landscaped spaces, beaches, boardwalks and the retail and leisure attractions of this mini-city. Access to these facilities will be by foot through pedestrian-friendly streets, open plazas and arcades, the intention being to discourage the use of cars for short journeys and support a healthy lifestyle.

Water is not just a theme but a focus of Durrat Al Bahrain Marina. The marina is the heart of the development, and the islands around it create a series of canals, lagoons and bays, and frame vistas of the open sea.

Sculptured bridges link the islands' pleasant residential streets, which are lined with trees. The waterborne inhabitants of the marina and the land-based urban community meet at the marina waterfront, the lively hub of the marina's retail and leisure precinct.

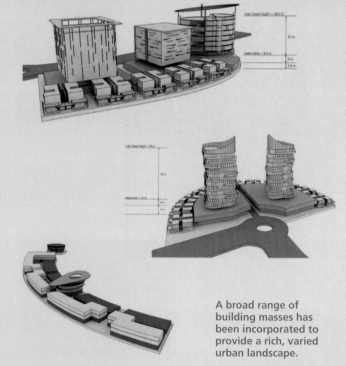

A broad range of
building masses has
been incorporated to
provide a rich, varied
urban landscape.

Durrat Al Bahrain North Horn
Bahrain

MASTERPLANNING
AND URBAN DESIGN

Client
Durrat Khaleej Al
Bahrain

Area
15.8 ha

Type
Residential,
commercial
and leisure

Status
Masterplan complete

Date
2008–2009

In marked contrast to the self-effacing structural development on the Durrat Al Bahrain islands, the treatment of the crescent North Horn will establish this area as a landmark and community focal point.

Its architectural forms and complementary landscapes are intended to set new benchmarks for Bahrain, yet be anchored to the sustainable themes that are an integral part of the main resort. North Horn aims to be the first development in Bahrain to obtain LEED Gold accreditation.

While connected to the mainland and providing access to the other islands via road bridges, the North Horn is designed to encourage green transport alternatives and is intended to be as vehicle-free as possible. Conurbations are concentrated in tall, slender towers that have relatively small footprints to maximise the spaces in between for green 'pockets'. Photovoltaic panels strategically mounted on buildings serve a dual function of providing shade at street level and generating renewable energy.

The landscape design is inspired by natural forms and, conceptually as well as physically, provides a transition zone between the inhabitants and the local environment.

Pedestrian routes are carefully shaded and integrated so as to make them an attractive alternative to motor transport.

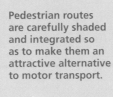

Euston Station Masterplan
London, UK

**MASTERPLANNING
AND URBAN DESIGN**

Client
Sydney & London
Properties

Area
17 ha

Type
Holistic redevelopment
of station

Status
Complete

Date
2007–2008

Euston has long suffered at the hands of the planners. The 1960s redevelopment is infamous for its disastrous demolition of the station's Doric gateway arch, and is credited with kick-starting the architectural conservation movement in Britain. The later 1980s scheme, interposing a commercial development between the station and Euston Road, created a depressingly downbeat entrance, at once concealed by unrelated buildings and exposed to the elements. Rail travel from Euston became something to be endured rather than enjoyed.

This new vision reintroduces the excitement that travel should evoke by reworking Euston Square as the forecourt to a new, confident station frontage. The station becomes a small but important part of comprehensive proposals for a mixed-use community of 350,000 m², combining commercial, retail and leisure facilities, residential buildings and high-quality public spaces below a series of terraced roof gardens and parks.

The new buildings extend into the flanks of the square, providing some much-needed shelter and containment and introducing a pleasing vertical counterpoint to the square's calm horizontality, while deferring to the star of the show, the station itself. Clever use of restrained landscaping delineates access routes and desire lines, while creating a blend of intimate spaces and open swards. The primary axis of the new Euston Square will be the station approach, in a move intended to provide the passenger with a significant arrival or departure experience and reintroduce the idea of travel as something to be enjoyed.

Part of the challenge was to achieve this apparently free approach to the area while accepting the limitations of the heavily trafficked site boundaries, the rail system, four London Underground lines and a protected overhead view corridor to St Paul's Cathedral. The result will not only make travelling through Euston attractive again, but develop it as a destination in its own right.

The design team saw the rehabilitation of Euston Square as a fundamental objective in the redevelopment of the station, reclaiming it from the wind and reintroducing it as a vibrant, bustling and comfortable urban space.

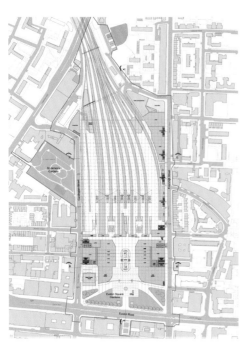

Ground floor plan

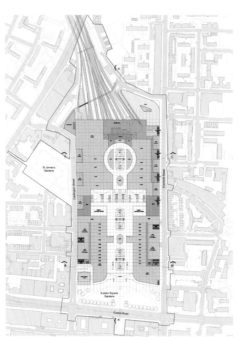

1st floor plan

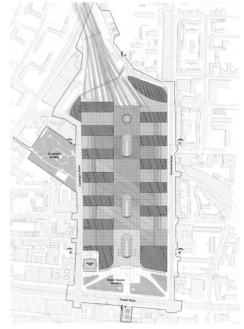

Roof plan

Euston Station

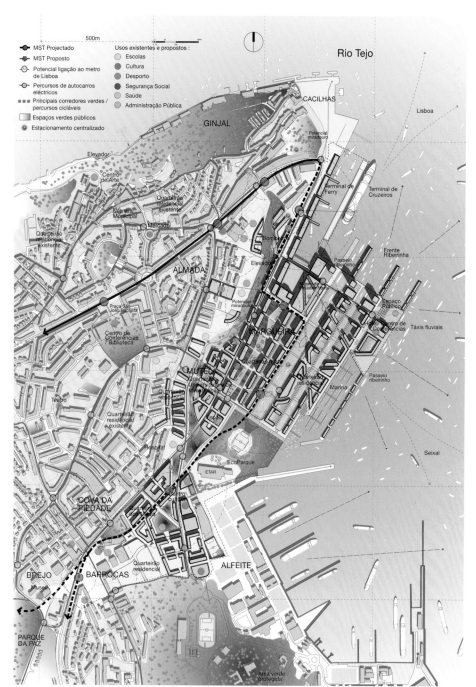

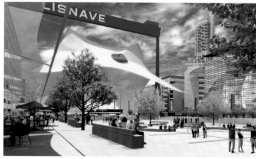

Almada Docks
Lisbon, Portugal

**MASTERPLANNING
AND URBAN DESIGN**

Client
Municipality of
Almada

Area
150 ha

Type
Dockland regeneration

Status
Complete

Date
2003–2004

The Almada Docks in Lisbon are the subject of one of the most extensive dockland regeneration projects in Europe. Covering a site of 150 ha, the masterplan has been developed on the most contemporary of sustainable urban design principles.

Directly across the Tagus Estuary from Lisbon, the Almada Docks are intended to become a model urban community that will pioneer new forms of employment. The design exemplifies the best of urban living, using buildings and landscaping to temper the exposed environment and foster an inclusive community.

The regenerated areas become the new waterfront district while the former linear docks become a central water park. The mixed-use plan reinvents the Lisbon *praca* to create streets and public spaces that are lively, intimate and secure, with pedestrians accorded priority over cars. Additional housing supports the attraction of the 'critical mass' necessary for the development of an active, enriching urban community lifestyle.

The project methodology was a model of best practice, with the aim of delivering a 'zero-carbon' development through an integrated strategy for energy efficiency, on-site energy production, renewable energy harvesting and carbon sequestration. Initial technical studies were carried out by both local and international discipline specialists.

Community involvement was central to the project, with a range of initiatives adopted to ensure that everyone who wished to could take an active part in the development of the masterplan. The process became and exercise in collective education for consultants, client and community.

Hornsea Promenade
Hornsea, UK

MASTERPLANNING AND URBAN DESIGN

Client
Confidential

Area
6,000 m²

Type
Renovation of public space and facilities along the seafront promenade

Status
Complete

Date
2002–2004

Following Atkins' preparation of a seafront masterplan for the Yorkshire coastal town, the firm was retained to implement the proposals. The award-winning design promotes Hornsea as a revitalised English seaside destination.

The principal features are a series of 'wave' lawns enclosed by solid granite walls, which provide shelter and enclosure and incorporate contemporary sunken gardens, a children's splash pool with interactive water jets, a new café and a parade of distinctive beach huts.

A sympathetic street lighting scheme and a new balustrade with 'crow's nest' lookout points have added to the regeneration of the promenade.

This comprehensive design project has boosted tourism and provided a lasting economic and environmental asset for Hornsea. Ecological concerns over travel to far-flung destinations have seen a revitalisation of the English seaside holiday for UK residents, something directly addressed and referenced in the details of this new scheme.

Hornsea Promenade has won a number of prestigious awards since it opened in the summer of 2003. These include a special category Civic Trust hard landscape award, East Riding of Yorkshire's Council's 'Chairman's Award', Landscape Institute North West's 'Best scheme by a north west practice award', and the highly commended 'Local Government News award'. Hornsea Promenade has also been recognised by CABE in its library of Britain's best buildings and public spaces.

Trafalgar Square, World Squares for All Masterplan
London, UK

Client
Greater London
Authority and
Transport for London
Street Management

Area
20,000 m²

Type
Redevelopment
masterplan

Status
Complete

Date
2000–2003

Trafalgar Square is the symbolic and geographic heart of London, but by the year 2000 it had been reduced to the status of a traffic gyratory system, providing few amenities for Londoners and even fewer facilities for the millions of people who visit each year.

Striking a balance between old and new and providing a more amenable space, an Atkins-led multidisciplinary team developed a radical plan that has now received over a dozen international awards for excellence.

Removal of traffic from the north side has transformed the square by connecting it to the National Gallery through a broad flight of steps, and replacing the cramped pavement with generous pedestrian space – the new North Terrace. This not only provides the National Gallery with an appropriate forecourt, greatly enhancing its architectural composition, but also transforms the square from an isolated traffic island into a truly grand urban space. Other pedestrian areas have been significantly enlarged

and further zones introduced, creating more dignified settings for the church of St. Martin-in-the-Fields and the King Charles I statue, as well as establishing safer vantage points for the best views along the historic thoroughfares that converge on the square.

Wherever possible and appropriate, traditional materials have been employed: historic 19th-century granite paving has been re-used, and York stone, granite and cast bronze utilised in the new features.

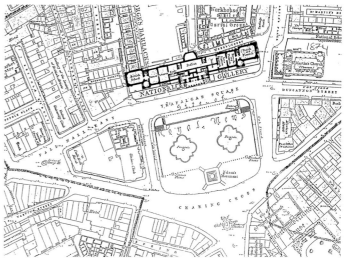

Oxford Circus
London, UK

MASTERPLANNING
AND URBAN DESIGN

Client
The Crown Estate
(in conjunction with
Transport for London,
City of Westminster
and the New West
End Company)

Area
5,000 m²

Type
Public realm and
pedestrian movement
improvement

Status
Complete

Date
2009–2010

Oxford Circus is the busiest crossing in London's West End – the busiest shopping district in Europe. Around 43,000 people and 2,000 vehicles pass through it hourly and its congestion threatened to undermine its reputation.

The Crown Estate was determined to address this problem as one of a number of initiatives under the Oxford, Regent and Bond Street (ORB) Action Plan. This is a scheme to revitalise the West End developed jointly by Westminster City Council, New West End Company and Transport for London. This aligned attractively with the Crown Estate's plans to revitalise the whole of Regent Street (*see overleaf*) in a phased development aimed at making the best use of buildings as their leases reached maturity with minimal disruption to life on the street.

Atkins was commissioned and developed a scheme to transform Oxford Circus from a frustrating bottleneck into a pleasant and lively interchange. The widely acclaimed results, like most good designs, were based on simple, but very carefully considered precepts. The innovative use of diagonal crossings, the removal of much of the clutter that blights British streets and the judicious widening of pavements cleared routes and significantly reduced congestion.

Westminster World Heritage Site
London, UK

MASTERPLANNING AND URBAN DESIGN

Client
English Heritage
Chaired Steering
Group including
ICOMOS and all
local landowners/
stakeholders

Area
10.5 ha

Type
Management
masterplan

Status
Complete

Date
2002–2006

The Palace of Westminster and Westminster Abbey were inscribed on the list of World Heritage sites in 1987 in recognition of the universal architectural, historic and symbolic significance of this group of buildings and spaces. But these are not museums – they are places of work, worship and education for hundreds of people.

The challenge is to safeguard the heritage of the site while facilitating the democratic function of the Houses of Parliament and the ever-changing needs of the Abbey, two institutions that date back a thousand years to the time of Edward the Confessor. Both buildings are icons. Atkins has prepared a management plan in accordance with UNESCO standards, and the team of conservation architects, urban designers, transport engineers and tourism and heritage specialists have addressed issues such as the setting, dignity and accessibility of the various elements of the site. Proper use of the management plan will protect the future of the site, ensuring that the significant and universal values attached to it are safeguarded and enhanced.

Regent Street Urban Design
London, UK

**MASTERPLANNING
AND URBAN DESIGN**

Client
The Crown Estate

Area
8 ha

Type
Public realm
improvement

Status
Partially complete,
phased development

Date
1995–2020

Regent Street is the UK's foremost shopping street. Atkins started work on reinvigorating it for the Crown Estate in 1997 – since that time the scheme has embraced other initiatives under the ORB Plan. The Regent Street element matured into Vision 2020, a series of phased developments centred on blocks of buildings for which leases have expired and which are being renovated prior to re-letting. Atkins designed and implemented street improvement schemes as part of the project, including New Burlington Place (the Crown Estate's new HQ), Heddon Street and Swallow Street (both in a new international food quarter). The Quadrant development is currently being implemented near Piccadilly Circus.

The phased approach prevents disruption of both traffic flow and the commercial life of Regent Street, enabling the best of contemporary architectural and technology standards to be applied as they develop. The project is making the street a more pleasant and functional place for pedestrians, transforming side roads into 'oases' of calm, providing better crossings (especially for those following east–west cross-routes between Mayfair and Soho) and introducing a central median to allow informal crossing. From a noisy, cramped thoroughfare, Regent Street is being transformed into a sequence of attractive, enticing places.

International Crab Market
Suzhou, China

**MASTERPLANNING
AND URBAN DESIGN**

Client
Suzhou Industrial Park
Yangchenghu Lake
Resort Development
Co. Ltd

Area
77,500 m² of total
built-up area over
19.38 ha

Type
Commercial complex
for wholesale and
retailing of crabs

Status
Design complete

Date
2008

This commercial complex operates
primarily for the wholesale and
retail of crabs, but, in providing
other facilities such as restaurants,
entertainment and exhibition areas,
extends the concept more towards
a crab-based theme park.

The five main blocks of the complex
are arranged horizontally from west
to east. Each of these blocks stretches
south towards Shuangyang Road and
north into Lake Donghu. Water from
the lake is brought into the site through
a network of canals and pools that link
the five blocks, recreating some of the
ambience of the Suzhou of times past.

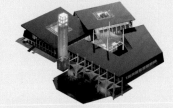

Tourist pier linked to the iconic tower
housing an exhibition centre and a
tourist service centre.

Double-level pods enclosing shops
and a market with courtyards that
are accessible via the canal.

Boat-like speciality restaurant
pods and a food fair connected
by the canopied tourist boat pier,
surrounded by landscaped plazas
and a waterbus stop.

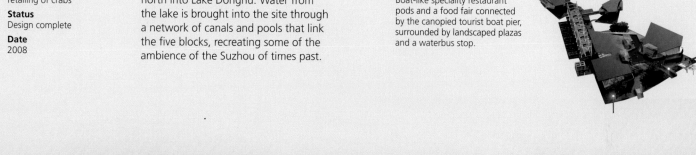

Xuzhou Railway Station Masterplan
Xuzhou, China

**MASTERPLANNING
AND URBAN DESIGN**

Client
Xuzhou Economy
Development
Committee

Area
900 ha

Type
Urban design
and masterplan

Status
Competition entry

Date
2007

Xuzhou High-speed Railway Station is one of the five main stations along the Beijing–Shanghai high-speed railway, which is due to be completed in 2012. The area surrounding the station is destined to become the core area of the Xuzhou Economic Development Zone and a major gateway to Xuzhou.

The masterplan is conventional, with the two landmark features – the station and an artificial lake – positioned at the ends of the new main axis. Connecting the two will be a mixed-use corridor. A separate network of pedestrian paths exists within a clear, three-level hierarchy of roads.

This provides convenient access for station commuters to the commercial, entertainment and community facilities sited around the lake, and to the government headquarters beyond.

Jiading-Anting New Town Masterplan
Shanghai, China

MASTERPLANNING
AND URBAN DESIGN

Client
Shanghai Jiading
District Government

Area
24,800 ha

Type
Masterplan

Status
Competition entry

Date
2004

Accessibility to public transport and areas of public open space are the driving forces behind the Jiading-Anting New Town Masterplan. With a target population approaching one million people, it is one of the three city regions (together with Songjiang and Lingang) that will play a key role in supporting Shanghai's booming development. Chinese cosmology, based on dualism in the form of 'yin and yang', plays a strong role in the masterplan, as does sustainability. The emphasis is on walking, linking paths to greenery and the canal network. The outcome is a strong diagonal axis through the town centre connecting the old town with the new.

Jiading New Town core is at the hub of the public transport routes. The plan is in the form of a 'key' that can be seen as a metaphor for the potential unlocking of the district, linking the old city to the new. Jiading is exceptional among the three urban centres in the Shanghai Metropolitan Region – it is the home of China's Formula 1 racing circuit and attracts thousands of visitors. Anting New Town is the centre of the automotive industry and home to the VW factory.

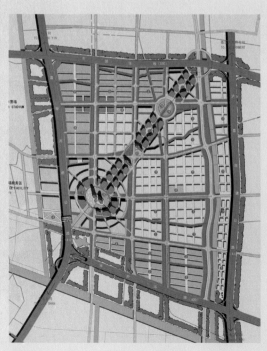

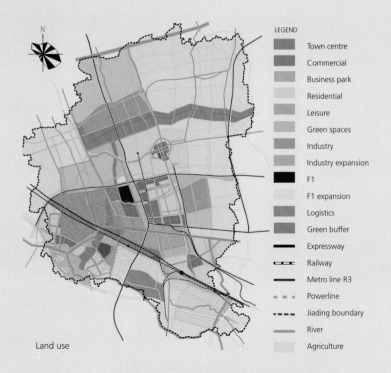

LEGEND

Town centre
Commercial
Business park
Residential
Leisure
Green spaces
Industry
Industry expansion
F1
F1 expansion
Logistics
Green buffer
Expressway
Railway
Metro line R3
Powerline
Jiading boundary
River
Agriculture

Land use

Colchester Garrison
Colchester, UK

MASTERPLANNING AND URBAN DESIGN

Client
Ministry of Defence

Area
303 ha

Type
State-of-the-art
military facility

Status
Complete

Date
2003–2008

Colchester Garrison is the home base of the 16 Air Assault Brigade, Britain's primary rapid reaction force. The Ministry of Defence wanted to relocate the garrison from the north to the south of its 303 ha site, releasing the currently occupied land close to Colchester town centre for redevelopment as an urban village. Under the PFI initiative, RMPA Services (a consortium including Atkins) was selected as preferred bidder to design, construct and operate the facilities within the new garrison and urban village.

The urban design of the garrison has a clear structure with a legible hierarchy of buildings, spaces, and linkages – all prerequisites for a military establishment. More than 95% of the redeveloped garrison is new-build, including 137 buildings. With a challenging timescale for design and implementation, a large part of the accommodation was prefabricated and assembled off-site.

The garrison is a state-of-the-art facility fit for the 21st-century army. Well-designed accommodation, messes, classrooms, working areas, training facilities and extensive sports facilities are provided, all within a high security single wire perimeter.

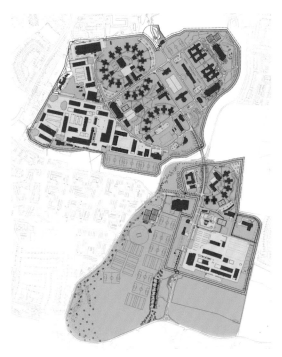

Malmö Plaza
Malmö, Sweden

**MASTERPLANNING
AND URBAN DESIGN**

Client
City of Malmö,
Sweden

Area
2 ha

Type
Public realm
improvement

Status
Competition entry

Date
2009

Malmö lies at the southern tip of Sweden on the coast of the Oresund, a narrow strip of water between Sweden and Denmark forming the main sea route to the fabled Hanseatic Baltic trading nations. It is a city of parks and squares and is home to a significant Muslim population, something of a pointer to a long trading relationship with the Arabian nations.

Stortorget, the central square, was established in 1536 as a reflection of Malmö's growing political and economic importance. The square was a precise rectangle, in contrast to the organic layout of the medieval city, and provided a venue for commerce and trade. In time the square's function, atmosphere and aesthetics changed, and today it has become an anonymous and unfocussed space with little relevance to the contemporary life of Malmö.

Atkins, in concert with landscape architect Kristine Jensen Tegnestue and heritage consultants Minne and Miljö, was invited in 2008 to participate in a design competition to revitalise the square. The proposal is to transform it into a magnificent European urban space, centred on a grand open square beneath the vaulting sky, with a patterned 'storytelling' floor surrounded by a sequence of intimate, peaceful spaces defined by trees, benches, furniture and lights.

The intention is to create a stimulating yet calm place to walk, sit, pause and contemplate, and at the same time provide a venue for the different events – concerts, theatre, flea markets – that combine to support a rich, modern urban life. The central floor takes its inspiration from the history of Malmö and its maritime traditions, communicated through the beautiful paving, which incorporates subtle variations in texture and colour to suggest sky and stars, astral navigation, sea patterns and trade routes.

During the long northern winter nights, and when the floor is under snow, the theme is continued by the lighthouse. This in itself inspires the concepts of way-finding and safe haven, using its beam to project an Arabesque pattern over the square – a lacework of maps and trade routes, constellations and currents. This calls to mind the important Arabian influence on a thousand years of trade, and gives the scheme its title – 1001 Nights.

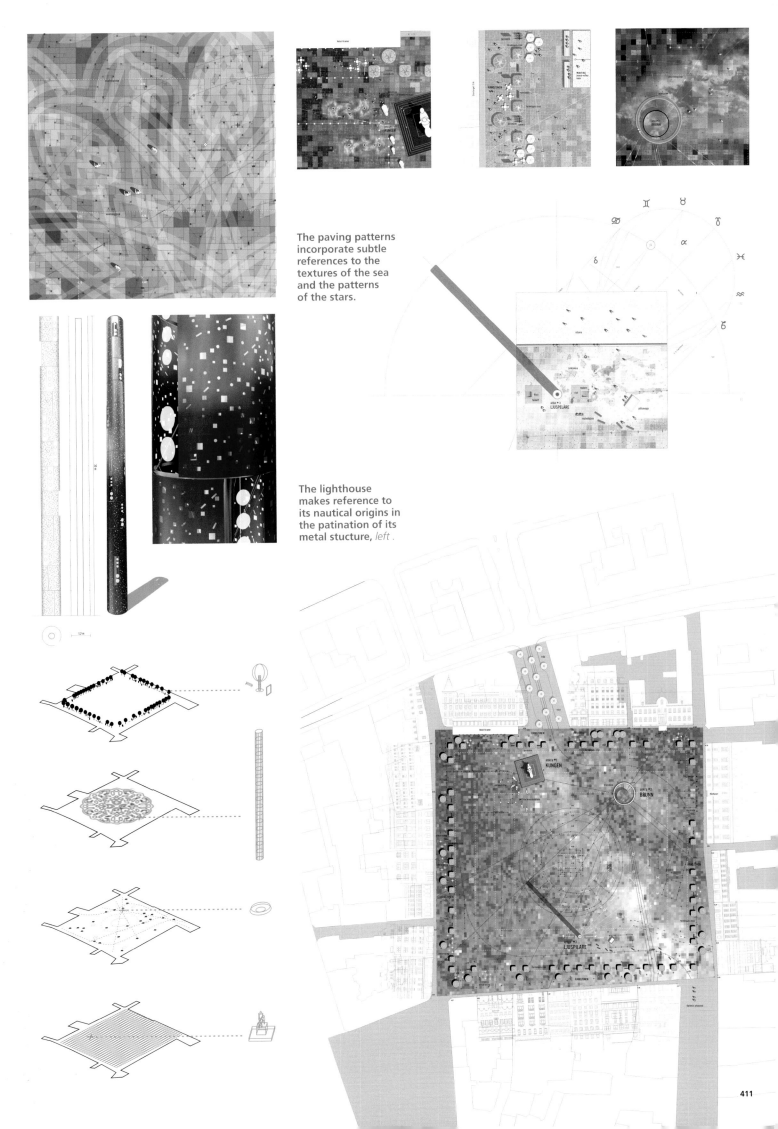

The paving patterns
incorporate subtle
references to the
textures of the sea
and the patterns
of the stars.

The lighthouse
makes reference to
its nautical origins in
the patination of its
metal stucture, *left* .

Shenfu Connection Area
Liaoning, China

**MASTERPLANNING
AND URBAN DESIGN**

Client
Liaoning Development
and Reform
Commission

Area
56,000 ha

Type
Regional development
planning/new
sector planning/city
masterplanning

Status
Competition entry

Date
2007

Shenyang and Fushun are already
connected by the River Hun. This
masterplan seeks to build on that
connection by combining the urban
resources of the two districts through
the placement of the new Shenfu
Connection Area midway between
the two, alongside the river.

The infill connection area will
support the urban functions of
both Shenyang and Fushun. It will

enhance the role of Shenyang as
the regional centre for northeast
China and boost the development
of industry in Fushun, facilitating its
transition into a modern city and
providing many job opportunities.

Although the two areas will now be
connected, their existing characters will
be reinforced by distinct treatments of
the existing border zones at the north
and south ends of the River Hun. The

north end will be transformed into
an ecodistrict, while the south will be
redeveloped as an industrial zone.

Despite the disparate functions of the
border zones, the entire plan is given
cohesion through the introduction
of rich landscaping. The scheme for
the green spaces makes much use
of water, building on the character
of the important river frontage.

Shiyan Syscan High-tech Industrial Park
Shenyang, China

**MASTERPLANNING
AND URBAN DESIGN**

Client
Syscan Technical
Holding Co. Ltd.

Area
19 ha

Type
High-tech
industrial park

Status
Masterplan
design complete

Date
1999

This masterplan addresses the development of a 19 ha high-tech industrial park for Syscan Technical Holding Co. Ltd., a Hong Kong listed electronics manufacturer holding a number of American patents. Sited in a valley embraced by orchard-covered hills, with access from the highway to the south, the plan defines three zones: manufacturing, administration/research and development, and residential quarters.

The intention throughout the masterplanning process was to retain the unique topographic character of the area and to dam the fast-flowing stream in the valley, thus creating a lake as the fulcrum of the plan.

Feng shui dictated an entrance gate that deviated from the customary orientation, in order to avoid looking at the tall chimney stack of a factory immediately to the south. The principal axis connects the entrance gateway to the research and development centre on a hilltop across the lake, and passes through the exhibition centre on the lake shore, marking it as an equally important focus.

Executive quarters are located on the lake shore and other dormitories in an adjoining valley, along with a canteen and sports fields. In total the plan provides 124,000 m² of high-tech manufacturing space.

Thames Town
Songjiang, China

MASTERPLANNING AND URBAN DESIGN

Client
Shanghai Songjiang
Planning &
Administrative Bureau

Area
100 ha

Type
New town urban
planning

Status
Complete

Date
2001–2006

On a 100 ha site in Songjiang, 20 minutes from downtown Shanghai, a simulacrum of an English town has taken shape. Aptly named Thames Town, it resembles in its urban form and individual building typologies a large English village. The project is entirely market-driven, commissioned by clients who wish to differentiate their product from the norm, to create a brand and to target a perceived niche in the real estate market.

The result is an organic urban form with streets, squares, a village green and a waterside promenade. Building types include terraced townhouses, detached villas, a town hall, a church (a replica of a church in Bristol, UK) and most importantly an English pub. It all looks uncannily close to the original and yet is very different. The structure of all the buildings is concrete with applied brick, tile and render finishes.

The ethos driving parts of this design is complete anathema to many architects, but it has proven extraordinarily successful and is driven by demand. Large, mass-housing developments are essential in China, where improvements in living standards are a priority and where the urban population is expected to grow by some 300 million during the next 30 years.

Using 100 ha of land so close to Shanghai for housing at such low density automatically limits its market to the newly wealthy, something that would be true whatever the style of housing adopted. Its pragmatic originators expect it to attract high-flying academics to teach in Songjiang's seven universities, as well as providing an interesting tourist attraction.

Bao'an Central Business District
Shenhzen, China

**MASTERPLANNING
AND URBAN DESIGN**

Client
Bao'an Central
Government Office

Area
110 ha

Type
New town urban
design

Status
Under construction

Date
2006–2009

More than 20 years ago, Shenzhen was a small fishing village called Bao'an. It was renamed when the Special Economic Zone was built next to Hong Kong.

The Shenzhen Bao'an masterplan stretches along a 4 km coastline, occupying 640 ha. Centred upon a reclaimed harbour, it will be Shenzhen's only waterfront CBD and the gateway city for the Shenzhen International Airport. The proposal is based on an award-winning submission for an international competition, which involved both

architectural and landscape disciplines within Atkins' China offices.

The plan transforms an urban zone into a water environment, incorporating local, national, cultural and historical references. It provides approximately 3,000,000 m² of accommodation for office, commercial, hotel and residential uses, all within a green and spacious environment in which arts and crafts will be able to flourish.

The focus is a central green axis for which the inspiration was the form of a dragon. The spine of the dragon

becomes a pedestrian route that links the significant parts of the site. In some places the spine is at ground level, in others it rises and falls above and below ground, reflecting the qualities of the Great Blue Dragon and in the process becoming a symbolically charged 'ribbon of discovery'. The torso of the dragon is transformed into a linear body of water connecting all parts of the site.

While a sense of civic formality generally underpins large-scale masterplans, individual buildings can explore more experimental and informal arrangements of mass and colour, as shown in the alternative layouts, *right*.

JGC Development
Dubai, UAE

MASTERPLANNING AND URBAN DESIGN

Client
Confidential

Area
250 ha

Type
Masterplan and urban design

Status
Concept design

Date
2008

JGC Development aims to improve one of the older areas of Dubai, a section of the city that has been somewhat left behind in development terms. The new plan incorporates the best of contemporary urban design and sustainability.

The plan is given structure by the careful placement of buildings – some very large, others significant for their striking design – and by the introduction of large swathes of water in the form of lakes and canals. The spaces between are given over to communication routes, play spaces and relaxation areas, all intensively landscaped.

The landscaping follows a hierarchy of formality with prestigious areas adopting elegant, spare layouts that become increasingly naturalistic the further one penetrates the parks and

gardens. The sustainability initiatives embrace this approach, using trees for shading, low-radiance materials for paving and salt water for the cooling fountains and lakes.

Concentration on pedestrian and cycle routes as a primary means of travel is bolstered by the integration of key worker housing and mixed-rent accommodation, shortening journey times for residents and reducing city traffic. This approach is fundamental to creating efficient, sustainable communities.

The cheering result of the design work is confirmation that rather than compromising standards and quality, incorporating sustainability brings clear, demonstrable improvements in terms of the quality of spaces, as well as reducing the burden they place on resources and the environment.

A fundamental aspect of the development is the encouragement of pedestrian rather than vehicular movement. Significant research was put into establishing the main pedestrian routes and desire lines, and adapting layouts to provide shelter, safety and good separation from those vehicular routes that are still required for service and access, while ensuring careful integration with public transport.

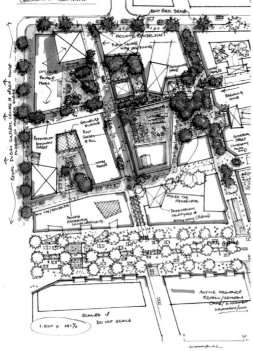

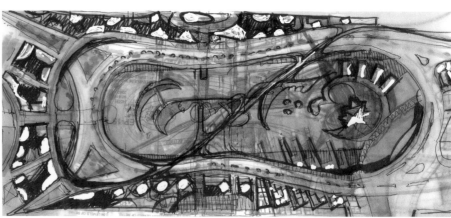

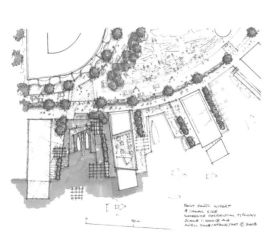

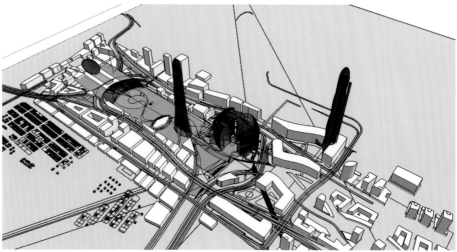

Western Marina Development
Abu Dhabi, UAE

**MASTERPLANNING
AND URBAN DESIGN**

Client
Confidential

Area
210 ha

Type
Mixed-use
development including
five-star hotel, aqua
park, residential
and retail

Status
Concept design

Date
2010

The Western Marina is a mixed-use development on a series of created isthmuses in the western region of Abu Dhabi. The scheme will focus on the integration of urban life with the Gulf seas – maximising the potential of the water for views, sport, leisure and relaxation.

Residents will have a choice of some 440 luxury villas, ranging in size between 500 m² and 1,000 m². Most have private jetties or direct access to private beaches, and great pains

have been taken to ensure that all have the best possible sea views.

There are also over 1,900 sea view apartments developed in combination with a retail mall. A boardwalk lined with cafés, restaurants and outdoor seating connects the mall with the residential areas and central marina, providing a lively social link.

A four-star, 250-key hotel is proposed as both a stand-alone location and a supporting facility. It will have a private beach and a direct access route

to separate it operationally from the other establishments on the site, but local residents and hotel guests will be able to use the fine dining and health spa facilities. In addition, a large water fun park is proposed for both residents and visitors, building on the theme of water in the Gulf.

The marina contributes to Plan Abu Dhabi 2030, an initiative intended to establish the UAE capital as an international marine centre, capitalising on its 200 natural islands and lengthy coastline.

Workers' Cultural Palace Redevelopment Masterplan
Hu Xi, China

MASTERPLANNING AND URBAN DESIGN

Client
Shanghai Ludi Sun
Lung Keo Property
Co. Ltd

Area
46 ha

Type
Redevelopment of
mixed-use masterplan
and urban design

Status
Competition entry

Date
2002

Following the Communist takeover of China in 1949, every city created a workers' cultural palace. It was the place to go for respite from work, and became the centre of urban cultural life.

The redevelopment masterplan for Hu Xi Cultural Palace is aimed at regenerating a 12 ha area beside a rare 2 ha urban lake. The 40,000 m² cultural palace will be relocated within this high-density mixed-use zone around

the junction of Wuning Road, Caoyang Road, Kaixuan Road and Puxing Road.

Other major components include a 10,000 m² commercial podium, and office and residential towers occupying 240,000 m². A spacious, 400-room five-star hotel is also included.

The masterplan exploits access to the new metro and light rail stations to the north and capitalises on views around the newly redesigned lake.

Guangzhou Underground
Guangzhou, China

An international competition for the civic centre of Guangzhou, a completely new city, resulted in this fascinating, vital scheme, bursting with excitement and creativity. Unfortunately it wasn't developed, but it provided a valuable opportunity for experiment.

The space under consideration had been set aside as a potential civic square, traversed by an underground metro system with five stations. The proposal dealt with highlighting the stations at the surface, and connecting them to their surroundings and other transport types through a woven network of sunken gardens, semi-submerged retail space, a park with sunken and raised landscaping, and a web of surface and sub-surface connections to roads, bus networks, cycle routes, paths and open civic spaces at all levels.

This playful approach to the earth's face – variously treating it as the 'ground', the surface of a bubble, a roof, a perforated layer of earth, an open hole, a planting medium or a body of water seen from above or below – gave the scheme an extraordinary richness, and investigated new ways of thinking about urban spaces below as well as above ground.

MASTERPLANNING AND URBAN DESIGN

Client
Guangzhou City Planning Bureau

Area
140 ha

Type
Masterplan and urban design

Status
Competition entry

Date
2005

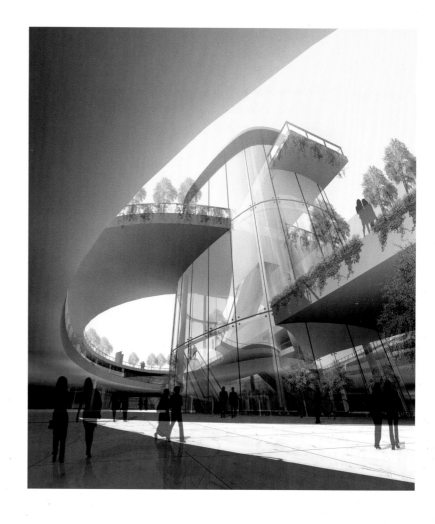

Dongjiu New District
Yixing, China

MASTERPLANNING AND URBAN DESIGN

Client
Yixing Planning Bureau

Area
4,600 ha

Type
Masterplan and urban design

Status
Competition entry

Date
2007

Dongjiu New District is located to the east of Yicheng City in Yixing and covers an area of 46 km², centred on Dongjiu Lake. The intention is to expand the city onto the banks of nearby Tai Lake and develop a new lakeside community.

The key challenge for the planning team was how best to integrate the city development and tourism functions with a lakeside landscape. The response is a proposal for a landscape corridor to link the old city with Tai Lake, around which three core areas are established, each with an especially compact structure to reduce the impact on the land and provide more potential for wetland conservation, recreation and scenic areas. Landscape corridors are also used to 'draw' the lakeside scenery into the high-quality residential areas, which are set back from the water's edge.

The Dongjiu New District plan was received with acclaim, and resulted in a further commission to design the first phase of the development – a 1 km² site at Chengdong. As well as meeting the obvious functional requirements, this development had two additional objectives: to act as a catalyst for future development in Dongjiu New District, and to promote the eastward development and improve the function of Yicheng City.

The Chengdong site will provide the main commercial and cultural facilities for the Dongjiu New District. It will incorporate a hotel, a conference centre, tourism facilities and residential developments.

Meishan Dao Masterplan
Ningbo, China

This masterplan was the winning entry in an international design competition to develop a port on Meishandao, an island of 29 km² with a deep-water coastline located some 25 km northeast of Ningbo. Ningbo is a city in the east of China, to the south of the Yantze River delta. The city as a whole has a population of about 5.6 million people, with the urban areas home to some 2.2 million people.

The plan is based on a comprehensive analysis of the economic positioning of the container port and the development of a land-use mix. These elements were used in the development of a masterplan and the preparation of an urban design scheme for the core business district, together with a phasing strategy.

The main elements of the plan include a bonded container port area, a value-adding manufacturing zone, a logistics park, an administration area, an exhibition precinct and core business district, a research and design park, leisure and tourism facilities and an ecoresidential area.

The key challenges were not only to develop the port, but to integrate it with the other zones on the island, including significant areas requiring ecological protection. Ecology also informed the landscaping, a significant component of the scheme.

**MASTERPLANNING
AND URBAN DESIGN**

Client
Administrative Commission of Meishan Island Bonded Harbour

Area
2,900 ha

Type
Urban design and conceptual planning for mixed-use container port

Status
Competition entry winner

Date
2008–2009

Shizimen New CBD Masterplan
Zhuhai, China

MASTERPLANNING AND URBAN DESIGN

Client
Huafa Group, Zhuhai Shizimen Business District Construction Holding Co. Ltd

Area
300 ha

Type
Masterplan

Status
Competition entry

Date
2009

This concept masterplan envisions a 'Zhuhai–Macao' city cluster centred on the Shizimen Business District. This new cluster is intended to complement 'Guangzhou–Foshan' and 'Hong Kong–Shenzhen' as a third engine for development in the Pearl River delta.

The design proposes a vibrant, liveable central business district on the waterfront, sensitive to the existing environment and providing a robust basis for economic growth. For example, a borderless relationship between Macao and Zhuhai intended to create a comprehensive and sustainable space for conferences, businesses, heritage and tourism within the Shizimen corridor has been proposed.

The proposed design features green and public open spaces, landmark buildings and public transport systems. All embrace the central principles of Carbon Critical Design.

Careful integration of a hierarchy of public transport and pedestrian routes through landscaped and green spaces is intended to help China avoid the traffic problems suffered in the West. The green agenda is now invariably at the heart of masterplanning on this scale.

Daqing West Rail Station Area
Daqing, China

This design was awarded first place in an international planning and design competition for the 720 ha Daqing West Station area in Heilongjiang Province, north China. The new station will form part of the high-speed rail line linking Daqing with its wider region.

The scheme develops the station as a regional commercial, business and entertainment centre, helping Daqing to diversify its economic base. The intention is to reduce reliance on oil exploration and develop instead a regional service function that will complement other initiatives within the city relating to information technology, new material industries and tourism. The urban design integrates an existing oil headquarters complex into the plan and provides a framework for future development to the north of the station.

The urban design specifically addresses the particular climate of Daqing, which endures long, cold winters. Accordingly, the plan provides underground retail links to the associated mass transit stations, as well as covered ground-level landscaped corridors into the surrounding residential areas.

MASTERPLANNING
AND URBAN DESIGN

Client
Daqing City Planning Bureau

Area
720 ha

Type
Masterplan and urban design

Status
Competition entry

Date
2008

Chengdu Sports City
Chengdu, China

**MASTERPLANNING
AND URBAN DESIGN**

Client
Chengdu City
Planning Bureau

Area
990 ha

Type
Masterplan and urban
design

Status
Competition

Date
2007

This scheme was awarded first place in an international planning and urban design competition for the 990 ha sports city in Chengdu, in Sichuan Province. The masterplan features a series of specialised stadiums specifically required to support the China National Games.

The new stadiums are designed to serve a number of sports and games, and are planned around a central axis linking them to an extensive riverside culture park containing Ming dynasty tombs.

A major component of the plan was the absorption of development pressure arising from Chengdu's continuing growth. Continuing the theme, new urban neighbourhoods were planned around community sports and recreation.

The integration of subtle lighting schemes and transluscent roof systems ensures that, if anything, the stadiums are more spectacular at night than during the day.

431

CITIC New Town Development
Changsha, China

MASTERPLANNING AND URBAN DESIGN

Client
CITIC Huizhou Real Estate Co. Ltd

Area
62,860 m²

Type
Masterplan and urban design for five functional districts comprising city and cultural plazas, ecological hotel, cyber port and residential units

Status
Competition entry

Date
2009

This new town development on the outskirts of Changsha, the capital of Hunan, consists of five districts: a city square, a cultural plaza, a sustainable hotel, a cyber port and an ecological residential district.

The masterplan places the active commercial functions to the west and the quiet neighbourhoods to the east. The first phase, mixed-use city square district faces the triangular parkland that is the focus of the V-shaped boulevards framing the new Central Business District.

Commercial activities are concentrated on the western boulevard, conceived as a 'Champs Elysee' in character. On this boulevard is centred a new hotel, standing on raised ground and overlooking the CBD and the residential valley.

To enhance the quality of life of citizens, the ecological principles of 'new urbanism' are applied to preserve the rolling topography and landscape of the site, with walkways along existing streams connecting the east and west districts. On the corners of the new town are four iconic gateways leading into the city centre.

Oceania Point
Xunliao, China

**MASTERPLANNING
AND URBAN DESIGN**

Client
Financial Street
Holding Company Ltd.

Area
2,000 ha

Type
Masterplan and urban
design

Status
Design ongoing

Date
2006–ongoing

Oceania Point is located to the east of Shenzhen City in the Pearl River delta of southern China. It is a new tourism and resort destination, designed to make the best use of 16 km of coastline, pristine sandy beaches and natural resources including mangroves, paddy fields and fishing villages.

The project incorporates plans for 10 international hotels and resorts, an international standard 18-hole golf course, yacht clubs and luxury villas with private marinas. The core township will provide a range of residential and visitor facilities including direct road and sea transportation to major cities such as Shenzhen, Macau, Guangzhou and Hong Kong.

The planned 60,000-person residential community will be based on family homes, holiday retreats, active-ageing communities and tourist accommodation, projecting the concepts of family values and healthy lifestyles, reinforced by a basic design approach that diminishes the need for transport to the distinct advantage of pedestrians.

Oasis City – Sub-centre East
Riyadh, Saudi Arabia

The ArRiyadh Development Authority (ADA) has proposed a long-term vision for the future planning of Riyadh, in which four urban sub-centres are to be created on the perimeter of the existing city. Oasis City is to be the new centre for the eastern sector.

As its name suggests, Oasis City aspires to be a haven, providing shelter and relief to its inhabitants and developing a modern concept of urban life by providing vibrant, interesting spaces. The plan takes its inspiration from the organic sculpting effects of water within a wadi and alludes to the historic origins of Riyadh as a garden city of canals and orchards.

It is dominated by a curvilinear, organically shaped public park that ties the north and south sides of the site together with a string of spatial experiences. These public spaces insinuate themselves into every aspect of the planning and use idealised aspects of Riyadh's history, spirituality, culture, tradition, ecology and future aspirations as themes under an overall approach of sustainability. The spaces within the park are based on themes of nature, religion, tradition, the souk, art and sport.

A network of landscaped pedestrian and bicycle routes connect the main public amenities of the site, set in organically shaped and spatially interesting wadis. These wadis vary in width and alignment and are strung with pocket courtyards and plazas to create a journey of discovery, a 'string of pearls', with new and wonderful experiences awaiting travellers around every corner.

MASTERPLANNING AND URBAN DESIGN

Client
Prince Faisal bin Turki Al Abdullah Al Saud and Al Mozaini Real Estate Development

Area
200 ha

Type
Masterplan and urban design

Status
Concept complete

Date
2009

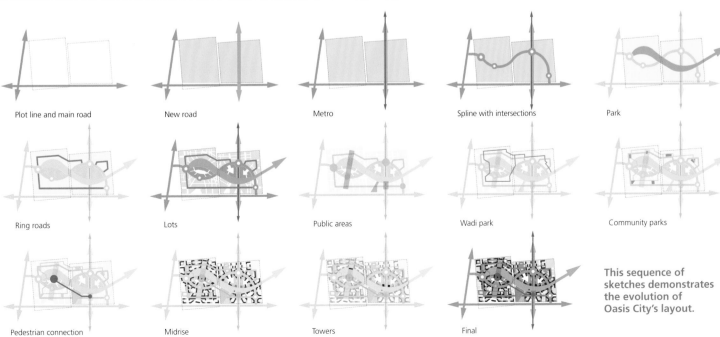

Plot line and main road

New road

Metro

Spline with intersections

Park

Ring roads

Lots

Public areas

Wadi park

Community parks

Pedestrian connection

Midrise

Towers

Final

This sequence of sketches demonstrates the evolution of Oasis City's layout.

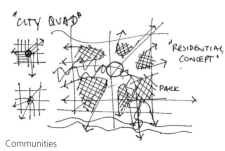
Communities

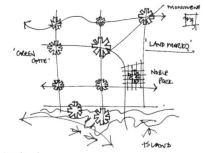
Landmarks

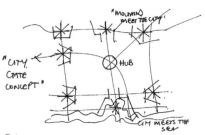
Gateways

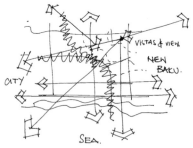
Views and vistas

White City
Baku, Azerbaijan

**MASTERPLANNING
AND URBAN DESIGN**

Client
Azerbaijan
Development
Company

Area
220 ha

Type
Strategic and detailed
masterplan

Status
Under construction

Date
2010

Located on Baku's east edge, White City is the largest urban development in the Azerbaijani capital and is a response to a significant annual influx of people. The site straddles Nobel Prospect, which is the main transport artery linking the capital to its international airport. It is named after the Nobel family who first exploited the natural oil reserves found in Baku in the early 20th century.

The White City masterplan sees this area transformed into a brand new environment made up of seven identifiable mixed-use urban districts. These are woven together in a hierarchy of tree-lined boulevards, public squares and landscaped parks and gardens that have been planned to make the most of the dramatic site topography.

Key civic centres of commercial, retail and leisure activity are strung along a central spine running north from the Caspian Sea coastline that provides the city's south boundary. Landmarks and gateway buildings have been carefully placed on high points and ridges, providing a legible visual structure, in between which residential buildings are carefully located to command the best views of the Caspian Sea.

The masterplan provides a total of 4,800,000 m² of gross floor area, of which 75% will be for residential use. The new development will be populated by a community of 50,000 people in some 19,700 households, and will provide jobs for almost 48,000 people.

Atkins' masterplanning team has been commissioned to lead the implementation of the plan, coordinating contributions from various architects and acting as the custodians of the masterplan vision. Work on the landmark buildings has already commenced.

Looking south towards the Caspian Sea.

Aypara Residence, *below left,* and the Gateway building, *below right,* can be seen towards the southwest corner of White City, and are discussed in more detail in the residential and mixed-use sections of this book respectively.

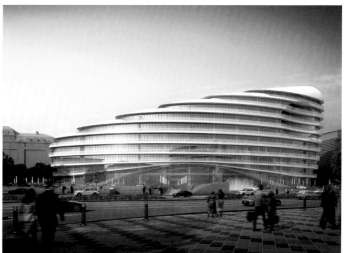

Nordhavnen
Copenhagen, Denmark

MASTERPLANNING AND URBAN DESIGN

Client
Udviklingsselskabet By and Havn I/S

Area
200 ha

Type
Masterplan

Status
Competition entry

Date
2008

The North Port is at present the largest and most ambitious metropolitan development in Scandinavia. It is a vision for living, working and playing in a new sustainable city by the sea, accessible to all – a dynamic place where energy, resources, transport and environment are green, healthy and sustainable.

The developer, Urban Development Port I/S, provided a creative and challenging brief based on a series of excellent contemporary precepts.

A green city – focusing on renewable energy and new energy forms, optimal resource utilisation, recycling of resources and environmentally friendly transport supporting a sustainable city and urban structure.

A vibrant city – open and welcoming to all, providing a rich urban environment and making the most of land and water, with a wide range of shops, cultural and sports facilities and urban spaces that invite enthusiasm and creativity.

A city for all – with varied housing types at all price levels, an integrated mix of residential and commercial buildings and a diverse range of spaces for everyone, including vulnerable groups, all offering a welcoming and friendly ambience.

A city by the sea – with housing and extroverted activities along the water, but with publicly accessible waterfront dock areas and coastlines, urban beaches, beach sport facilities and a port.

A dynamic city – providing a wide range of institutions, shopping and experiences, new jobs and initiatives, and attractive environments for knowledge workers and students, supporting the realisation of Copenhagen as a significant international knowledge city.

A city with green traffic – with urban areas developed primarily to meet pedestrians' and cyclists' needs by providing a dense network of comfortable bicycle and pedestrian connections supported by a single network of efficient public transport.

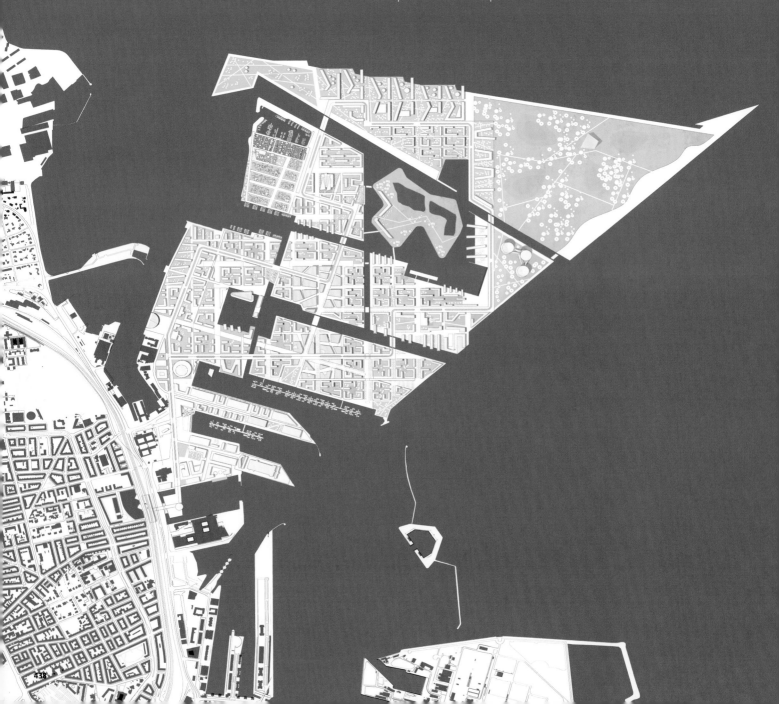

Movement framework

- ▬ Bicycle tracks
- ― Pedestrian sidewalks
- ▬ Public promenade

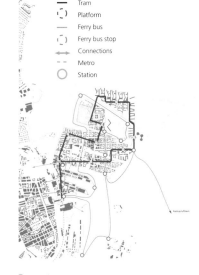

Transport

- ▬ Tram
- Platform
- ― Ferry bus
- Ferry bus stop
- ↔ Connections
- --- Metro
- ○ Station

Car transport

- ↔ Car traffic
- ↔ Car tunnel
- ▪ Parking structures

Views and vistas

- ― Sightlines and view points
- ⌄ Strategic views / panoramic views

Open space

- Open space
- Landscape / green space
- ― Significant waters edge
- ✳ Habour basin and water activities

Preserved heritage and buildings

- Nordhavnen local farmers market
- Heritage buildings
- Special habour environment
- Nature reserve
- Water and harbour preservation

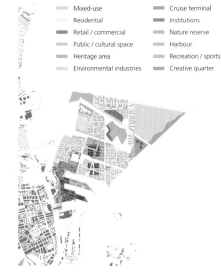

Land-use

- Mixed-use
- Residential
- Retail / commercial
- Public / cultural space
- Heritage area
- Environmental industries
- Cruise terminal
- Institutions
- Nature reserve
- Harbour
- Recreation / sports
- Creative quarter

Character areas

1 Nordhavnen gate
2 commercial pier
3 Aqua stadium and marina
4 Sund quay and oriental quay
5 Cultural centre
6 Integrated communities
7 Greentech experimental dwelling
8 Nordhavnen market
9 Nordhavnen business centre
10 Nature reserve
11 Cruise terminal
12 Fishing habour
13 Residential neighbourhood
14 University
15 North forest
16 Environmental bio-clusters

Creating a masterplan on this scale requires a tremendous amount of research. This forms the basis for the development of elemental plans that are integrated by overlaying and refining the concept until a harmonious solution is achieved. This sequence of sketches illustrates just part of the approach.

Panama Pacifico
Panama

**MASTERPLANNING
AND URBAN DESIGN**

Client
Confidential

Area
1,500 ha

Type
Masterplan

Status
Concept complete

Date
2007–2008

The vision for Panama Pacifico is of a world-class commercial and business hub, with desirable residential areas among the best of tourism and leisure facilities – all within an ecologically managed landscape of lush, tropical forests, hills, mangroves and wetlands. In this thriving, high-quality new community, people can do it all – live, work and play. The development is intended to create 40,000 jobs, 20,000 new homes and apartments, and 1,000,000 m² of commercial space.

The setting for Panama Pacifico is the 1,500 ha site of the former Howard US Air Force Base. This sits at the west mouth of the Panama Canal, and features shorelines of both the canal and the Pacific Ocean, with spectacular views and a tropical climate.

Panama Pacifico is one of 17 large-scale urban developments on six continents selected by the Clinton Climate Initiative, in partnership with the US Green Building Council, to demonstrate that cities can grow in ways that are 'climate positive', striving to reduce emissions of CO_2 to below zero.

Panama Pacifico's masterplan involves careful integration of new development into the beautiful natural environment of the site. Conservation plans recognise the importance of individual trees, as well as preserving wetlands, mangrove swamps, forests and native habitats.

Surely one of the world's more spectacular sites, Panama Pacifico is bordered to the south by the Pacific Ocean and to the east by the Panama Canal.

441

**MASTERPLANNING
AND URBAN DESIGN**

Client
Confidential

Area
400 ha

Type
Vision masterplan

Status
Concept complete

Date
2007

V&A Waterfront
Cape Town, South Africa

As with docklands all over the world, the coming of containerisation saw the traditional Victoria & Alfred Waterfront port in Cape Town lose much of its commerce. Although still a working port supporting a large offshore fishing fleet, much of the cargo-based activity had shifted to the adjacent Duncan Dock by the late 1980s. In 1990 the city initiated a scheme intended to

revitalise the V&A Waterfront by reconfiguring it as a mixed-use and tourist zone, building on the attraction of its historic maritime character.

Following a change in the ownership of the waterfront, Atkins became involved in 2007 as part of a new initiative to reinvigorate this process. Working closely with the owners and

management and in conjunction with local firm GAPP, Atkins undertook a deep analysis of the waterfront, and used the results to inform a comprehensive vision masterplan, a highly detailed proposal building on the success of the initial schemes, but providing a reconsidered and refined concept and detailed guidance on how best to improve the waterfront

The revised strategy centred on careful improvements to the existing buildings, the judicious insertion of new buildings, improvements in public access to the water's edge and the creation of new links with Cape Town's central business district, previously cut off from the sea by a new city arterial road. The new buildings envisioned in the plan are contemporary existing buildings and to dovetail with the existing historic context. A vertically integrated mix of residential, commercial and leisure uses was adopted to support the 'work/live/play' ethos that underpins a lively, ecologically aware development.

A significant but subtle enlargement of an existing retail mall is proposed, while used to improve links between the site's extremities and centre, reconnecting the area to the sea and the city. Taken together, the new proposals add life to both the land and water, and enhance the V&A Waterfront's growing reputation as being among the world's foremost dockland developments.

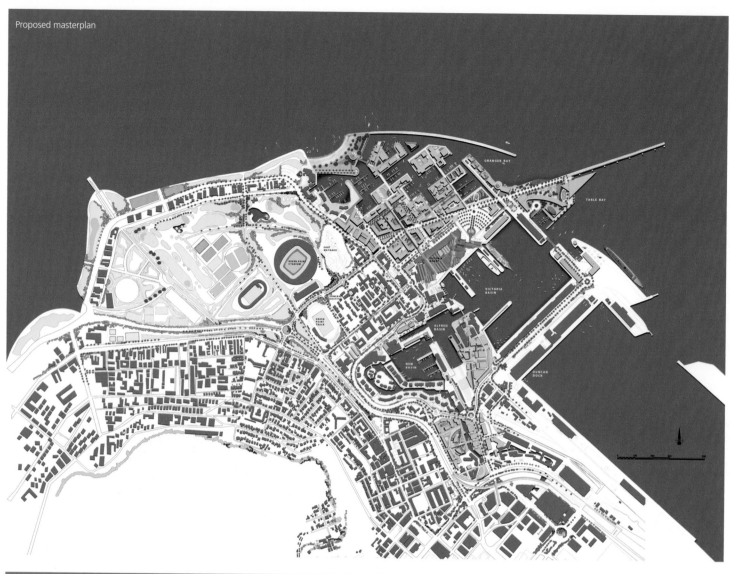

Proposed masterplan

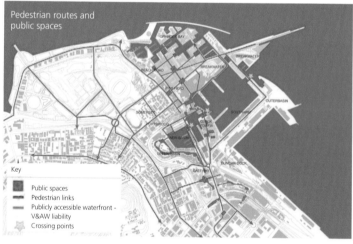

Pedestrian routes and
public spaces

Key

- ■ Public spaces
- ━ Pedestrian links
- ━ Publicly accessible waterfront -
  V&AW liability
- ✦ Crossing points

Vehicle movement
routes

Key

- ━ Highway
- ━ Major arterial
- ━ Minor arterial
- ━ Local roads
- ━ Tertiary - pedestrian and access routes
- ◉ Public parking
- ◉ Private parking

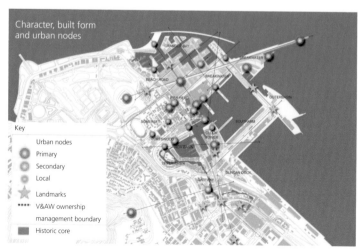

Character, built form
and urban nodes

Key

Urban nodes
- ◉ Primary
- ◉ Secondary
- ◉ Local
- ★ Landmarks
- ••••• V&AW ownership
  management boundary
- ■ Historic core

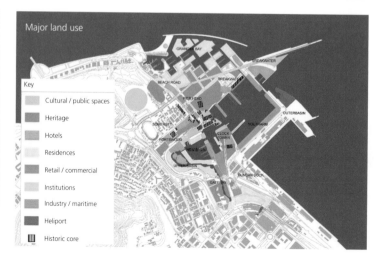

Major land use

Key

- Cultural / public spaces
- Heritage
- Hotels
- Residences
- Retail / commercial
- Institutions
- Industry / maritime
- Heliport
- ▥ Historic core

445

Index

Selected Awards

Atkins

Consultancy of the Year Winner 2010 – CIBSE Low Carbon Performance Award

Specialist Consultancy of the Year 2009 – MEP Awards

Engineering Firm of the Year 2009 – Construction Week Awards

Economic Excellence Award 2009 – Sharjah Chamber of Commerce & Industry

Best Consultancy 2009 – EDIE Awards for Environmental Excellence

Top Consultant (shared) 2009 – Construction World Awards

Engineering Consultancy of the Year 2009 – Gulf States Building Awards

Top Consultancy in Middle East 2009 – *New Civil Engineer*

Most Influential Planning & Design Institution 2009 – CIHAF China

Civil Engineering Award 2008 – British Construction Industry Awards

National Award for Value 2008 – Constructing Excellence Awards

Specialist Consultancy of the Year 2008 – MEP Awards

Local Landscape Planning Winner 2008 – Landscape Institute

Award for Structural Excellence 2008 – IstructE East Anglian Branch

Best Consultancy 2008 – EDIE Awards for Environmental Excellence

Middle East Architect and Young Architect of the Year 2008 – ME Architect Awards

Innovation and Best practice Award 2008 – AGI Awards

Engineering Consultancy of the Year 2008 – *Building* magazine

Specialist Consultancy of the Year 2007 – MEP Awards

Best Consultancy 2007 – EDIE Awards for Environmental Excellence

Consultancy of the Year and Supreme Judges Award 2007 – MEP Awards

In addition Atkins consistently appears in *The Sunday Times* list of 'Top 20 Companies to Work For', and *The Times* lists of 'Top 50 Companies Where Women Want to Work' and 'Top 100 Graduate Employers'.

Al Sharq Office Complex

Future Architecture Awards MIPIM 2007 – *Architects Review*

CNBC Arabia Property Awards 2007

Ashton Market

Greater Manchester Chamber Building of the Year Award 2009

Burj Al Arab

'Tallest All Suite Hotel in the World' *Guinness Book of World Records 2003*

Retail/Offices/Commercial Development – Cityscape Awards 2003

Business Bay Sales Centre

Small project of the year 2006 – Construction Week Awards

Al Sharq Office Complex

Bahrain World Trade Center

Burj Al Arab

Chancellor Park Primary School

Chepstow High Street

Bahrain World Trade Center

Best Use of Exterior Lighting
2010 – PALME Awards

Innovations Award in
2009 – NOVA Awards

Best Tall Building Award for Middle
East and Africa 2008 – CTBUH (Council
Tall Buildings & Urban Habitat)

Tower Project of the Year 2008
– Construction Week Awards

Innovations Award 2008 –
BEX (Building Exchange)

Sustainability Award 2008 –
BEX (Building Exchange)

Architect of the Year 2008
– *Building Design*

Environmental Excellence
2007 – EDIE Awards

Best Use of Technology
2006 – LEAF Awards

Chancellor Park Primary School

Best School – Essex Civic
Trust Commendation Award
2008 – Civic Awards Trust

Chepstow High Street

LGN 2005 Street Design Award

Paviors Award 2005 – The Worshipful
Company of Paviors

Runner-up in the ICE (Wales) Award

Clerkenwell Village Renaissance

Local landscape planning award 2008
– Landscape Institute Awards

Dubai Metro

Mega Project of the Year Award
2009 – Kingdom Expansion Awards

Durrat Marina

Best Marina Development – Bahrain
2008 – CNBC Property Awards

Enchantment of the Seas

Shippax Awards for Outstanding
Sundeck 2005

Hornsea Promenade

Special mention – Hard Landscape
Award 2003 – Civic Trust Awards

Chairman's Award 2003 – East
Riding of Yorkshire Council

Best Scheme by a North West
Practice Award 2003 – Landscape
Institute North West

Highly Commended Local
Government News Award 2003

Jumeirah Beach Hotel

Best Hotel in the Middle East
2009 – *Business Traveller* Award

Best Hotel in the Middle East
2009 – Virgin Holidays UK

Top Hotel in the Middle East 2009
– *Business Traveller* Award

Lighthouse Tower

'Bronze Award' 2008 –
The Holcim Awards

Dubai Metro   Durrat Marina   Hornsea Promenade   Jumeirah Beach Hotel   Lighthouse Tower

Selected Awards

Northumbria University

Best Building Overall and
Best Public Building 2007 –
Journal Landmark Awards

CIBSE Low Carbon Awards
2007 and 2008

Low Carbon New Build Project
of The Year 2008 – Construction
Excellence National Awards

Sustainability, Design and Innovation
and overall Building of the Year Award
Northern Region 2008 – RICS Awards

Innovation Award Winner
2008 – Cardiff University

**Northumbria University
Sports Centre**

Community Benefit Award – RICS
North East Renaissance Awards
2011 – *Estates Gazette*

Northwood Primary School

Shorlisted for The Legacy Award
– Sustainability and Client of the
Year (Darlington Borough Council)
2010 – Constructing Excellence
in the North East Awards

Oxford Circus

CIHT/WSP Award for
Urban Design 2010

Regatta Jakarta

Bali Congress Award 2010 – FIABCI
Prix d' Excellence Awards

Regent Street

Mayor's Award for Excellence 2010
– London Planning Awards

Seven Dials Project, Covent Garden

1st PRIAN award for outstanding
achievement in the public realm 2007

Taiyuan Wusu Airport

Lu Ban Award (for completed
project) 2009 – Ministry of
Construction of China

**Trafalgar Square, World
Squares for All**

RIBA (Royal Institute of
British Architects) Awards
for Architecture 2004

Thames Town

Excellent Residential Quarter (for
completed project) 2006 – Shanghai
Municipal Housing, Land and
Resource Administration Bureau

Songjiang New Town District in C
Category (75K to 200K population)
Gold Award – The International
Awards For Liveable Communities

The Address, Downtown Dubai

Best New Hotel 2009 –
World Hotel Awards

The Hub

Sustainable Development of
the Year 2009 – South West
Insider Property Awards

Shortlisted for New Building
of the Year 2010 – CIBSE Low
Carbon Performance Awards

Northumbria University   Northwood Primary School   Oxford Circus   The Address, Downtown Dubai   The Riyadh Tower

Building of the Year, Best Corporate Workspace 2010 – British Council for Offices (BCO) annual awards

The Riyadh Tower

Best Developer – Commercial/Office/Retail (Future) award 2009 – Cityscape Saudi Arabia Awards

Whitehall Streetscape

Security in the public realm award 2008 – Institute of Highways and Transport awards

Wild Wadi Aqua Park

Industry Innovation Award for Outstanding Design & Theme 1999 – World Water Park Association

Willenhall Primary School

Sustainable Design 2007 – Coventry Design Awards

Zhanjiang Minda Sheraton

Human Habitat Classic Award (for design) 2009 – Architectural Society of China

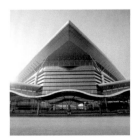

| The Hub | Taiyuan Wusu Airport | Regatta Jakarta | Wild Wadi Aqua Park | Zhanjiang Minda Sheraton |

Atkins Design Studios

As with any profession, the practice of architecture requires considerable commitment in terms of education and investment, and brings significant responsibilities with respect to both clients and the public. The reward is the opportunity to make a mark on the world in a way that few people do.

Atkins' architects are given that opportunity at all levels. Atkins is a large multidisciplinary practice that attracts exciting and challenging projects. The firm's ethos is fundamentally egalitarian, and within a simple organisational framework the studios are open and collaborative. Large projects often form the basis for internal competitions, with all designers, regardless of seniority,

encouraged to submit proposals provided they demonstrate creativity, innovation and excellence. This opportunity for fresh, creative thinking, refined through a significant body of experience, keeps Atkins architecture at the forefront of contemporary design.

Furthermore, the conscious avoidance of a house style ensures that each project is considered in terms of true design parameters – brief, context, and project aspirations – and not artificial constraints. Add to that a real commitment to excellence, which extends to every part of the organisation, and Atkins has the means to attract designers from all over the world to work on projects of which they can be justifiably proud.

This approach is applied through a fine network of international studios. Design teams have the benefit of being multi-local; they are able to provide immediate support to clients, but also enjoy international access to diverse sources of creativity and knowledge. Design teams are generally multidisciplinary, composed of experts from the wide range of professions and skills within the Atkins portfolio. Working in this way engenders real respect for colleagues, confidence in the team and a determination to excel, which is the foundation for everything Atkins does.

Acknowledgements

COLLEAGUES

It is impossible to mention everyone in the Atkins design community who has contributed to this book. At the risk of offending those we may have missed, the authors would like to acknowledge the assistance of the following individuals who suffered a barrage of requests and, on behalf of everyone, supplied narrative information or project data:

Hussam Abdulghany, Obada Adra, Dalia Al-Ajrami, Tim Askew, Peter Balana, Richard Barrett, Jaron Brender, Jie Cai, KY Cheung, Keith Clarke, Manoj Cletus, Alex Cochrane, Adrian Cooper, Helen Cooper, William Cooper, Andy Crabb, Simon Crispe, Duncan Cryer, Brian Daly, Helen Dixon, Valerie Evans, Simon Fairhurst, Lee Ferris, Geku George, Prodipto Ghosh, Lindsay Glendinning, Lee Glover, Venu Gopal, Susan Grant, Chris Greenwood, David Hamer, Mark Harrison, Helen Hasted, Peter Heath, Keith Hill, Irene Ho, Marcus Horning, Venetia

Humble, Abdul Jalil, Martin Jochman, Richard Johnston, Hakim Khennouchi, Sanjeev Kumar, Stephen Lang, Adrian Lindon, Hala Lloyd, Kate Lockey, Philip McGuiness, Joseph McLaughlin, Susanna Mendonza, Ruby Montalbo, Peter Morley, Paul Oburu, Ben Piper, Hannah Pyper, Sharif Rahmani, Leanne Ramshaw, Paul Reynolds, Paul Rice, Peter Ridley, Michael Ross, Janus Rostock, Kylie Schumacher, John Sincioco, Richard Smith, Colin Sweby, Joe Tabet, Shona Tait, Shadi Talaat, Lesley Taylor, Ian Tempest, Ludwig Tewksbury, Ben Thompson, Colin Tierney, Matthew Tribe, Davina Tyler, Phillip Watson, Yan Wong, Lei Ying, Loubna Al Zalek, Grzegorz Zimnicki.

CLIENTS

Atkins acknowledges with gratitude the many clients whose generosity and cooperation have made this book possible.

PHOTOGRAPHS

Atkins acknowledges with gratitude the following people and firms for allowing us to use their images:

The image of the Burj Al Arab® is reproduced under licence from Jumeirah International LLC.

For the interiors of The Address, Downtown Dubai – WA International.

For the panorama and detail of Trafalgar Square – Nigel Young, photographer, Foster + Partners.

For the aerial view of Westminster – Simmons Aero Films.

AUTHORS

Atkins is pleased to acknowledge the efforts of the following people who were involved in the production of this book:

Mukund Agarwal, Edwina Askew, Vadim Charles, Will Grime, Donna Hawkins, Shaun Killa, Gareth Kirkwood, Martin Pease, Maya Thomas, Tom Wright.

UK & Europe

Euston Tower
286 Euston Road
London
NW1 3AT
United Kingdom

+44 (0)20 7121 2000
info@atkinsglobal.com

Middle East

Al Rostamani Building
Khalid Bin Al Waleed Road
PO Box 5620
Dubai
United Arab Emirates

+971 (0)4 405 9300
marketing.me@atkinsglobal.com

Asia Pacific

21-22F, No 388
West Nanjing Road
Huangpu District
Shanghai, 20003
People's Republic of China

+86 (0)21 6122 5100
info.cn@atkinsglobal.com

North America

4030 W. Boy Scout Boulevard
Suite 700
Tampa, Florida 33607
USA

+1 (813) 282 7275
Buildings-NorthAmerica@atkinsglobal.com